THE MODERN SPIRITUAL SERIES

A COMPILATION OF THE BOOKS HEALING MANTRAS, MODERN CHAKRA AND MODERN TAROT

VERDA HARPER

WRYTING LTD

CONTENTS

HEALING MANTRAS

SIT BACK, TAKE A DEEP BREATH, AND EMBRACE
THE VIBRATIONS OF THE GODS THEMSELVES...

This checklist includes:

- 10 ways to prepare for the successful use of healing with Mantras and Chakras.
- The highest quality items.
- Where you can buy these items for the lowest price.

The last thing we want is for your healing start to be delayed because you weren't as prepared as you could have been.

To receive your checklist just scan this code with your phone camera or go to:

www.verdaharper.com/10-ways-to-prepare-checklist/

INTRODUCTION

It was over five years ago when a somewhat eccentric friend of mine started raving about a spiritualist she had visited. After two sessions, my friend had become an expert on mantras and was determined to use spiritual healing to transform her life.

As with anyone who takes up a new interest, she went on about how I need to do this and that. She could see the darkness of my aura and warned me that I needed to do something about it. I giggled a little and assumed it would be another passing phase she was going through.

At first, I admit I wasn't too keen to delve into the depths of the subject, probably because of the way my friend was portraying her new passion. We would be out for coffee and she would lay her healing crystals out and start chanting things that only she could understand. Along with a few "Oms" and "Shanti" (which I later learnt means 'peace' in Pali, an Indian language), the only thing she seemed to achieve was some strange stares from the adjacent tables.

So, as I was trying to convince my friend that mantras were not going to transform her life, I found that they would transform mine. I read one anonymous quotation that hit me with such an impact:

"The quieter the mind, the more you can hear"

— ANONYMOUS

There was nothing complex about the theory, but when I tried to put it into practice, I simply couldn't. My mind was racing with things I had to do, worries, and problems. It was impossible to break from the hectic world. But I loved the idea so much, I had to learn how to do it.

Needless to say, my friend's interest soon faded as she moved on to tarot cards, a whole other experience to which I have also dedicated a book. But I must thank her, because it was her experience that led me to begin my spiritual journey. Like many, I thought that the concept of spirituality was a bit of a con and, looking back, this is probably because of how it has been commercialized. Every time I made the awful journey into the hectic city, I would pass a holistic shop with dream catchers covering the windows. Aside from never having the time, there was something that was putting me off going in. Long-haired, mysterious women with healing powers have appeared in numerous films and have become a stereotype, far from reality. My interest began by trying to poke holes in the concept. The complete opposite happened as I started to see the great sense in the original teachings, the parts that we rarely see on films and TV.

It wasn't that I was unhappy with my life. I was blessed with two amazing children and a husband who worked hard so that I could stay at home to be with the kids. However, there was something off, something missing. I was stuck in a rut, mentally and physically. Being a mum is the best job in the world, but there comes a point when you lose your sense of being and struggle to find purpose in your life.

This is the point that I had reached. Every mother will be able to relate to this at some point, but it felt like my destiny featured a vacuum cleaner and several loads of washing. I fell into depression, unhealthy habits and a lack of interest in the world. I knew something had to be done and I wanted to better my life, but I wasn't sure that Western traditions held the right solution for me.

I realized that in order for me to change my life, I didn't need gimmicks or tricks: I needed guidance. I needed to find peace. From encountering that first quotation, I saw that I would have to empty my mind of trivial things, like household budgets and meal planning. This would allow me to truly hear what my mind and body required.

This quotation started my thirst for learning. I became a student again, with a fresh notebook and a Google history filled with searches on Eastern philosophies. I was bursting with energy when I signed up for my first online course in

Buddhism. In just a few short months, I felt like a different person and I had only scratched the surface.

I took up yoga and meditation, neither of which was as easy as I had thought. I had become physically out of shape in my state of depression and I soon learned that yoga was far more than just a bit of stretching. The backache that had prevented me from other exercise gradually eased as I found myself becoming physically fitter. I knew I was getting a better night's sleep, because I wasn't waking up tired. I had more energy and with a little weight loss, I felt far more confident.

Meditation took time and effort to master, a process that I will share with you throughout this book. Cleansing the mind brought about a new way of thinking for me and a higher level of clarity, but as someone whose brain had been constantly interrupted, I had put in the effort to see the results.

These two practices are just a small part of my learning. I took to travelling so that I could gain first-hand insights from spiritual leaders and masters. I left no stone unturned. I read books and watched videos. I ignored what I felt to be too forced, and followed gurus who didn't impose their teachings, but who instead showed me the teachings so that I could draw my own conclusions.

While reading this book, I have three hopes. The first is that you are able to learn about mantras the same way I did—in a way that is in no way pressurized. Second, I want you to gain understanding of the principles and philosophies going back to the earliest mantras in Vedic Sanskrit. My third hope is that together, we can work on removing negative thoughts, in order for you to connect with your inner self and enhance the quality of your life.

Part of our educational path will be concerned with how to create mantras that are meaningful to you, as well learning as some of the most powerful mantras for various uses. We will discuss how to use mantras correctly so that you can refocus your mind, heal your body and realign your energies. I have chosen to include some recommendations for what not to do. As I have said, I don't want to impose my journey on you, but there are some lessons I wish I hadn't had to learn by myself over the years and I feel it's important to share them with you.

If you have practised a little yoga or meditation and would like to take that to the next level, the information in this book will allow you to build on you the knowledge you have. If you are feeling lost in life and have no experience in spiritualism, that is fine—there is no better place to start than here.

It is understandable if you are sceptical. You might be doubting just how far mantras can help you. Many have asked me: "What if it does more harm than good?". Even more have felt that they aren't capable of healing, or that they don't have time for spiritual practices. It's important that you realise that we can integrate mantras and healing into your daily life so that you can completely benefit from the positive changes that are about to occur. I too was full of self-doubt, but these philosophies have been practised for thousands of years for a good reason. You just need a pinch of faith.

Finally, I promise to make this an enjoyable experience for you. After all, introspection and self-realization can be an intense experience, so it's important for me to share my passion and learnings in a way that will put a smile on your face. I may even share the odd faux pas I have made along the way.

Nobody's life is the same. Some of us have high-demanding jobs, others are poor, some might be going through a divorce, mourning the loss of someone they loved, moving home—the list of our stresses and strains can go on. I am not here to compare my pains to yours or tell you that your problems can be fixed. One man's heaven is another man's hell and people view and handle problems differently. The one thing we have in common is that the problems you are suffering with are going to have a huge negative impact on your life, as did mine. What I aim to do is to guide you to a better life, the same way others have guided me. At the end of the day, we all need a little help sometimes, and this book is my help to you.

PART I

———

Not everyone will feel so eager to jump straight into the practice of mantras. Like many others, I needed time to explore the concepts, and more than anything, I wanted to find out if there was any truth or scientific support behind the use of mantras for healing.

Your beliefs are reflected in your intentions, and your intentions are governed by your goals. On a larger scale, your goals are set depending on what you want from life. Every aspect of who you are will play a role in the mantras that you choose. At this point—and this is perfectly normal—you may have chosen this book without intentions or expectations, or you may have your heart set on changing something in your life that will then lead to even better things.

Because I was a sceptic at first, I wanted the focus of Part 1 to be on the history of Hinduism and Eastern philosophies that are relevant to mantras. I want to share my passion for the

Sanskrit language and explain why is it so important. I want to share my findings regarding the certain correlations between science and mantras. And we will begin to look and some mantras that can be used to prepare ourselves in order to get what we want from life.

Part 1 is like a history, science, and foreign language lesson from a teacher who never went to university, but who taught themselves through love of the subject and by learning what works and what doesn't. The best thing is, although the lesson isn't compulsory, I am fairly sure you will get caught up in the fascinating complexities of healing mantras.

THE UNIVERSAL PRIMAL SOUNDS

I started my journey into mantras fairly early on into my spiritualism research. While I understood the theory behind them and even the science, it wasn't until I started practising yoga that I began to fully appreciate their meaning and power. The great thing is, you don't need to have any background in mantras to start benefiting from them. You don't need to be religious; you don't need to have a certain way of thinking. Mantras are used by students, businessmen, single mums, and everyone in between.

Hinduism and spiritual teachings are steeped in tradition and I feel that it is necessary to gain insight into the history of the religion, not only to respect it, but also to learn the intricate depths of the origins of mantras. For me, my experience was enhanced when I started to fit all of the puzzle pieces together. I realized how certain scriptures were used for different teaching methods, just like certain mantras were developed for certain purposes. I also grew to appreciate that the ways that this knowledge was passed on throughout the centuries has impacted the effectiveness of the mantras and spiritual healing.

These are the areas we will focus on in this chapter. It's about learning the foundations, in order to gain a higher sense of one's self. Equally important is that while Hinduism is a religion, there is also a side to it that doesn't call on the gods for enlightenment, but which requires a personal, internal focus to lead you to the place you feel you want to need to be.

THE SOURCE OF HINDU KNOWLEDGE

To keep the ancient traditions alive, scriptures of Hindu texts have been kept. However, as the teachings are predominately oral, there is little information on the original authors of the texts. They are considered to be a collaboration of teachings from both men and women and may have been added to over time.

These scriptures are either *shruti*, to be heard, or *smriti*, to be remembered. The oldest scriptures of Hinduism are the four Vedas, which are shruti. The four Vedas, all written in Vedic Sanskrit, are the Rigveda, Yajurveda, Samaveda, and Atharvaveda.

Rigveda: This is a collection of 1,028 hymns and 10,600 verses that were composed between approximately 1500 and 1200 BCE. The teachings aim to answer questions regarding existence and are heavily based on the concept of universal vibrations.

Samaveda: The majority of the Samaveda was taken from Rigveda and then expanded with 75 mantras. Many of the scriptures were meant to be sung and were likely to have been danced to.

Yajurveda: The 1,875 verses are ritual offerings. There is a strong element of worship and religion in these teachings.

Atharvaveda: These scriptures also have elements of ritual offerings. There are around 760 hymns and 160 of those have similarities to teachings in Rigveda. It is composed of chants, hymns, and prayers that are intended to keep danger and evil at bay.

Each collection of Veda books contains four types of texts. Aranyakas are texts of rituals and Brahmans are further interpretation of the rituals. Samhitas are the prayers and mantras within the Vedas. Upanishads are the philosophical works, of which there are 108. The Upanishads, which deal with meditation, philosophy and spiritual knowledge, are the best-known parts of the Vedas, and play a central role in Hinduism.

Upanishads- meaning by (upa) and ni-sad (sit down) or 'sitting down near'

Hinduism stands out from many religions. There isn't one God that you must follow, but a broad set of deities who may be called upon for their particular areas of power. There is also a great deal of focus on rituals, mantras, chants and prayers, and not necessarily and overtly on the deities themselves. Some of the Hindu teachings are easier to master, others are complex and require time and practice. You will notice that not only are the scriptures and teachings different, but so too are the ways in which knowledge is shared.

A STYLE OF LEARNING EMBEDDED IN TRADITION

There came a point when I had to move away from what I had considered the best way to learn. As western tradition teaches us, we are accustomed to a student-teacher relationship where the teacher recites learned knowledge and the student takes down as many notes as possible to study later on.

I was both the student and the teacher when it came to my research and I felt that I needed to write down mantras and learn them by heart. This was my first mistake, as I had pages of phrases with little pronunciation hints in the margin, but I didn't feel like anything was particularly sticking.

The student-teacher relationship in Hinduism is still an important one, but the dynamics are different. Mantras were handed down to students as, say, a grandmother would pass on her favourite recipes. She has practised her recipes over the years and doesn't need the ingredients to be written down. Her recipes are a part of her, like muscle memory.

Yoga, one of the six orthodox philosophical schools of Hinduism, involves a wide set of physical, mental and spiritual practices. In the West, we tend to think just of yoga postures, or *asanas*, but really this is just one part of yogic practice. An adherent of yoga is called a *yogi*. Yogis have great wisdom, which has come from the teachings they received and the experience that those teachings have given them. Knowledge is not forced on you, but rather offered. As the student, you need to take the parts of the teachings that relate to you. And this is the same with mantras.

Across all of the Vedas, there are 20,379 mantras. They are not all going to be necessary for your healing. Some may be relevant for a part of your life, while others can be used to overcome a specific issue that you have. Never should you feel that a mantra is forced upon you or that you should feel obligated to try something, as this goes against the tradition. Mantras, like Hinduism, are a way of life.

WHAT CAME FIRST—THE VEDAS OR THE MANTRAS?

Both Vedas and mantras have been around for thousands of years. The Vedas are the teachings of Hinduism and are among the oldest surviving religious works in the world. They are written in Sanskrit, a language with 3500 years of history. Many believe that even before writing, the Vedas were practised in profound meditative states until they were written down somewhere between 1500 and 900 BCE.

Veda- meaning 'knowledge'

As language was far from developed, the Vedas focused on silence, in order to gain knowledge of the energy pathways in the universe. Most specifically, yogis concentrated on vibrations and their patterns. When in silence, it is thought that you are able to sense the universal vibrations. These vibrations led to sounds but not to specific words, so the sounds became mantras. Each sound is a way of connecting with the divine and has specific healing abilities.

Mantra- meaning 'mind' (man) and 'liberate' (tra)

Words and meaning came later, as did translations and the ways we use modern mantras. Yet, when we say words aloud, the sounds are still vibrations that propagate as waves. Vac is a Vedic goddess and the mother of Vedas. She is the goddess of speech and the mother of emotions. As human brain function began to develop along with language skills, Hindu tradition teaches that it was Vac who enabled those she loved to put words to sounds and emotions.

The key takeaway is that the power of the mantras does not come from pen and paper. As soon as you start to write mantras down, whether as transcriptions of sounds or words, they start to lose their quintessence. Unlike the Bible, Vedic mantras are written down so that the tradition can stay alive, not as a teaching tool.

THE USE OF MANTRAS IN OTHER RELIGIONS

As Hinduism is the oldest religion in the world, there is no great surprise that younger religions and belief systems have borrowed aspects from it. The rosary of the Virgin Mary in Catholicism is a set of prayer beads, and prayer beads also have significance in Buddhism, but the idea was probably borrowed from their use for Hindu prayers in India.

Mantras are no different. Chinese Buddhists include mantras in their spiritual practice, but as their culture has been more focused on the esteemed written language rather than the sounds, it has become normal for Chinese Buddhists to write mantras as their spiritual practice.

Sikhs use mantras to concentrate their minds on God and making sure God is an integral part of their daily lives. Jews repeat phrases from the Hebrew Bible in the form of song, and some Islamic communities chant the 99 Names of Allah.

The Hail Mary in Christianity is a mantra, a prayer that is repeated! In the modern world, the idea of a mantra as a repeated phrase has been more loosely applied in other contexts, especially in support of a particular philosophy or cause. The Vietnamese War led to the emergence of a number of New Age groups that looked for a world of peace, leading to the modern mantra "make love, not war". Transcendental Meditation is another spiritual group that uses simple mantras in its meditation, although its mantras are silent, to be spoken only in the mind.

Many of the modern mantras are not related to religion at all, but they are still a crucial part of the person using them and lead that person to a better understanding of themselves. Whether you feel connected to a religion or not is obviously entirely up to you, and not the purpose of this book.

Each mantra calls on a distinct attribute associated with a deity. Deities in Eastern traditions can be gods, goddesses, or a creator or a supreme being. There are the gods of fire, of animals, of light, of the weather, Mother Nature and the Furies. However, you do not necessarily need to believe in and worship the gods directly to benefit from mantras, and the deities need not be a focus in finding the right mantras. We will cover a range of mantras that are connected to deities but have deeper meanings than what you may see on the surface.

SO, WHAT EXACTLY IS A MANTRA?

This may be no surprise, coming from a religion where words are not the core of the lesson, but there is no single definition of a mantra. Some will see words or sounds that allow themselves to free the mind. It can be described as the appreciation of sounds and vibrations in order to aid your concentration and focus on a particular idea. Others use it as a form of prayer and some people who see mantras as a form of positive reinforcement through chanting.

Yogis will agree that a mantra is a blend of Sanskrit sounds that purify the mind, body and soul, allowing the mind to experience peace, in order to reach a higher self, or Purusha. As this is a detailed subject, we will discuss it more a little later on.

The reason I like to start by going into the history and traditions of Hinduism is that mantras will generally only work when combined with the right understanding. Regardless of how determined you are, repeating a phrase is not enough.

It reminds me of when I was a kid and learning to dive. My father stood next to me and told me to say out loud, over and over again, "I can dive". The theory seemed to be that if I said it loud enough, I would glide into the water with perfect elegance. The truth is, I belly-flopped. Telling myself (and embarrassingly, half the pool) was only going to provide me with the confidence to dive; beforehand, I still needed to learn the stages of how to do a dive.

The words and length of a mantra will vary greatly. It is the purpose of the mantra that will remain consistent. We use mantras to declutter our mind from the trivial aspects of our daily lives. They will enable us to silence the buzz in our brains that occupies so much of our energy. Once your mind is quieter, you will be able to reach a state of self-awareness and empower yourself with the ability to make necessary changes. With that in mind, let's continue by understanding the three main types of mantras.

THE THREE TYPES OF MANTRAS

Before choosing a mantra or even a collection of mantras, you need to understand how each type has a certain purpose. One type has the power of healing, another allows for spiritual development, and finally, there is a type of mantras that enables you to attain worldly desires.

Saguna mantras are used to personalize aspects or powers of God, whereas Nirguna mantras are based on the principal truths of yogic philosophies and are not related to deities. Both are complex concepts to grasp and I didn't introduce these types of mantras into my routine until further on in my education.

I began with Bija mantras, which draw on the tradition of expanding the mind by using the power of vibrations. These mantras allow us to grow our physical, emotional, and spiritual sides as if flourishing from seeds. Bija mantras are written in

Sanskrit. The sounds are each just one syllable and so are easy to pronounce, yet have a great amount of power.

Bija- meaning 'seed'

Here is where the subject of mantras began to make a lot more sense to me. There are numerous studies and opinions regarding the Big Bang—again, nothing that we are going to debate. However, some believe that the universe was created by cosmic sound energy and light energy, which created life. From this perspective, cosmic sound energy, or vibration, is directly related to life. By tapping into vibrations, we can connect with our energies and encourage balance within our mind and body.

For those who may need further convincing, you only need to look at the benefits of psychoacoustics and the psychological responses to sound. For example, listening to soothing music has been shown to reduce stress, blood pressure and post-operative trauma in hospitals when compared to silence.

If you take each syllable, or seed, from Bija mantras, you are able to combine them to form longer mantras. Imagine each sound as a letter of the Sanskrit alphabet. This is how the yogis developed mantras with certain purposes.

There are seven Bija mantras that are used in yoga and meditation. When practising the following mantras, you can be lying down or sitting cross-legged—whichever position you feel comfortable in.

The seven mantras are each associated with a chakra, a spinning wheel of energy, and each one will control a different aspect of your life:

- **Root Chakra**- at the bottom of your spine, near the coccyx. It keeps us grounded and controls the things we need to survive, for example, money and food.
- **Sacral Chakra**- in the lower abdomen area. It controls our creativity, sexuality, and can help us maintain control of our lives.
- **Solar Plexus Chakra**- found in the upper abdomen area. This chakra enables you to be yourself and be confident in doing so.
- **Heart Chakra**- slightly above your heart. It enables us to experience love, happiness, and inner peace.
- **Throat Chakra**- in our throat, or vocal cords. The throat chakra is essential for us to speak the truth and let others know how we feel.
- **Third-Eye Chakra**- located between the brows. The eye to our soul, it lets us connect with our instincts and wisdom, and helps us to see the bigger picture.
- **The Crown Chakra**- the highest part of our body, the top of the head. Its location is significant in spiritual connection and higher consciousness.

Chakras are fascinating and complex, and while I want to briefly touch on them here and elsewhere in this book, book two in this series is dedicated to this wonderful subject and the associated healing benefits.

MEDITATION AND MANTRAS

You may have already discovered a type of meditation that suits you. I have tried various forms of the most popular forms and found positives and negatives in each and it will be a personal preference. For me, I struggled with movement meditation: I felt that I was too easily distracted. It could be a very simple movement like rocking in a chair or going for a walk.

I fell in love with mantra meditation, because I was able to repeat mantras aloud, which helped me to focus more. Once I learnt how to control my focus better, I could repeat my mantras in my mind and take advantage of complete peace.

HOW CAN YOU USE MANTRA MEDITATION?

Mantra meditation is perfect for people who struggle to focus. When I felt like the world was on my shoulders, I couldn't see a solution that would relieve the pressure. Mantra meditation requires you to repeat a word or phrase. It is not the word that you need to focus on, but the sounds that you create. When you think of a word, your brain tends to start linking it to another and then another. You may have chosen the number one— simple, right? But when concentrating on one, you might associate it with one thousand, then the money that you need to get your car fixed and stay on top of the bills.

Instead, concentrate on the sound of one, notice the vibrations of the first "w" sound, the openness of the "uh", the strength of "nu". Notice the difference in the sounds as you inhale and exhale, not forcing the emphasis of any of the sounds, but letting them flow.

Repetition is crucial. Your mind will start to stray, and this is perfectly normal, but by repeating your sounds, you will gradually regain your attention. A busy mind takes time to settle and you may find that takes a while before you start to feel inner peace. Even if it is difficult to slow the mind down, you will notice very quickly that it is harder for you to let negative thoughts into your mind when you are focusing on sounds. So, mantra meditation is a way to protect your mind from damaging emotions while you are mastering a deeper spiritual connection.

WILL MANTRA MEDITATION HELP ME PHYSICALLY?

Perhaps the reason you are reading this book is that you need help resolving your problems, either physical, mental, or a combination of both. Or maybe you feel like your problems are under control, but you are looking for something more in life. A healthy mind is essential for a healthy body. Once you begin to focus your mind, you will begin to see what it is that you need in life. Mantra meditation brings about a positive sensation that will encourage you to make the necessary changes. It's not just used for finding a higher spirituality: it will also give you the energy you need to improve your physical self.

Over the last few decades, more and more scientific research has been carried out on the physical benefits of mantra meditation. The results are mixed, and the experiments hard to adequately control in a scientific setting, but there is some evidence that mantra meditation can have positive effects on health and wellbeing. For example, one study found that transcendental meditation can reduce trauma symptoms and perceived stress in prison inmates. There is also some evidence that mantra meditation can reduce blood pressure, as well as lowering cholesterol and blood sugar. Much of the existing research concerns silent, transcendental mantra meditation, so much potential remains for new studies on spoken mantras.

It is always necessary to practice mantras with a purpose and this applies to mantra meditation too. Before you begin, make sure you are aware of why you have chosen this type for spiritual growth. Is it because you want to improve your physical self? Do you need to quieten the mind? Or do you feel the need to create a stronger connection with the divine? Unfortunately, I often hear the answer "a little bit of everything" and although this is probably true for all of us, we need to tackle one aspect at a time.

BIJA MANTRA MEDITATION

Here are seven very simple Bija mantras that can be used to improve the chakras that we covered before and some tips on how to pronounce them so that you get the right sound:

- **Root Chakra** – "Lam"- said as /lum/ like plum
- **Sacral Chakra** – "Vam" said as /vum/ like ovum
- **Solar Plexus Chakra** – "Rum" said just like the drink
- **Heart Chakra** – "Yam" said as /yum/ like yummy
- **Throat Chakra** – "Ham" said as /hum/ just like the sound
- **Third Eye Chakra** – "U" said as /oo/ like the long sound in uber

- **Crown Chakra** – "Om" said as /aum/ as if you were feeding a toddler

Notice the major difference in the vowel sounds.

HOW CAN YOU USE THE MANTRAS IN THIS BOOK?

Hopefully, at this point, you have learnt some key concepts about mantras that will help to answer this question. In the first place, I am not going to impose any mantra on you. The mantras you read in this book have been selected based on their traditions and teachings and on how they can help certain issues you may have. You won't find a listicle of my top 10 favourites that transformed my life.

Different mantras should be repeated in different ways so that you can really benefit from them. Most are repeated 108 times. Why 108? You may encounter several different explanations. One is that the diameter of the Sun is approximately 108 times bigger than the diameter of Earth. The distance between the Earth and the Moon is, on average, around 108 times the diameter of the Moon. Hindu astrologers have also divided the ecliptic—the path that the Sun and the Moon take—into twenty-seven equal sections, and each of these into four equal steps, marking the 108 steps that the Sun and Moon take across the sky. 108 sounds a lot, but as most of the mantras in this book are short, it will only take around ten to fifteen minutes. Chakra mantras are repeated from the bottom to the top one to three times but can be for longer.

Read all of the mantras in the book; say them aloud; say them to yourself; concentrate on each sound. Decide if the mantra has meaning for you. If you need to write it down, it probably means that it doesn't have enough significance to become beneficial for you. The mantras that stick in your head are the ones that you should keep using. Those that don't light a spark inside you should be forgotten or kept to one side in case a situation arises where they could become relevant. Use the mantras that feel right.

SACRED WORDS TO MANAGE YOUR LIFE

This history lesson is complete, but forgive me if I pop back to the subject here and there, as I find it truly fascinating and I found great benefit in learning about how we came to today's mantras. Now, we are going to delve into the four main goals in life and look at which mantras will allow you to achieve them. Before that, I want to discuss the significance of mantras to our karma.

WHAT IS KARMA

Most people see it as "what goes around comes around"—you laugh at someone who falls over, only to go and fall over yourself. More so in the Western world, we wrongly associate karma with bad luck or destiny. In reality, it is just as possible for karma to lead you to good things, if your actions merit it.

Like mantras, people use the word karma in all walks of life regardless of religious or spiritual beliefs, but it is one of the principal concepts of Hinduism and Buddhism, as well as other Eastern philosophies. It symbolises a life-cycle that is dominated by cause and effect. One action you take now will impact your life later on. Karma literally means 'action', but it's not limited to actions in the narrow sense: karma can be influenced by your words or even your thoughts, as these are also considered kinds of karmic actions.

Karma- meaning 'action'

It's also worth noting that the intentions behind each action can influence the karmic result. A poor person who steals to feed their children is doing so out of necessity. Nevertheless, it is still stealing and will result in bad karma, because it is morally wrong. Throwing a surprise party for your friend is a lovely idea, but if you are doing it for the recognition, your intentions are still wrong.

Mantras are mainly connected to yoga, meditation, and spiritual practises and these are good places to start, because you are in the right setting. But the ultimate goal is to practise mantras in our daily lives so that we can develop higher awareness and optimise our karma. As karma is a continuous cycle, we need to use mantras more frequently than our weekly yoga class.

There are four different types of karma. which are then defined in 148 subtypes. The four types are:

- **Sanchita karma**- the karma that has accumulated over

all our previous lives (Hindus believe that the soul returns to the physical realm in a new body after death).

- **Prarabdha karma**- the karma from our present birth. It cannot be changed, as its built into who we are from birth.
- **Agami karma**- the karmic results from our willing actions. These actions impact our future karmic returns.
- **Kriyamana karma**- the more immediate results from our actions.

The subtypes range from higher to lower. Higher karmas are associated with the soul, knowledge and perception. Lower karmas include emotions, fear, anger, and false beliefs.

When we suffer from problems in our lives, it's the lower karmas that take control. If we want to reach a higher place and start to enjoy life to its full potential, we need to remove the lower karmas and encourage the higher karmas. By adjusting our karmic patterns, we can start to move forward.

HOW CAN MANTRAS IMPACT KARMA?

Mantras will change our Agami karma. The correct use of mantras allows higher karma to flourish, while gradually reducing lower karma. With enough practise, we are able to eliminate the lower karma.

We have talked so far about the role of mantras in Hindu practice, but they are also important for Buddhists. In Tibetan and Chinese Buddhism, one of the most popular and powerful mantras is "Om mani padme hum".

Om Mani Padme Hum- meaning 'I prostrate to the Buddha Great Compassion/ Hail to the jewel in the Lotus'

Om Bhrum Ayu Hum No Jah- meaning 'I prostrate to the Buddha Detached Lotus One'

Om Ami Dhe Wa Hrih- meaning 'I prostrate to the Buddha Limitless Illumination'

The lotus is a sacred flower in both Hinduism—where it is associated with the god Vishnu and goddess Lakshmi—and Buddhism, where it is a symbol for the Buddha and for purity. According to legend, the Buddha's first steps made lotus flowers appear wherever he trod. It is an aquatic flower, and it floats to the surface of water, so it symbolises elevation above material attachment and physical desire.

When combined, these three mantras are the ultimate way of destroying all negative karma. If you are still relatively new to using mantras, it might be worth starting with one and then building up to the mighty three. Even one of the mantras will start removing negativity and some believe that this can be carried on into future lives. It will open up your inner mind and help you to reach a higher state of being.

MANTRAS FOR MENTAL WELLBEING

Like so many people, I felt like I was plagued by stress and problems and it was a huge upheaval just to try to organise my mind. I didn't want to try medication and I wasn't the type of person to discuss my problems with a specialist. My yoga instructor had briefly taught us how mantras would improve our physical and mental wellbeing, and this was enough to spark an interest for me to investigate further.

The twenty-first century has seen an abundance of studies connecting mantras to psychological wellbeing. One that caught my eye was from the US-based Alzheimer's Research and Prevention Foundation and involved Kirtan Kriya, a type of meditation. It is Sanskrit song that is used in conjunction with finger positions for each syllable in the mantra, Saa Taa Naa Maa.

Saa, Taa, Naa, Maa- meaning 'my true essence'

Kirtan Kriya, when practised over an eight-week period, improved the psycho-emotional and cognitive health of a trial group of subjects with mild cognitive impairment, decreasing tension, hostility, confusion and anxiety levels.

As I read about the benefits of these four simple sounds, I felt as if they would provide the help I needed to start overcoming my problems. I included Kirtan Kriya as part of my morning meditation ritual and soon noticed that the outside world was becoming less of a burden, and although, at first, the negative thoughts still rose up in my mind, I was better prepared to not let them affect me.

If you don't feel a connection with Kirtan Kriya, you could also try the following:

Om Gum Ganapatayei Namaha- meaning 'salutations to the remover of obstacles'

Om Shanti Om- meaning 'infinite peace'

Bear in mind that though you will probably feel the psychological benefits fairly quickly, our problems, like karma, are cyclical, so it is best to keep practicing your chosen mantra, even when you feel that your problems have been resolved. Our journey to higher self-awareness is a continuous one.

DEFINING OUR GOALS FOR A BETTER LIFE

The old saying, "you only have one life" is a bit of a contradiction when talking about Hinduism, but for the sake of this part of the book, we are going to focus on the life we are leading at present. It's true that only with age do we generally start to appreciate the fact that we need to get the most out of this life. Time slips by and before we know it, we have sent a large portion of life doing what is expected of us, rather than what we actually want. Generally speaking, our goals will change with time. Who didn't want to be rich when they were growing up? As adults, the goal might shift to 'financial stability'.

In Hindu teachings, there are four main goals according to Vedic tradition that can be found in the Upanishads. They are collectively known as Purushartha, which is a concept that helps us determine our purpose in life. In order to achieve the four goals, excellent health is required.

Purushartha- meaning 'primaeval human being as the soul and original source of the universe' (Purusha) and 'purpose' (artha)

Arogya translates as 'without disease' and refers to the good health we require in order to go about our daily lives and for us to have a greater experience of life. A healthy lifestyle leads to a healthier body and mind. A healthy mind is necessary for the ability to think clearly about the goals we have in our life. For our physical health, we have to appreciate a zest for life and the energy we need to achieve our goals.

The main focus of this book is to reduce our ailments, and promote a healthier self all round, which is why the mantras are related to Arogya. That being said, I want to provide some background into mantras for the four goals of Vedic tradition, because you might find ties between the health and other goals, which are not limited to reduced stress when we are able to solve some of our financial issues.

WHAT ARE THE FOUR GOALS OF PURUSHARTHA?

Dharma- the goals related to our life purpose. They include our responsibilities, laws, and the proper way of living. The point of Dharma is to use the laws and structures in the world to reduce the chaos and remind yourself of who you truly are. It teaches you to be aware of your words, actions, and thoughts, highlighting the importance of karma.

Artha- related to material and financial prosperity and incorporates our career or how we earn our living. Artha incorporates human dignity and having sufficient material goods to enjoy a fruitful life, but not to lead us to become greedy. Artha is about finding a career that both serves the community and makes you happy.

Kama- the pleasure acquired through non-material gain, our happiness, love, and the enjoyment of life. It's the beauty of life that we seek to find in art, literature and music. It is also the beauty we seek in relationships and intimacy. You might have associated the name with Kama Sutra, and while we can still experience pleasure from sex, the Kama Sutra is about experiencing sexual pleasure rather than being a how-to guide.

Moksha- the freedom we seek to live and liberation from the cycle of death and rebirth so that we can reach our potential.

Originally, there were only Dharma, Artha, and Kama in the Vedic scriptures and in many ways they entwined and one may depend on the other. Later on, Moksha was introduced as a way to balance the connection between the three earlier concepts. When you follow all of the values of the Purusharthas, you will be able to assess your current situation and make better decisions for your life.

HOW CAN THE PURUSHARTHAS BENEFIT YOUR LIFE?

Take a moment now to review your goals, and you must be honest. Don't adjust your goals so that they fit into one of the four goals mentioned above. This isn't a test to see if you pass or fail. Some people don't have clearly defined goals, or they assume that goals just apply to the grander aspects of life. Think about what you want to achieve or gain to make you happier.

We will use the example of 'Jessica' to put things into context.

Jessica is a 57-year-old teacher who wants to lose weight. She is completely stressed out at work because of senior staff telling her how to run a classroom. Her goals are to retire in 3 years and go to the gym three times a week, and she also wants to decorate her bedroom, but has very little time to do it.

Jessica's goals are what she thinks will make her happy, and on a superficial level, they will. But there is no balance between the goals, so it will be difficult for her to improve herself as a whole. Once she has retired and decorated her bedroom, what will she be left with? Her job is one that contributes greatly to society, but it no longer makes her happy. A fresh coat of paint and some new sheets on the bed are certainly not too much to ask and won't make her greedy. She will appreciate the beauty of her room, but it's unlikely that this will aid her in discovering the beauty of the world.

For Jessica to find inner happiness and peace and to discover purpose in her life, she will need to reassess her goals in order to make sure they incorporate Dharma, Artha, Kama, Moksha, and of course Arogya for the mental and physical strength to bring to light all of her new goals.

Before you begin to practice mantras to accomplish your goals, you need to ensure that there are objectives for each of the five elements. Begin by writing the five words (Dharma, Artha, Kama, Moksha, and Arogya) on a piece of paper. See where your current goals fit and try to expand on them so that you have a balance of all five.

A MANTRA FOR EACH OF YOUR GOALS

Mantra masters encourage repeating a mantra 108 times between sunrise and sunset. Don't feel that you have to do this in one sitting. Some people will spread this out into two or three meditative sessions throughout the day. The most important thing is that your goals are clear and balanced and that the mantra you choose can be incorporated into your daily life.

Dharma

To discover your purpose in life, you first need to remove the obstacles that are blocking your path. Ganesh is a Hindu deity and the remover of obstacles. There is no coincidence that in some parts of India, Ganesh is thought to be married to Buddhi (intelligence) Siddhi (success), and Riddhi (prosperity).

Om Gum Shreem Maha Lakshmiyei Namaha- meaning pure force (Om), removal of obstacles (gum), the sound of abundance (shreem), increased energy (maha), life purpose (lakshmiyei), and completion (namaha)

Artha

For prosperity, there is a popular mantra that is actually a prayer to the earth goddess, Vasundhara, the divine female or the bearer of treasure. It is also commonly known as the Buddha money mantra.

Om Vasudhare Svha- meaning 'stream of treasure'

While being blessed with prosperity and wealth, the ancient teachings were not designed for you to win the lottery. You should be blessed with enough to let you follow your spiritual goals without distractions from financial issues.

Kama

For increased pleasure as well as peace of mind and even reducing sins, this mantra has various translations relating to the adoration of Lord Shiva.

Om Namah Shivaya- meaning 'O salutations to the auspicious one'

In Hinduism, Lord Shiva is one of the three most important gods. His role is to destroy the universe so that it can be recreated. He is also the patron of yogis and the protector of the Vedas.

Moksha

Becoming free and liberating yourself makes space for superior knowledge. This mantra isn't only about freedom, but it is also a message about how we treat others. It highlights karma and the fact that our thoughts, words, and actions should bring happiness into our lives and the lives of those who share our universe.

Lokah Samastah Sukhino Bhavantu- meaning 'may all beings be free and happy'

In Western philosophies, we probably use the phrase 'treat others as you would want to be treated'. You can see how the Moksha mantra can be used for more than one aspect of your goals.

AROGYA: MANTRAS FOR HEALING

When we talk about healing, we could mean a great number of different things. You might have the flu or a backache. You could be suffering from depression or addiction. Your healing might be for something obvious, or something subtle, and it could be something general or specific. So, when it comes to healing mantras, there are plenty.

Remember that the chakra mantras we have discussed are also used in healing. If you feel that you are lacking a sexual appetite, the "Yam" mantra will help to unblock your Sacral Chakra, allowing you to heal. With other healing mantras, you can use a specific sound that will correct the imbalance in that area, for example:

> "Mmmmm"- the vibrations are directed towards the
>   sinuses
> "Nnnnnn"- to alleviate problems with your ears
> "Eeemmm"- for problems related to the eyes
> "Gaa Gha" - to heal your throat
> "Yaa Yu Yai" – this will help with any issues in the jaw

Alternatively, the five vowel sounds are non-local, which means you can choose one and mentally send the vibrations to the area of the body that requires healing. You will notice that although there are longer mantras for healing, most of them are Bija mantras, the seeds we need to replenish our health and align our energies.

Longer mantras do exist, even as long as thirty or more syllables and needless to say, to repeat these 108 times takes almost an hour. I discovered a healing mantra that ticked all of my boxes, and probably will for you too:

> Om Ram Ramaya Namaha- meaning 'relieve pain, deep healing'

This is actually a Rama mantra and Ram is also the seed sound for the Solar Plexus Chakra, which unlocks a large amount of dormant energy.

Another benefit of this healing mantra is that as a Rama mantra, it has great power in uncovering negative karma and eliminating it.

Without wanting to sound like a broken record, these mantras are only ideas. If you hear a mantra that has a striking significance to your goal, then you should use it over the ones mentioned. Mantras are very personal and although many can be used for different purposes, it's the person who is using them who must understand the purpose.

As soon as I figured out my new set of goals and began using specific mantras, I noticed something that went beyond healing. My husband commented that I was more communicative, not about my day or what had happened with the kids, but about my feelings. This is something that had probably been blocked before. It didn't mean that I was spreading my negativity—quite the opposite. I started to talk about the holidays we could take together, new restaurants we could try. It was when he mentioned this that I realized that I was beginning to see life from a different point of view. It wasn't a certain number of years that we had to try to survive, but instead a gift that we could use in any way we wanted to.

A MODERN TAKE ON MANTRAS

There is no doubt that as mantras have become more popular in Western cultures, they have been adapted and perhaps to an extent, modernised. This has included translations into English

We also live in a world where results are required almost instantly and not everyone has the time to learn about the philosophy behind a new concept. Personally, I found that using mantras in Sanskrit opened my eyes to the culture and I felt more connected to the traditions of Hinduism, Buddhism, and Eastern philosophies that I learnt about.

Nevertheless, I appreciate that not everyone has the time to Google Translate every Sanskrit mantra that they come across. Not only this, but there are also mantras that can't be directly translated or that may have two translations with similar meanings.

HOW ARE ENGLISH AND SANSKRIT DIFFERENT?

You probably think I have lost the plot bringing up such an obvious question, but the answer is more about their purpose than what you see on paper.

English and Sanskrit were constructed for very different reasons. Sound and oral communication were valued qualities in ancient India, so in Sanskrit, the sound of the word mattered, rather than just the semantic meaning. In English, each word has a purpose. In Sanskrit, each sound has a purpose. The alphabet, words and grammar of the vernacular languages of the region (*Prakritic* languages) were polished quite deliberately into a more refined form in Sanskrit. Professor Shlomo Biderman of Tel Aviv University's School of Languages describes Sanskrit as a 'collection of sounds, a kind of sublime musical mold'. The perfection of language through Sanskrit was viewed as part and parcel of the perfection of thought that could lead to spiritual liberation. Sanskrit also became a language of the social and political elite, and the language developed over time. The earlier Sanskrit found in the Rigveda was further refined and homogenised into a stricter grammatical form, known as classical Sanskrit, by about the first century before the Common Era.

A lot of the mantras we have already seen are clear examples of how Sanskrit and English vary, particularly in sounds and syllables. Here is another of the most powerful mantras.

Nam Myōhō Renge Kyō – meaning 'devotion to the Mystic Laws of the Lotus Sutra', or 'glory to the Dharma of the Lotus Sutra'.

Nam Myōhō Renge Kyō is a five-syllable chant. The English equivalents have twelve or fourteen syllables, depending on the translation.

How Are English and Sanskrit Similar?

One of the oldest written languages in the world, Sanskrit descended from the ancient Proto-Indo-European language. Classical Latin, Germanic language and Old Norse belong to the same language family, ultimately sharing the same ancestor language. As a Germanic language, English is also part of the Indo-European language family, so is a very distant relative of Sanskrit. In addition, a small number of words of Sanskrit origin have made it into the English dictionary. These include 'cheetah' (meaning 'uniquely marked'), 'avatar' (meaning 'descent'), 'bandana' (meaning 'a bond'), as well as of course some terms we have been using, such as yoga and karma.

The English language has very rich and complex vowel sounds. With twenty vowel sounds (*phonemes*) in total, it is one of the most intricate spoken languages in the world. With such an extensive range of sounds, English is almost the logical language to choose over Sanskrit.

If you look at the following list of Sanskrit words and their English translations, you will see how there are clear links between the two.

Gau- cow
Matr- mother
Navagatha- navigation
Manu- man
Danta- dental

Naama- name

Maha- mega

That being said, a fat-free donut just isn't a donut, and while mantras in English can still have a profound impact, they will never be quite as powerful as those in the original Sanskrit. Let's take a look at how we can use the English language to gain personal empowerment.

HOW ARE AFFIRMATIONS DIFFERENT TO MANTRAS?

Affirmations are short expressions that have a powerful meaning to the speaker. By repeating an affirmation, you are able to tap into your conscious mind and alter your way of thinking and your behaviour. Affirmations are generally used along with positive mental imagery of the words you are saying.

"I think, therefore I am"

— *COINED BY RENÉ DESCARTES*

Descartes used this phrase as a way to prove his existence when others tried to convince him differently. Today this has become an affirmation used for a number of different reasons and can be adapted for any speaker. If you need to become more confident, you would repeat the words and imagine yourself full of self-esteem. When your brain hears it enough, it starts to act in this way. This affirmation can be used for people who want to improve their physical appearance, become stronger, more content, or more relaxed.

The majority of our daily thoughts are often negative. If we think of our perspectives in this way, we can see that we could all benefit from choosing an affirmation.

The main difference between an affirmation and a mantra is that when using an affirmation, it is the words that provide power and energy, rather than the sounds and vibrations. Although, that's not to say that the vibrations won't help.

HOW CAN YOU BENEFIT FROM AFFIRMATIONS?

In many ways, the benefits of affirmations are similar to those of mantras. They can be used to find motivation, whether that's for large or small activities. How many times have you got off the sofa saying "I can do this" as you look at the mountain of ironing? While providing you with energy to overcome the woes of day-to-day life, they can also make you more active about personal development and the transformation of yourself and the world around you.

By activating a more positive brain, affirmations will help you to see the world differently. The person you have been putting off seeing all of a sudden doesn't appear to be that bad. In turn, communication becomes easier, and even more enjoyable.

With the additional energy and motivation that you discover from using affirmations, you will be able to tackle your goals with more gusto. Your goals become easier to achieve as concentration is elevated. As you become more open, you can meet new people, and as your circle of friends grows, you benefit from more wisdom and more connections that will also help you to reach your goals.

When I first started to use affirmations, I was reminded of the infamous scene from the film, *Jerry Maguire*. This film left us with a legacy of affirmations, the most obvious being "Show me the money". Tom Cruise starts the film being stressed and unwilling to play the game, uttering the words with a complete lack of spirit. Even Cuba Gooding Jr. claims that this is a very personal and important thing for him. As Cruise is forced to repeat the four words, he becomes louder, more convincing, and more determined, finally reaching his goal.

Relax, there is no need for you to shout your affirmations to the world—unless, of course, you want to. But I liked the scene, because it was a clip that many of us can relate to, moving from frustration to achievement with the help of simple words.

HOW TO USE AFFIRMATIONS IN YOUR DAILY LIFE

There are so many affirmations to choose from; some are longer, others shorter. Like mantras, it is important that you choose affirmations that ring true to you. Discover what you want to gain from your affirmation before you begin your search. Keep the ones you like; discard the ones you don't. Even if you start with an affirmation and you feel like it doesn't strike the right chord, don't be worried about changing it. Here are some ideas for inspiration:

- I love my job and the tasks I perform
- I am valued
- I am loving and lovable

- Life is full of love and I find it everywhere I go
- I love everything about my body
- Everything I think, say, and do makes me healthier
- I am enthusiastic about every second of my life
- I am beautiful
- I set myself free

If you feel that you have multiple areas that you need to work on, you can choose two or three affirmations to create a set, but again, make sure each one is specific to a certain area. If you are new to affirmations, stick to one to start with, so that you can focus more easily.

Affirmations need to be repeated daily and with consistency, so it is important to try to incorporate them into your daily routine. It could be as you exercise, shower, drive to work, or any time that you have five or ten minutes without interruptions (so keep the mobile away from you).

It is always best to repeat your affirmations in at least two sessions. I find the best time of the day for the first set is first thing in the morning, as the first thing you tend to do is start thinking about your goals for that day, so this way, you can begin with a positive mind.

The time I like to say the second set is just before going to bed. It was that time of the day when I used to struggle with anxiety, and this would lead to a sleepless night. If you repeat your affirmations before going to sleep, they become ingrained in your subconscious while your mind is resting.

Keep going for at least thirty days. By then, you will be comfortable with your words and will have found the best times to repeat them. At this point, they will have become as natural as brushing your teeth and easier to maintain in the long run.

AFFIRMATIONS TO STEER CLEAR OF

You may talk to a few friends about how you want to use affirmations and naturally, they may want to help and could mention a few that they have heard. The first suggestion is "I will be happy". The problem here is that the affirmation is in the future, and your subconscious doesn't understand this.

Our subconscious works in the present and has no concept of the past or the future. Even if your goal is to be happy in the future, you need to use the present tense so that your subconscious understands that this is happening now. If you hear an affirmation that you like but is in the past or the future, keep the same vocabulary and change it into the present.

Another problem I have come across is that some people use negative affirmations. Even to the untrained eye, this seems illogical. Unless your goal is to become weak, repeating the words "I am weak" is only going to reduce your strength. Choose affirmations that are positive, that make you smile, or that make you feel warm inside. A good affirmation should make you feel like you can climb Everest.

HOW CAN YOU FIND THE RIGHT MANTRAS WHEN YOU DON'T HAVE A FAITH?

Not everyone believes in one god or many gods. Whether you believe that a man sits in heaven watching down on us, or that the gods are walking among us, or that there is nothing beyond what we experience in this life, there is a mantra for you.

There are even Buddhist teachers who recommend mantras for those who don't belong to any faith. Animals too have been known anecdotally to heal from mantras. We can only assume that animals are not concentrating on the sounds of the mantra, which suggests that mantras will have a positive affect even for those who don't consciously believe in a higher being. This has further encouraged the use of mantras in the modern world.

I am trying not to influence your mantra decision in any way, but I do have one particular non-religious favourite that people often feel comfortable saying:

`Lokah Samastah Sukhino Bhavantu- meaning 'may all beings everywhere be happy and free'

The following two non-religious mantras can be used to instil confidence and self-belief, or to liberate yourself from the mental or physical problems you are facing:

So Hum- meaning 'I am that'
Om Gate Gate Para Gate Para Sam Gate Bodhi Swaha- meaning 'gone, gone, way gone, beyond gone, awake, so be it'

The ancient traditions of Hinduism are closing the gap between science and medicine and allowing people to improve their physical and mental health regardless of their stand in society, their age, gender, or beliefs.

DECIDING WHAT TO SAY WHEN YOU MEDITATE

We have touched on this before, but it's an area to revisit, because the more you read on it, the more insight you will gain into finding mantras that work for you. We know that mantras have to be for a specific purpose and used with focus. And we have reassessed our goals in life and chosen mantras that will help us to achieve them. It is also necessary that your mantras are in line with your personal and religious beliefs.

Many people start to feel overwhelmed when it comes to finding a mantra, like they are about to take an exam or like the rest of their life depends on it. Granted, your life will be greatly impacted, but there is not a single mantra that is going to harm you. Deciding on the right words, you will enable yourself to feel a stronger connection to what is important in life.

To help you choose the right mantras, I have put together a list of related vocabulary for various mantra purposes. Each group is based on common issues we face or goals that we want to achieve. This is by no means a complete list, but just another tool for inspiration.

Mental wellbeing—stable mindset /emotional stability /inner balance /mental balance /health of mind /peace of mind /mental soundness

Physical wellbeing—physical form /body state /physical condition /fitness /physical status /weight /ache /pain /physical suffering

Career vocabulary—employer /employee /work skill /qualifications /ethics /values/ income /salary /learning styles /time management /promotion /career ladder

Relationships—partner /family /friends /love /marriage /communication /ties /loved ones /romance /kinship /bonds /matters of the heart /commitment /faith /security

Tangible and non-tangible attainment—fulfilment /realization /winning /acquirement / completion /gain / reap the efforts /reap the rewards

Higher state of being—higher power /spirituality /subconscious /inner thoughts /empowerment /acceptance /liberty /wisdom

Stress—anxiety /nerves /patience /lack of hope /depression /strain /worry /unease /irritation /sadness /guilt

These words should start you on your path to understanding what your mantra should be for. It should have the same effect as your favourite song—calming, motivational, inspiring and happy. It might be the words that you connect with or the rhythm, but as soon as you hear it, you feel the benefits.

CREATING YOUR OWN MANTRA

Because what holds us back is often very individual, you might find you need your own mantra. You may have been searching for a while and found that the mantras are too specific, or not specific enough. Your mantra should represent the way you want to live your life, acting as a sign of your values and ethics that are related to your goals.

Anything can be a mantra—a set of words, sounds, hums, so there is no reason for you not to blend your own words for the perfect, unique mantra. You may find you can combine words from the different lists if they work to achieve one purpose; for example, "I have the confidence to carry out my work". Notice that this is still a specific mantra with a motive.

Regardless of whether you choose Sanskrit or English mantras, you should focus on the individual sounds of each syllable. Appreciate the vibrations and imagine the area of the body that is healing.

Mantras shouldn't be distracting, which is why, ideally, they are kept short. It shouldn't be difficult to remember a mantra, as the words and sounds are supposed to be natural. Chanting your mantra aloud will help to centre your concentration. Chanting in silence brings forward a greater sense of peace. It's a personal preference and there is no right or wrong way.

A summary of what to remember when creating your mantra:

- They must ring true to you and be used for a specific purpose
- Mantras should be in line with your goals and your beliefs
- They should bring you peace, motivation, and happiness
- They should be short and contain either words or sounds
- They need to be in the present tense and positive
- You can be sitting or lying, chanting, or in silence; it's most important that you are comfortable

- Mantras will be most beneficial when you use them consistently and incorporate them into your daily life

When I created my own mantra, I decided I wanted a combination of the ancient and the modern. Sanskrit gave me a deeper connection with the philosophy and original teachings. At the same time, I had found a lovely English mantra that helped me to pull my attention to the present and appreciate just being:

"Om Shanti, I am here"

This was the first mantra I developed for myself. It was the starting place for my own journey. Using mantras before had most definitely helped me get out of the rut that I was in and helped me feel more positive. It was true that I was beginning to appreciate the simple things in life, like the warmth of the sun on my face. When my children started to argue, I used to get frustrated and escalate the situation, but now I just feel grateful that I have children, as others can't. It wasn't until I started repeating my own mantra that I felt that instead of following other people's paths, I was creating my own, and I needed this to discover my purpose in life.

THE SIGNIFICANCE OF LANGUAGE AND INTENTION WHEN USING MANTRAS

For me, it's quite upsetting that the language of Sanskrit is slowly becoming extinct. I have had the privilege of being able to travel quite a bit in my life and I find that exploring the less touristy areas really forces you to try to speak even a few words of the language. It provides a closer connection and appreciation of the culture. Going to China and ordering fried rice is no different than popping down to your local takeaway, until you try saying 'Chaofan'.

Travelling through India, Thailand and Sri Lanka probably allowed me to learn more about mantras than I ever would from trying to learn by myself. This is not because I took part in classes or had one-on-ones with yogis and buddhas willing to share their wisdom, but because I had the opportunity to experience the languages of those countries.

In 2011, it was estimated that Sanskrit was spoken by less than 1% of the Indian population and mostly used by Hindu priests.

It is only the official language in one Indian state. This decline is not new, starting in the eleventh century, if not before, and linguists believe that Sanskrit was never ubiquitous across all of India. Nonetheless, given its supposed spiritual importance and power in mantras, it makes me sad to think that Sanskrit might die out altogether.

Hearing this, I felt a sudden urge to learn at least some Sanskrit in a naïve attempt to spread the word and keep the language alive. In this chapter, I want to follow up on the importance of correct pronunciation of mantras so that the most can be gained from each one, so that you too can get a touch of the culture, and so that the strong traditions can continue to be passed on from person to person as they were intended to be.

It was my first trip that filled me with determination and enthusiasm, though I will confess, I soon reverted back to the shy student from school who couldn't pronounce a single word in French. I am going to assume that you aren't one of the less than 1% who speak Sanskrit, and it is quite possible that you will feel the same way as I did when learning how to pronounce mantras. The trick is to overcome your fear of getting it wrong. As with meditation and yoga, the Sanskrit pronunciation takes a little time to perfect.

WHY IS SANSKRIT PRONUNCIATION SO IMPORTANT?

We have already touched on this, so now you know that if your yoga instructor is stringing together a bunch of sounds, there is actually great significance behind them. Each sound in a mantra will produce a vibration that leads to healing a certain area or help you to reach a particular goal. Our Chinese example of fried rice (*Chaofan*) is also slang for "have sex" in Cantonese. The wrong pronunciation or even intention could lead you to get something you hadn't expected!

Sanskrit has been regarded by Hindus as the language of the gods, and this might put some people off from the start. It is necessary that we understand the translation so that we can select the right mantra, but it is also important to remember that you aren't necessarily praying. Look at it like how some say, "Thank God". They aren't literally thanking God: they are expressing relief.

In a way, mantras are the same. If you want to connect with the gods, the best way is to use the oldest, divine language. On the other hand, each letter or bija is created by a sound, and it's the sound that we will focus on, rather than the words.

What I am trying to say, without offending the religious or the non-religious, is that although some of the most powerful mantras were originally prayers, they also serve another purpose. Whether you want to practice because of curiosity, spiritual enlightenment, healing, or just to escape from the turmoil of life, it's the sounds and vibrations that we are going to concentrate on.

SHOULD YOU CHANT MANTRAS?

There is no simple answer to this. I know from experience that in the beginning, you feel a bit of a fool, especially if you are practising as part of a group. I can also tell you that silent mantras encourage a greater sense of peace. Finally, I can reiterate that Hinduism encourages students to find their own path and so nobody will tell you whether you should or shouldn't chant.

While yogis and even advanced students are able to benefit from Nada yoga, it does require more concentration. Nada yoga uses the power of sound or the conscious use of sound. Instead of words, the person pays close attention to every sound they hear while meditating, from the sound of your breathing to a footstep in the distance. Nada yoga is about inner sound rather than a chant.

Nada- meaning Sound

Traditionally, mantras were meant to be spoken, some even sung with music. It is how they still remain so meaningful today in a language that is far from common. Your body and mind will be able to absorb the vibration without a conscious effort to direct the sounds.

Take the words "We will, we will, rock you". Read them in your head as you would any other written sentence. Now read them aloud. Which feels more powerful? Which gives you more motivation or gives you a greater 'can do' attitude? Now hum the tune and focus on getting the exact pitch. Notice how even humming the right tune makes you feel better than simply saying the words in your mind. This is the reason that despite experience, I still chant mantras.

HOW TO PRONOUNCE SANSKRIT WORDS

If you have ever seen the International Phonetic alphabet (a little bit like Jolly Phonics in schools) you will know that each sound is represented by a symbol. The pronunciation of a word is transcribed between two forward slashes. When you translate a word online you have probably seen the forward slashes and symbols.

Vowels

In English, there are long vowel sounds and short vowel sounds, as with Sanskrit. The long vowel sounds have a colon after them. So, the word ship is represented as /ʃɪp/, with a short vowel sound. Whereas sheep is /ʃiːp/. In Sanskrit, the long vowel sound is represented with a macron (horizontal line) above. The Sanskrit i is produced like the English i in bit. The Sanskrit ī is longer, as in the i in twice.

Diphthongs are blends of two vowel sounds. Here are some examples of Sanskrit diphthongs:

- e- /ei/ like in wait
- ai- /ai/ like in my
- o- /əʊ/ like in show
- au- /aʊ/ like in cow

Consonants

Retroflex sounds are consonant sounds that are made with the tip of the tongue rolled back towards the top palate. This produces a deeper sound than is found in English. The positioning of the tongue in this way isn't used in English and it might take a while to get the hang of. Let's look at some words to help:

- d- /d/- like in dog
- n- /n/- like in never

Then there are what's known as the dental sounds. Here, the tongue is very close to the front teeth and you may even detect a vibration that you wouldn't in English.

- t- /t/ like in team
- n- /n/- like in never

Notice that the t, n, and d can either be retroflex or dental and you can tell the difference with the Sanskrit symbols:

- त् - the dental t, ट - the retroflex t

Other sounds

When an r is followed by another consonant in Sanskrit, it is pronounced as /ri/. The first sound in the word Vrksansana would be said like /vrik/.

Sh and Sa are both pronounced in the same way (one less to remember): /sh/ like shoot or shut.

Va is pronounced the same way as we would in English, for example, vain, unless it is followed by a consonant, when it can sometimes be pronounced like a w. The Sanskrit word for master is svāmi and it could be pronounced as svami or swami.

Words that contain pha or bha are also pronounced in the same way and with an exhale on the p sound—imagine you are saying pathetic.

Luckily, there are also a good number of sounds that we would pronounce in the same way as in English, such as k, g, ch, and j, sky, chain, god and jump. It is also worth bearing in mind that there will be different native pronunciation depending on regional dialects.

HOW IMPORTANT ARE THESE SOUNDS?

Very important! Just as they are in English. Sheet has a long vowel sound, but for a foreign speaker who pronounces it as a short sound, they may well make a bit of a social blunder. The Sanskrit short *i* vowel is used to enhance energy, focused around the right eye, and to encourage will power. The long *i* vowel is concentrated around the left eye and helps with emotions, creativity, and understanding. Once again, it goes back to the purpose of the mantra and each sound that is produced.

THE INTENTIONS OF MANTRAS

In Hinduism, all matter in the universe comes from Prakriti, a fundamental layer that provides us with three qualities of energy known as gunas and all three are constantly present in the living. Our energy, matter, and consciousness can be altered depending on our thoughts and actions.

Prakriti- meaning nature

Sattva, Rajas, and Tamas are the three gunas that we are able to control, but we can never completely remove one. We can, however, use yoga, meditation, and mantras to adjust the gunas and as a guide to achieving a better understanding of ourselves and the universe.

Sattva is a state of harmony. It is the intelligence we are able to acquire and the pleasure we get in giving. Sattva is also associated with liberation, kindness, helpfulness, love, and a sense of balance. It's the gratitude we feel and the self-control we have. We should intend to enhance our sattva, as it will diminish the other gunas.

Rajas is a state of action and change. It's one that is easy to understand, as it is what draws us to our careers, but unfortunately, it is reaped with worry, stress, irritation and aggression and it is also linked to the chaos we have to try to survive.

Tamas is a state of inertia. It fills us with self-doubt and guilt, and it is what makes us ignorant. Laziness, boredom, addiction and apathy all arise from Tamas. When you feel like you are lacking energy, or you are confused and hurt, it means that Tamas has too strong a hold on you.

It is easy to say that tomorrow I am going to wake up in a better mood. "I will be more positive." We are hoping that Sattva will be more present. And while you don't literally cry over the spilt milk that didn't make it into the coffee, the first sign of a bad day and your good intentions disappear.

Mantras can be used for good and for bad. There are some people who will practice Tamasic mantras in order to manipulate others or even for destructive purposes. No, it's not black magic, but it does appeal to the dramatic side of some people. While negative energy may be projected onto others, it may also bounce straight back to you and increase your negative karma, so it is highly recommended not to practise these mantras.

Rajasic mantras are used for gaining status, money, career opportunities, and they will feed the ego. You still need to be careful with these intentions, as although your goal might be to improve your career, it is possible that there will be a negative impact on your karma.

With the help of Sattvic mantras, we can focus on the fundamental things we need in our lives—a roof over our heads, our family around us, freedom and good health. When you are choosing your mantras, always make sure that there is good intention behind them.

Sattvic Samkalpa- meaning 'good intention'

Our use of mantras should not only be with good intentions for ourselves but also for others. Your spiritual path or the journey to your inner self will be more fruitful when you can help others along the way, and this will help with your good karma too.

Fun fact: to increase your sattva, it is worth trying to adjust your diet. Try to decrease your meat intake as well as your consumption of processed foods, stimulants and hotly spiced foods. Replace them with whole grains and fresh fruit and vegetables, and when possible, those that are grown above ground.

Your lifestyle plays a crucial role in the balance of the gunas. Overworking and even taking part in excessive amounts of exercise and listing to loud music can increase your rajas, while overeating, sleeping for too long and living in fear will increase the tamas, neither of which is what you should be aiming for.

HOW LONG SHOULD YOU USE MANTRAS FOR?

This is another question that doesn't have a simple answer. Most of the traditional mantras are repeated 108 times. The number 108 is a sacred number in Hinduism, not only for the distances in our solar system but also because there are 108 sacred sites in India, 108 Upanishads, and 108 scared places of the body (marma points). 'Japa' refers to a type of meditation which requires the repetition of mantras a certain number of times.

In my early days, I felt it was impossible to keep count. It was like trying to count sheep while trying to sleep. I would get to the thirties and my mind would start to drift, debating whether or not I had missed one. That was when I was introduced to malas. A mala is a string of beads. Different malas have different numbers of beads, typically 108, 54 or 27. These beads are a tool that helps you to follow the number of times you have said your mantra, without focusing on the actual number. You simply slide your finger over a bead.

Mala- meaning 'garland' or 'wreath'

A mala is very similar to a rosary in Christianity. Some historians believe that when the Romans explored India, they came across the words 'jap mala'. As 'jap' meant rose to the Romans, then mala became the rosarium and, as English developed, rosary. An alternative theory that rosary derived from the French, 'rosaire', as in a rose garden, as a figurative term for a sacred and beautiful collection of prayers. What is certainly true is that malas, prayer beads, have a very long history in India.

Like a rosary, the mala will have a head bead, known as the 'guru' or 'meru'. The guru bead can represent a higher power for some. Others see it as the greater connection to the universe. One common rule is that the guru bead is never counted, and therefore it is the 109th bead. The guru bead is rotated when the japa is complete, so the person knows to start the process again.

When I was travelling, I was tempted by beautiful beads and my eye would fall on the materials and colours that I liked. But needless to say, the material of which the beads are made also has its own purpose and intention. I used this as the perfect excuse to start an amazing collection! Moonstone is a good material choice if you are looking to calm your emotions, onyx for self-confidence, and rose quartz helps to remove negative energy.

Colour can have an effect too. Purple represents spiritual values, yellow inspires creativity, and orange will help you to find more enthusiasm for things. Obviously, malas are going to be a huge benefit in helping you to focus. My advice would be to have your intentions clear before finding out the best colour and material for your mala.

The other thing that will determine the length of time is how many mantras you have chosen, and whether you want to use one mantra or a combination. Ideally, you should aim for two sessions a day of about ten to fifteen minutes—don't worry if it's less or more. But please make sure you are giving yourself enough time to complete the correct number of japas. Each repetition should be slow and calm, and you can't speed up towards the end as you see the hands on the clock spinning round.

PREPARING TO START YOUR MANTRAS

The time has finally arrived! You have reassessed your goals and you have a clear idea of your intentions. You have either selected a mantra that you feel a connection with, or you have created your own. Even if you haven't found the perfect mala, there will be time for this. A plain beaded mala will serve for the right purpose. Now it is time to begin.

Decide on the right location

Half of me would giggle while the other half was envious as I looked at some of the images of mums sat in the typical yoga position with kids running around, washing flying all over the place, but they have this perfect poise about them. Perhaps those closest to attaining enlightenment may succeed in this environment, but I still find it impossible.

I need to know that the basic jobs in the house are done, at least those that you can see. Even if I'm in the living room and there are dirty dishes in the kitchen, I know I won't be able to focus.

I also find that it helps if I am alone. Not so much now, because I feel more confident, but in the beginning, there was still something that made me feel a little silly to be chanting. I suppose it's no different to the first time you run a meeting or try a new sport. Being alone removed the distractions and allowed me to really feel a connection with the sounds I was making.

I have tried sitting on a chair, standing in the tree pose, sitting crossed-legged, walking—you name it, I have tried it. I still find sitting cross-legged to bring the best benefits. It's comfortable, it improves your posture, and it allows for deep breathing. Grab a few cushions for support under your knees or ankles if you prefer.

For me, the best place is my living room or the park, as long as there aren't a lot of people around, only because I want the peace that those fifteen minutes bring. There is enough hustle and bustle in our daily lives, and this should be time for just you.

Decide on when to start

Now this is an easy question. Today, now, tonight, tomorrow morning. There is no time like the present and you already have the most important thing you need to start practising mantras —your mind. Cushions and malas will help, but if you don't have them, don't let that be an excuse not to start improving your life.

MANTRA PURUSHA AND THE BODY OF SOUND

It was so valuable for me to learn about the Sanskrit alphabet. I am by no means fluent, but the mantras I use I can use to the greatest potential because I decided to take the time to perfect the sounds. Sanskrit is a beautiful language, one of the angels and gods. It is relatively unusual as a language in that it transmits its meaning through sound and vibration, rather than placing an emphasis on the meaning of the word.

At the same time, it provides incredible healing powers and not only for those with religious beliefs. The Hindu gods will not show their wrath if you use the power of Sanskrit for healing rather than to communicate with them. While our aim is to reach enlightenment, this can mean different things to different people.

I used to think that enlightenment was a mental state that allowed a level of spirituality that was closest to God. It was something that was almost unattainable, for not even the Dalai

Lama was there yet. If he hadn't reached this spiritual bliss, then what hope did I have?

Then I felt the need to decide what enlightenment meant to me. The word itself made me feel that it was about lightening my load. And this was one of my main intentions, not to palm my responsibilities off to other people, but to mentally relieve some of the things that were weighing down on me.

Another of my intentions was to learn more about myself. Without sounding theatrical, I wanted to learn what my life was about, what I hoped to achieve from it, and what I was still capable of achieving, so enlightenment also became about self-realization. Because mantras don't require a religious belief, I appreciated that this was how I was going to improve my physical self and achieve my own definition of enlightenment. We have briefly talked about chakras and how each area has a mantra that will increase the energy flow into the spinning chakra. In this chapter, we are going to look at Mantra Purusha and the joining of the healing belief of the mantras with marma therapy.

WHAT ARE MARMAS?

Ayurveda, meaning 'knowledge of life', is the traditional Hindu system of medicine. It defines 'marma' as a medical term referring to the vital parts of the body. Marmas can be categorized as relating to muscles, veins, ligament, bone and joints and each one is located at junction points in the body, where two or more meet, for example, the wrist, neck, elbow, knees, even finger joints. When using mantras for marma therapy, the idea is that you are able to alter frequencies in the body, which can help remove negative thoughts from the mind and improve karma and sattvic qualities.

Marma- meaning 'vital parts'

Imagine these marma points as bus stops and the passengers on the bus being the energy in your body. As the bus transports passengers around the town, it drops people off and picks others up, connecting the town. The marmas in our body help to connect the body, mind, and conscious. They join the physical and the non-physical, the matter and the energy.

A marma is not the same as an acupuncture point. There are more than 400 acupuncture points, and in China, they were traditionally believed to be minute holes in the skin that could allow energy to flow. Now they are defined as specific anatomical points. A marma is an area that can be from approximately one to four inches in size.

THE THREE ENERGIES OF EACH MARMA

All of the 108 marmas in our bodies contain three energies or doshas, Vata, Pitta and Kapha. These biological energies inside the marma are what makes us individual in terms of our mind and emotions and if you consider yourself. You may see if and how your energies are not balanced and within Ayurveda medicine, Vata, Pitta, and Kapha are incredibly important.

Dosha – Meaning 'fault' or 'disease'

The doshas are derived from the five elements: space, air, water, fire, and earth. One of the three will be more apparent, but at the same time, it is possible that you notice certain qualities from a second dosha, known as a dual-doshic constitution.

Those who have strong Vata energies have qualities that reflect the elements of space and air and will sometimes have dry skin. They usually have a slim physical appearance and fine bones. They are fast, both in the mind and with their actions. Pitta dominance will see a person who might have an oilier complexion, be warm to touch, be quick to fly off the handle, and have a fiery personality, as their elements are fire and water. Finally, Kapha represents water and earth. These individuals are calm and often have a more solid body frame and may also have an oily complexion.

Our thoughts and actions play a role in the balance, increase or decrease of our doshas. Doshas are also impacted by the food we eat and the physical activities we participate in. The ideal balance of the doshas is more often found in newborns, those who are still innocent to the negativity in the world and the attraction to the things we like that are no good for us. The more stress we find ourselves under, the greater the imbalance becomes.

During the time that I was learning about doshas, I found myself thinking how awfully I treated my body. This is not the road to go down: there is no point in feeling guilty for the bar of chocolate and the glass of wine you had last week. It does go to show, and it is worth remembering, that how we treat our body has a huge effect on our physical and mental health. We already know this: the glass of wine may have given you a hangover and made you grumpy; however, I'm referring to a bigger picture.

While there are some things we can do to help encourage a balance of the doshas—

exercise, relaxation, a balanced diet, etc.—there are other things in today's world that are almost impossible to avoid. The stress of commuting to work, getting stuck in traffic, the constant buzzing of mobile phones with things that need to be handled straight away, money, the kids... it all builds up within us and it's only when you are on the brink of burnout that you realize the extent of the imbalance.

The phone isn't going to stop ringing and the traffic, unfortunately, isn't going to just disappear. So, this is where we can use Mantra Purusha and the marmas in our body to begin to correct the imbalance of our doshas.

HOW ARE THE SANSKRIT SOUNDS RELATED TO MARMAS?

The Sanskrit alphabet reflects the prime powers of creation. Aside from our bones and organs, Hindus believe that we have a life force energy called 'Kundalini'. This energy sits at the base of our spine and as we become more awakened and our bodies are more in balance, this energy passes in an upward flow, almost activating each chakra until reaching our mind. For me, the unpoetic version of this is the game at the fairground where you have to swing a mallet so that a bell rings at the top. By using the sounds of Sanskrit, you are able to encourage the flow of Kundalini and heal parts of your body.

Kundali Shakti- meaning 'serpent power'

There are fifty sounds in total, and each sound or seed has a specific location on the body. Before we go into the body parts, I wanted to explain more about how the mantras are created. There is a short mantra and a long mantra for each marma. The short mantra begins with Om (the source, or sacred sound), followed by the bija sound. The longer versions begin the same way, but they also include the word namah (salutations) and the part of the body. Let's use the first vowel sound as an example.

- Om Am- the short mantra
- Om Am Namah Sirasi- the vowel sound that relates to the head (sirasi)

You will notice that an *m* has been placed after the sound. This occurs with all of the sounds so that the bija becomes a mantra.

The sixteen vowel sounds all relate to the head. I won't list them all, but I will include a few so that you get the idea. I will include the long mantra and you can decide which version you choose to use.

- Om Im Namah Daksina Netre – the right eye
- Om Ūm Namah Vāma Karne – the left ear
- Om Rm Namah Vāma Nāsapute- the left nostril
- Om Om Namah Adho Dantapanktau- the lower set of teeth

You can see how specific the marmas are. We aren't just saying that you can chant a mantra if you have a bit of a cold. There is a specific mantra that can alleviate congestion in the right nostril and another for congestion in the left nostril. In Western medicine, you would be given a nasal spray, if you haven't been told the usual "take paracetamol", which apparently fixes anything.

Moving onto the consonants. There are three groups—ten for the arms, ten for the legs, and five for the abdominal area.

- Om Kan Namah Daksina Bāhumūle – the right shoulder
- Om Nam Cam Namah Vāma Kūrpare – the left elbow
- Om Jham Namah Vāma Hastāngulyagre – the tips of the left fingers
- Om Tam Namah Daksina Pādamūle - the right leg
- On Dham Namah Daksina Pādāngulimūle – the root of the right toes
- Om Pam Namah Daksina Parsve- the right side of the abdominal area
- Om Bham Namah Nābhau- the navel

As well as picking up some anatomy vocabulary, you may have worked out the words for left and right too, which is something I struggle with even in English!

Finally, there are the semi-vowels and sibilants that focus on tissue, mind, and soul:

- Om Lam Māmsātmane Namah Kadudi- the soul of the muscles and the palate
- Om Van Medatmane Namah Vāmāmse- the soul of the fat tissue and the left side

- Om Sam Asthyātmane Namah Hrdayādi
  Daksahastantam- the soul of the nerve and the heart to
  the end of the left hand
- Om Sam Sukrātmane Namah Hrdayādi Daksa
  Pādāntam- the soul of the reproductive tissue and the
  heart to the end of the right foot

Please don't confuse the mantra, the Sanskrit name of the body
and the name of the marma. With all the new vocabulary it can
be overwhelming, but nobody is expected to remember everything. It's unlikely that you will need to try and learn all of the
Mantra Purusha. You only need to focus on the areas where
you wish to see an improvement.

If you are determined to chant the long mantras, that is great,
but don't forget the traditional method of teaching and learning, through words and sounds, not pen and paper. Luckily, we
have so much technology that can help us with this, so my
advice is to record the mantra on your phone so you can listen
throughout the day and practice the pronunciation before you
begin your japa.

HOW TO USE MANTRA PURUSHA FOR HEALING

Through meditation, we are able to develop a connection with
our consciousness, our 'Purusha'. Meditation lets us remove the
negativity in our minds and the source of our pain. By using
mediation and Purusha mantra, we can work towards healing
both the mind and the body. It provides an opportunity for us
to detach ourselves from the body, which can then offer us
some freedom from our pain.

It would be an insult to science to state that mantras will cure cancer or treat heart disease. Never should any reputable spiritualist recommend meditation and mantras as an alternative to the treatment that a person is receiving. What one should hope to achieve is some form of relief.

"Repetition of mantras is the best means for the alleviation of all diseases."

— *KARMATHA GURU*

The emphasis here is on the word alleviation. The best way to demonstrate healing with mantra Purusha is to tell you about a friend of mine and her experience.

Unlike my eccentric friend who we met at the beginning of the book, I have a friend who probed me about my learnings. She knew I had started using mantras and she was interested after seeing a difference in me. I wouldn't have called myself an expert at this point, but I had learnt enough to explain how our energies worked and which mantras could be used for different purposes. It took her a few more weeks to open up about her problem.

The poor thing had been trying to get pregnant for a couple of years and with no luck. She and her partner had tried a round of IVF and still she wasn't pregnant. She was due for her next round of IVF in five weeks and she was convinced it wasn't going to work. As she told me her story, I could feel her pain and although I had never used mantras to boost fertility, the mantras I was using were reaping wonderful rewards and I was convinced they could help her.

She was tied up in so many emotions that when she began talking, it was like opening the washing machine door when it was still on full spin. I think even she was lost in so many feelings, most of which were guilt, anger, the envy of mums, fear, and loss.

As my friend was open to the idea of meditation and mantras, I started to share my morning sessions with her. She learnt "Om Sam Sukrātmane"; she chose to chant aloud and I marvelled at her bravery for a newbie. We sat side by side for forty-two days, as she repeated her mantra and I created my own that I felt would help her.

Today, she has two boys and has said she has experienced more joy in these years as a mother than she had in all of her life before. She continues with her mantras, but now for other purposes.

My friend went through with her second IVF treatment. The mantras helped to alleviate her pressure, her tension, her negativity, and her conviction that the IVF wouldn't work. In our time together, my friend was able to learn that her goal wasn't to get pregnant. Instead, it was to be a good mum and to learn what unconditional love felt like. If you are a parent, you probably know that there is no other beauty in the world like your child smiling—a true beauty.

During her mantras, it was hard for her not to think about the idea of being pregnant. It was a challenge for to take her mind off the idea of a baby and concentrate on the sounds and vibrations she was creating. I believe that it was a combination of the IVF and the alteration of her energies through mantras that made her a mum. Perhaps for those who are sceptical, mantras are a little bit like the divine: until you experience it, you can't appreciate it.

HEALING PARTS OF THE BODY

Mantra Purusha can be used to heal a great number of physical pains. If you want to relieve the pain in your lower back, you can work with "Om Bam". If you have had a car accident and you want to help the recovery process of a broken shoulder, there is "Om Kam". My eczema has completely cleared up since chanting "Om Yam", and I had tried multiple ointments, but still, I used them alongside the mantras.

HEALING THE MIND

Have you ever reached a point in your relationship where you have tried everything, but you can't find the words to get your point across? You blame the other person for not understanding, whether it's your parents, partner, or colleague. Can you remember the frustration of not being able to see the solution?

While each of the marmas has physical healing abilities, they can also have psychological benefits. Again, I'm not going to list all fifty of them, but these are some key marmas that will lead to mental healing:

- Am- feelings and expression
- Im- judgement and discrimination

- Um- listening and comprehension
- Rm- will power
- Dam- primary focus
- Dham- adaptation
- Nam- a higher mental connection

What happens if my right nostril is blocked but I don't want to increase my will power?

I'm not kidding, this was a question I was once asked, and you can probably see why! By now you have a good understanding of the intricacies of mantras and purpose, of how one sound can lead to mental and/or physical healing. The question really should highlight the importance of your intention. Mantra Purusha, along with all mantras, will have the most benefit when combined with intention. If your intention is to heal congestion in the right nostril, you need to focus your energies on this. On the other hand, if you want to increase your will power, then this is what your intention should be.

The Use of Mantra Purusha to Overcome the Pain of Our Past

There are some circumstances and experiences where no matter how hard we try, we can't seem to let things go. Even though decades had passed, the death of my grandfather haunted me. Childhood fears, which may seem stupid to some, will still affect the lives of many adults. Despite wanting to move forward, there are things that happened in our past that we can't let go of, and until we do, the possibility of moving forward and creating a better life will be more difficult.

Our liver is said to hold unresolved anger. That family argument might be resolved in your mind, but your liver may still struggle to break down the fats you absorb. Similarly, the gall bladder holds on to feelings of hatred. If you feel like you can never get enough air, bear in mind that your lungs retain grief and sadness. Rather than our kidneys focusing on cleaning our blood, they also have to battle with our fears.

None of us actively seek to hold on to these emotions. More often than not, we assume that they have been dealt with, until we hear a song, or somebody mentions a name, and they all come flooding back. Even those who are healthy, strong, and in a good place in their lives can have a moment from their past that can metaphorically 'bite them on the bum'.

Learning how to use Mantra Purusha can help individuals recognize the pain they have suffered in their past and let go of this pain, even that which is subconscious.

As you can see, these seed mantras have immense power, either used individually or combined, by alleviating your physical and mental pains, past or present. We all know how a toothache can be enough to stop you in your tracks, or backache can make it impossible to get out of bed, let alone make it to work. Learning about marmas and understanding your intentions can start the process of healing, clear away the negativity, and allow you some freedom from suffering. You will be able to clear the path so that you are ready to achieve your goals.

THE SOUND TO YOUR ENERGY CENTRES

W hile I wouldn't want to call one of my chapters 'heavy', I do understand that there was a lot of information in the previous chapter, lots of Sanskrit to pronounce and connections to parts of the body. We have learnt how crucial bija sounds are for certain healing purposes. This chapter will continue with the same theme, but with a simpler set of mantras—the monosyllabic Shakti mantras.

Shakti- meaning 'to be able' or 'empowerment'

Shakti is the personification of energy, the energy that is used in creation and change. Essentially, everything we see is energy, whether that is, for example, gravitational, matter or thermal. In Hinduism, Shakti is sometimes known as 'The Great Divine Mother'. As the primordial cosmic energy, Shakti has the power to be good, creative, and to heal, but she also has the power to do bad or create destruction.

Shakti mantras are widely considered to be some of the most significant and can be used in many ways: in yoga and meditation, for healing or energising, and more frequently in Hinduism, to worship the gods and to protect the different energies in the universe, the Shaktis.

WHAT ARE SHAKTI MANTRAS?

As monosyllabic mantras, they are words that contain vowels and consonants but only one sound; take, for example, cat, heat, knees, stretched, etc. In order to unlock the power of a Shakti, they must be repeated with incredible focus and an awareness of a power greater than we experience in our day-to-day lives. Though they are easier to chant, they can be more challenging to use, because of the concentration required. For this reason, we are only looking at them now, after first learning about the importance of sounds, vibrations, and intentions.

There are ten primary Shakti mantras, each linked with a chakra. By practising Shakti mantras, one is able to begin the process of unblocking the energy wheels in our bodies. These mantras are:

- Om/Aum
- Aīm
- Hrīm
- Shrīm
- Krīm
- Klīm
- Strīm
- Trīm

- Hum/Hūm

I will discuss each one in much greater detail, but first, I want to go over the various applications of the Shakti mantras, so that you are aware of their uses and abilities.

THE USES OF SHAKTI MANTRAS

Deciding on the appropriate Shakti mantra will first depend on your goals, dharma, artha, kama, and moksha. Then, you need to consider the three gunas that will be used to provide the mantra with energy—sattva, rajas, and tamas. Finally, you need to think about how you intend to use them, whether it's with yoga, Ayurveda, Vastu (the study of direction and balance), or Vedic astrology.

We will use the example of 'Shrīm' to demonstrate the different uses and show just how the Shakti mantras are able to develop, maintain, and even diffuse the patterns and forces that we possess.

In terms of goals, Shrīm is used for the aid of financial gain and to advance our career, and it connected with dharma and artha. It will also assist with our kama goals by enabling us to achieve what we desire.

When looking at gunas, if you chose to use Shrīm with the intention of sattvic, you will encourage harmony and nourishment. With rajas, your aim will be to improve your outer self and accomplish more. However, tasmic intention, the one not to be strengthened, has the ability to cause great destruction.

When used with yoga, Shrīm helps to fortify our devotion to the gods and gurus. With Ayurveda (the practice of medicine), one can benefit from healing. Vedic astrogeology ties Shrīm to the Moon and will help you to boost your strength. And finally, when used in Vastu, it is for increased happiness and wealth in the home.

It truly blows my mind how much can be achieved with just one Shakti mantra. Now consider the applications of the nine other words and, at least for me, it's impossible to imagine not experiencing some form of healing when using them.

As we are focusing on healing and yoga, there is no need to burden yourself with all of the uses, but it just goes to show how one monosyllabic word can have such extensive capabilities. Again, it's when I look at the whole picture, I realise that although my eccentric friend may have been going the wrong way about it, her appreciation of the sounds was far more beneficial than either of us could have imagined at the time.

THE MEANING BEHIND THE SHAKTI MANTRAS

Om and Aum

Whether on TV, in films, at your yoga class, or on noticing the chanting playing in the background of a holistic shop, it is likely that you have heard this sound prior to reading this book. Om is the prime mantra of the Purusha. It represents the essence of the ultimate reality, the universe. It enables us to connect with our true selves and the higher spirit. Om is the sound of the cosmic lord, Ishvara. He is an inner guru, a prime yoga teacher, and more importantly, the creator, preserver, and destroyer of the universe.

More often than not, you will hear Om chanted as Aum; the *A* signifies the creator and the waking, the *u* represents the preserver and a dream-like state, and the *m* calling to Shiva, the cosmic masculine force and a deep-sleep state.

Om helps us to clear our minds in preparation for other things, particularly meditation. Many of the mantras begin with Om, as it is said that with a clear mind, the rest of the mantra will have a greater effect. Om allows our energy to grow and it takes the energy that sits at our spine and pulls it upwards, passing through our chakras and flowing out of our body at the highest point. Aum will achieve the same thing, but with a stronger force to move the energy up through our body.

In terms of healing and Ayurvedic medicine, Om encourages harmony within the body, the mind, and across the senses. Healing energy is drawn into the subconscious and overpowers our negative thoughts, even alleviating addictions.

Despite knowing how much power is associated with the vibrations produced with Om and Aum, some still find it hard to imagine the extent of its healing abilities. There are Upanishads and books dedicated to this sound alone.

Aīm

Pronounced /iaem/, Aīm is the feminine sound of Om and is the second most common bija mantra. The masculine and feminine sounds are often chanted together, because this represents an understanding of all sounds.

Once our minds have been cleared after using Om, we are now prepared to centralise our mind and heart in a certain way. While we hear the sounds of Om, we visualise Aīm. As this mantra is the cosmic feminine force, there are plenty of mantras that are used for a greater connection with Shakti, the Divine Mother.

Aīm is also the seed mantra of the goddess of knowledge and speech, Sarasvati. It will, therefore, help us to find the right words when we struggle to communicate. It is a wonderful sound to stimulate learning, the acquisition of wisdom and all kinds of knowledge, but particularly to gain a better appreciation for the arts. It can also guide us in finding direction and motivation.

For healing, Aīm is still related to words, knowledge and speech. With concentration and awareness, Aīm can invigorate our vocal cords and allow our voices to be better heard.

Hrīm

The three sounds that make Hrīm are the Ha and Ra. *Ha* points to life forces, space and light while *Ra* has ties to fire, light, and dharma goals. *Ā* is the sound associated with energy, concentration and incentive. It is pronounced /hreem/ with a soft first sound and the tongue close to the top palate.

The use of Hrīm is more specific than Aim. As the prime mantra of the goddess and therefore the main Shakti mantra, Hrīm connects with the goddess across all of her principal powers—creation, preservation, and destruction. Its use is not limited to the goddess, but for spirituality, it can be used with any of the gods or even objects that we wish to bring closer to our hearts. It helps us to become humbler prior to receiving our hearts' desires.

Hrīm is predominantly Pitta energy: it's fiery and intense, but tamed down with a little air from Vata.

Speaking of the heart, Hrīm is the Shakti mantra for the heart. This means that it can help us with our emotions and feelings and to open up the Heart Chakra. It's that warm feeling when you see someone you love, the bliss you feel when you hear that person after a long absence, and overall, it is the Shakti mantra that allows us to experience joy.

For the physical heart, the actual organ, Hrīm can help to relieve the symptoms of heart disease and with the promotion of energies, it is believed that it can increase blood circulation, which brings about a number of health benefits, including stronger lungs and an improved nervous system.

Shrīm

The Shrīm Shakti mantra is highly adventurous as it is the seed mantra of Lakshmi, the goddess of prosperity and abundance, and it bestows numerous blessings on her. She is also the wife of Lord Vishnu and provides him with his power and strength. Another name for Shrīm is Rama bija, worshipping Lord Rama, dharma personified.

Shrīm is pronounced /shreem/ with very little emphasis on the *m* sound. As the mantra of faith and devotion, it can be used to express your dedication to any of the deities, as well as seek refugee with them. When used with religious intention, you may find yourself in favour with the deity you chant to. Like Hrīm, it relates to the heart, but instead of the life force, it has more relation to one's feelings. The two can be used together, not just for the benefits to the heart, but also because of the link between the Sun and the Moon in Hindu Astrology, Hrīm being solar and Shrīm, lunar.

Shrīm is primarily a Kapha mantra, the dosha of water and earth. It can be used to strengthen overall health, especially for women, as it can improve the circulation to the reproductive system and enhancing fertility. It is a mantra to calm the mind, but also has some pitta, a touch of fire to brighten our complexion.

Krīm

The first of the consonant Shakti mantras, those with an initial hard sound, Krīm is pronounced /kreem/. Broken down, there are three key sounds: *Ka*, the presence of life force and the first stage of energy, *Ra*, which indicates the seed of fire and *Ā* as the concentration of power. This mantra produces light and intention, much like Hrīm and Shrīm, however Krīm has a more precise use involving a grander presence and stimulation of nature.

Kali is the goddess of time and change. She is one of the ten tantric aspects of Parvati, the wife of Lord Shiva. Krīm is the seed mantra of Kali and with it, we can activate Kali's power. This power can in turn increase vibrations and give energy to everything. For this, we can see Krīm as the mantra of transformative energy, as well as the mantra of work and yoga.

Krīm calls upon the electrical energy that is present in the universe and it promotes action. Using Krīm allows us to take more control over our karma, both good and bad. When used internally, it arouses our serpent power (Kundalini). This results in greater perception, concentration and a deeper state of meditation.

When applied with Ayurveda intention, Krīm can produce a feeling of adrenaline, as the sound is a fusion of Vata, wind and electrical energy, and Pitta, fire. While prompting action with the biological fires, the physical benefits may be noticed in the circulatory system and the nervous system, and still more so in the heart and the liver.

Klīm

While Krīm is electrical, Klīm /kleem/ is its more feminine counterpart, the gentler side. If used correctly, Klīm can pull things towards us as if magnetized. Another quality is its ability to keep things in place, though if used with the wrong intention, Klīm may keep things down with power, rather than choice.

As with many of the Shakti mantras, you can use Klīm to reach a deeper connection with any of the deities as it has a special relationship with Sundari, the goddess of love and beauty. It is also the seed mantra of desire and may help us to get what our heart honestly wishes for, by reaching out to the deity that is able to help us attain our desires.

Klīm is the mantra of love, filling our hearts with this critical emotion. The benefits of Klīm are extensive and it is a popular mantra because it is so safe to use. As a watery Shakti mantra, and mostly Kapha, it is good for healing plasm and the skin. It can stimulate the digestive fluids and help us to absorb more nutrients. As a source of happiness, Klīm can have a calming effect, reducing nervousness and boosting the immune system.

Strīm

Along with the Ā vowel we have seen before, Strīm contains Sa, the sound of stability and Ta, providing extension. Pronounced as /streem/ it has qualities of peace, as well as movement and the spreading of energy.

Some believe this is the Shanti bija, the seed of peace, but it will also offer the power of the divine feminine, aiding in childbirth, the ability to nourish and provide direction. Strīm is rooted in the words for 'stand', 'spread', 'take a step', and 'the elevation from one level to another', and so our energy can extend horizontally or vertically.

With strong ties to the goddess of higher knowledge, we can connect with her or any of the deities to increase our energy for creative purposes. It can help us with poetry and art, but also creativity with our language (not for telling lies), our ability to argue our point of view and to debate.

Though not limited to women, for Ayurveda, it is a significant mantra for women's health, specifically for helping with childbirth. With the right focus, you can experience both healing and empowerment, along with a stronger circulatory system and healthier bones.

Trīm

When you take away the *Sa* sound, you remove the element of stability and this increases the *Ta* energies for horizontal and vertical expansion. In Trīm, /treem/, when you highlight the Tri, you see the relationship with the number three and the bringing together of contrasts.

Trīm is the seed mantra of the Trishula, another connection to Tri. Trishula is the trident of Lord Shiva, his most powerful weapon that fights off evil and negativity. It is also believed to represent the three gunas.

This is an ideal mantra if you need help overcoming difficulties and harmful forces. The strong levels of pitta energy enable us to rise up into a higher state of awareness. The fieriness of pitta can also help us to feel braver, have the confidence we may need to be just a little more daring and take away some of the fear that prevents us from moving forward.

Hum

Said as /hoom/, Hum is another of the more important Shakti mantras next to Om and Aim. It is believed to be both the primal sound of Lord Shiva and the transformative character of the Divine Trinity. The trinity, or *trimurti*, is the supreme triple-deity in Hinduism, consisting of Brahma (the creator), Vishnu (the preserver) and Shiva (the destroyer).

Hum with a short vowel sound /hom/ is used when we want to relight fire, from the fire in our consciousness to the fire in our life force and breathing. It is good for removing negativity, burning it with lightning fire. As the seed sound of wrath, it can cause fiery energy too.

When pronounced with the long vowel, it can stimulate the ferocious manifestations of the goddess, like Kali and Chandi. On the other hand, its softer side is the seed of the sound of the Mother (Parvarti), with the ability to summon as well as avert.

Hum in its short and long vowel sound can uplift our Kundalini. It will kick our Tejas and Pitta into action, aiding everything from our digestive system up to our mind. In terms of Ayurveda, it can boost the immune system.

This is enough information for you to be able to use Shakti mantras in the right way, knowing how the energies will affect your body and mind. I love them all because they are easy to learn and to pronounce, so you really can turn your attention to the feelings that each one awakens and be more aware of the force that each one produces. Needless to say, you can combine any of these mantras with other Sanskrit words and sounds to form longer mantras, but don't feel that this is essential.

HOW DO BLOCKED CHAKRAS IMPACT THE BODY AND MIND?

It is believed that there are energy centres all over the universe, also known as vortices, swirls of energy. When these swirls are related to the body, they are called chakras. These are not like your pulse, which you can feel beating, nor are they something you can see. What you will notice is an improvement in your wellbeing when you start to unblock your chakras. In the most commonly-used system in the West, there are seven chakras that follow the path of your spine and each will reflect a certain quality in your life. In the first chapter, we concentrated on the location of the chakras, now let's see how they relate to areas in our life, starting from the bottom and working our way up.

Root Chakra

When your Root Chakra is blocked, you may find that you don't feel stable in life and that you lack security. It's normal for you to worry about the essentials in life, like money, your home, food, etc. Physically, you may show problems with your legs, immune system and digestive system.

Sacral Chakra

This is linked to your creativity, your love for life and has deep ties with your sex life as well as your ability to enjoy yourself and have meaningful relationships with others. You may worry about being betrayed. Aside from imbalance affecting your sex life, you might have problems with the urinary system, lower back pain, and irritable bowel syndrome.

Solar Plexus Chakra

You will sense when this chakra is unblocked, as you will have more self-control and self-acceptance. Your increased confidence will allow you to feel more optimistic. When blocked, you will worry about how you look and about being criticized or even rejected. In terms of health, you might experience problems with your liver, stomach ulcers, high blood pressure and chronic fatigue.

Heart Chakra

As one would assume, it has a profound connection with love and relationships. When not balanced, this chakra can lead to feelings of jealousy, a sense of being suffocated or a fear of being alone. Heart problems may present, along with pain in the shoulders, arms and wrists. Asthma and allergies are also common.

Throat Chakra

So close to the vocal cords, this chakra deals with communication, the ability to express yourself with self-esteem. You will know how to let others know how you are feeling when the Throat Chakra is unblocked. However, when blocked, you may doubt your creativity. You may also be susceptible to ear infections, thyroid issues, sore throat and laryngitis.

Third Eye Chakra

When balanced, you will be able to enjoy clear thoughts, strong instincts and more wisdom. You will be focused and determined. If your Third Eye Chakra is blocked, or even unbalanced, you might notice that you are moody, confused, and unable to see things from another person's point of view. You could suffer from headaches, blurred vision, a loss of hearing, and even hormone imbalances.

Crown Chakra

You will gain from a close connection to your inner self; you will be aware of your abilities and see the bigger picture. There are strong negative emotions when the Crown Chakra is blocked, such as anxiety, depression and feeling a lack of power. Physically, you may be very sensitive to your environment, particularly light and sound, and you might have dizzy spells.

It is not uncommon for people to have blocked or unbalanced chakras. We often put these symptoms down to the stress in our lives, or say "I must go on a diet, start eating healthier". It's true, these things will help, but if we allowed ourselves to explore mantras to unblock our chakras, the benefits are almost unbelievable.

SHAKTI MANTRAS TO UNBLOCK YOUR CHAKRAS

Do not panic, there is not another list of mantras to decide from. The mantras are the same as the seven bija mantras we have already seen. But the importance now, and where your intention lies, is in the Sanskrit sounds and seeds to open up your chakras. Now you will have a better understanding of how to pronounce them, so we will just quickly revisit them with a better understanding of their association:

- Root Chakra – "Lam" – opening up your survival instincts
- Sacral Chakra – "Vam" – allowing you to feel more sensual and find your motivation
- Solar Plexus Chakra – "Rum" – gaining more personal power, detaching from the ego
- Heart Chakra – "Yam" – appreciating unconditional love
- Throat Chakra – "Ham" – boosting imagination and creativity
- Third Eye Chakra – "U" – fostering a stronger sense of wisdom, finding your inspiration
- Crown Chakra – "Om" – engendering the connection with the spirits and your inner self

As with some of the literal translations in Sanskrit, you may hear different mantras for the same chakra. For example, I have heard "U" and "Kshaam" for the Third Eye Chakra. They will both achieve the same result, it's just a question of the regional dialect.

ARE THERE ANY ENGLISH MANTRAS I CAN USE TO UNBLOCK CHAKRAS?

Yes, there are. But remember that a mantra has to have meaning for you. I'm going to include an English version for each chakra, but you now have the knowledge to create your own mantras too. I wanted to give you a little challenge, not a test, but just to show you how much you have learnt so far. If you feel like it, cover up the names of the chakras, read the mantra, and see if you can associate the words with one of the chakras. To make it an actual challenge, the order isn't from the root of the spine to the head like before.

- **Heart Chakra** – "I am love, I give love, I am open to love."
- **Root Chakra** – "I am strong, supported, and abundant."
- **Solar Plexus Chakra** – "I am worthy of pursuing my passion and purpose."
- **Crown Chakra** – "I am one with the divine. I honour the divine within and around me."
- **Throat Chakra** – "I am in alignment with my truth. I speak with clarity and intention."
- **Third Eye Chakra** – "I am in connection with my spirit and I trust my intuition."
- **Sacral Chakra** – "I am the creator of my entire reality."

Even if you can't get them all, I'm sure you will be able to relate some of the English vocabulary with the appropriate chakra.

The Shakti mantras are the mighty sounds, the kiss that brightens your entire day, the complement that makes you feel sexy, the pat on the back from your boss, or the spare seat on the underground when you've had a long day. These are the Hindu versions of the small things in life that make such a big difference.

Mantras are mighty sounds that have mighty power and with the wrong intentions, they can cause harm. There is so much negativity and destruction in the world, there really is no sense in using the Shakti mantras to cause more. Not only this, but there is still a chance that Shakti mantras used with negative intentions will reflect back on you. Don't waste your time trying to seek revenge. With all my honest intentions, you have so much to gain when your chakras are unblocked and balanced, you will never want to waste your time with negative intentions. Healing is about you; let that be the focus of your intentions.

PART II

Part 1 of this book has been a rollercoaster ride of history, tradition, pronunciation and learning about the use of both Sanskrit and English mantras. We have dug deep into who we are and what we want to achieve from life and clearly defined our goals.

Though not discussing the religious aspects of mantras and healing too much, we have briefly discussed the great number of deities and how each one has its own mantra that will bring about certain benefits depending on the deity.

Throughout this section, we are going to look closer at key areas in which people feel they might need assistance, whether that's to heal emotions that they are suffering from, to discover new opportunities, or to relieve themselves from physical ailments.

You may find that I talk about certain deities in more detail here, but this is not because they are more religious or because you need to believe. It is simply because I love the history and tradition behind each mantra, and I feel that a greater understanding behind them allows for a closer connection to the sounds.

I understand if you want to skip straight to the mantras that lead you to a more fruitful life; the temptation to get started as soon as possible is strong. Don't forget to go through the others, so that you are fully prepared for any ups and downs life may throw at you along your journey to a higher self.

BEFORE ALL HEALING; MANTRAS TO PREPARE YOURSELF

To an extent, you are have already made great progress with your preparation. You might have chosen some mantras and are putting them into practice, but most importantly, you have discovered more about your true self. This is not the person you feel you have to be for those around you or who you should be to fit into social settings. So, in this sense, you are prepared.

In this chapter, we are going to discover some of the ideal ways to prepare your mind. For the maximum benefits of a mantra, you need complete focus and concentration. This is a struggle when there is so much for us to contemplate in life. Whether we are employed, self-employed, working from home or retired, each of us has stress and problems and I know just how heavy a head we all lay on our pillows at the end of each day.

Now is the time to start clearing some of this emotional clutter. Before we look to achieving our goals and starting to heal physically, it is crucial that we prepare our minds and our emotions and lift ourselves out of the fog and into clarity.

With the example of one of my first healing groups, we are going to practice some mantras that will allow you to appreciate living in the moment, heighten your concentration, and discover harmony in your life and within yourself.

My first group wasn't really a professional group. I had begun an online community and there were a few ladies in my city who had shown an interest. It was simply a coincidence that we were all female and has no reflection on the use of these mantras. Looking back, perhaps my first website was a little feminine, but we all live and learn.

Anyway, I loved my first group. Really, at that stage, I was more of the organiser than the expert, but being able to share the knowledge I had gained filled me with hope and confidence and I started to see my goals coming to light. We were also a very mixed bunch, so we were able to explore a range of mantras.

A SHANTI MANTRA FOR FINDING INNER PEACE

Jane was the youngest member of our group. She had been a single mum for a few years and now has toddler twins with her new partner. It was impossible for her to get any sense of peace and it was hard for her to keep being the glue in what sometimes felt like two families living under one roof. There were jealous tantrums and not only from the children!

We began with the simple form of the peace mantra, Om Shantih Shantih Shantih Om because Jane felt overwhelmed by the full mantra. After just a couple of weeks, she was into the full swing of it and the long version had become part of her morning ritual.

It is recommended to chant this mantra first thing in the morning. As the twins were up (and fortunately going back to sleep again) at 6.30 am, Jane changed her morning routine and when the boys were back asleep, she chanted the longer version:

Om Dyau Shanti-Rantariksha-Gwan Shantih
Prithvi Shanti-Rapah Shanti-Roshadhayah Shantih I
Vanas-Patayah Shanti-Viswed Devah Shanti-Brahma Shantih
Sarvag-Wan Shantih Shanti-Reva Shantih Sa Ma Shanti-Redi
Om Shantih Shantih Shantih Om II

May there be peace in the whole sky and in the whole external, vast space
May there be peace on Earth, in water, in herbs, trees and creepers
May there be peace in the entire universe. May peace be in the Supreme Being, Brahman
Also, may there consistently exist in all peace and peace alone
Om, peace, peace, peace to us and all creatures

After just one month, Jane looked like a new person. The grey circles under her eyes had faded and you could see a fresh sparkle. She felt that the slow repetition of this Shanti mantra enabled her to concentrate on the word 'peace' and its meaning to her. She felt that as her mind became calmer, so did her home.

THE MOTHER OF THE UNIVERSE TO HELP US CONCENTRATE

Susan was all over the place and I mean this is the nicest possible way. She entertained the group with her numerous stories and often appeared to start another one before finishing the last. She had a teenage daughter who needed a lot of help with her studies, and rather than just concentrating on the particular topic they were studying, Susan felt she needed more focus on her life in general, as she didn't know how to compartmentalise.

The Durga Mantras are used to worship Goddess Durga, who is also known as Shakti or Devi. As the protector of the universe, Maa Durga is incredibly powerful and can help protect us from negativity. As a mother, she shows great love, but also has the ability to lose her temper.

Susan wanted to be more like Goddess Durga. She wanted to eliminate the negativity that was coming from her daughter and find the ability to focus on the different parts of her life.

Sensibly, she chose a relatively short mantra to help her remain focused, the Maa Durga Dhyan Mantra:

Om Jataa Jut Samaayuktamardhendu Krit Lakshman
Lochanyatra Sanyuktam Padmendu Sadya Shan Naam
I bow to the Supreme Power and urge you to help me concentrate on
my goals
and thus, help me to achieve them.

As I have said before, mantras aren't magic spells, and this didn't transform her daughter into a straight-A student. It helped Susan to focus on her work, then her daughter's studies, then her hobby, instead of getting flustered by doing everything at once. The time she spent with her daughter was dedicated to studying and they both saw the positive results.

TUESDAYS FOR ELIMINATING OBSTACLES

Sophie was a sweetie. She worked in customer services for a supermarket chain and though she had tried some mantras before, she didn't feel like they were having the right impact. From talking to her, I got the feeling that the challenges she faced in her daily life were blocking her mind and that it was important to remove these obstacles before she could see the other mantras take effect.

Lord Ganesha is the magnificent deity with the head of an elephant. In Hinduism, many of the Gods have a day dedicated to them and Lord Ganesha's day is Tuesday. This isn't to say that you shouldn't chant it every day, but some will also choose to fast as well as pray to Lord Ganesha on a Tuesday.

Vakratunda Mahakaya Suryakoti Samaprabha
Nivighnam Kuru Me Deva Sarva-Kaaryeshu Sarvada
O Lord, with a curved trunk and a huge body, you emit the radiance
of crores of suns.
Remove all obstacles and bless me, so that I succeed in the task that I
undertake now and in the future
Crores- Ten million in the Indian numbering system

This was a favourite for the whole group, as it wasn't often in our Western culture that we were able to celebrate a larger body and it gave us a chance to forgive the little extra weight we were carrying.

Sophie was able to handle her challenges at work, so that when she came home, she wasn't plagued by the stress of work. She chose to chant this mantra the full 108 times in the morning and evening and on Tuesdays, she repeated the japa a second time, which she said was "just in case he is listening".

A TASTE OF REALITY TO APPRECIATE THE PRESENT MOMENT

Emma was a bit lost in life. She was caught up in her past and regretted a lot of her decisions. At the same time, she was putting an awful lot of pressure on her future and where she was heading. She too had tried some mantras, but hadn't realized the importance of using them in the present tense.

It's something that we can probably all relate to. Even now, I can still find myself carried away with the stress of the day such that I feel guilty taking five minutes to just sit down and have a coffee and to use that time to be grateful for today.

Satchitānanda can be broken down into three words that also help with the pronunciation. Sat means being, chit means consciousness, and ānanda means bliss. As a mantra, it relates to the ultimate reality and can help you to pull your focus to the here and now. It was first mentioned in the Brihadranyaka Upanishad, one of the earliest Hindu texts.

Satchitānanda- meaning 'reality consciousness bliss'

Representing the absolute reality, some say this concept is the same as God, while others say it's an experience beyond enlightenment that only a small group of masters have been able to achieve.

I felt that by using this compound word, Emma would be able to start enjoying her life in the present so that she could gain some strength and perspective. Emma repeated Satchitānanda in the morning and evening, but also during the day when she felt her mind would drift back to her past or future. It particularly helped to prepare her mind for mantras that she would then use to heal things that were bothering her from her past.

The four of us were nothing but dedicated to our progress. There was no such thing as group WhatsApp chats in those days (I say with a youthful smile) so the times that we got together were full of positive recollections of the week that had passed, of where we had seen the benefits and what we wanted to continue to work on.

I suggested that we practised two mantras together, as I wanted to get a sense of the power of the group while not in a yoga class. Plus, I thought that both of the following mantras we suitable for all of us.

THE LIGHT OF THE SUN TO BEGIN OUR HEALING

In one way or another, we were all suffering and I knew we would all benefit from more positivity and warmth. While being lifted into the light of the sun, I also wanted to begin to heal our bodies and our minds.

The Hindu god of the sun is the Surya Devta. The sun is essential for life and growth and by worshipping Surya Devta, you will be able to gain from his light. As the god of the sun, it is best to start this mantra on a Sunday and then continue as part of your mantra routine.

Namah Suryaya Shantaya Sarvaroga Nivaarine
Ayu Rarogya Maisvairyam Dehi Devah Jagatpate
Oh Lord Surya, you govern the universe and treasure peace. You remove all kinds of diseases. Bless me with long life, good health, wealth and prosperity.

My aim for this mantra was to remove negativity and then replace it with positivity, or, if we weren't to get there straight away, at least to be able to experience a bit more of a balance. To appreciate that taking a wrong turn and getting lost at least led you to find a new restaurant you would like to try, instead of getting lost and the entire day thereby being a disaster.

In my mind, this mantra would create the feeling of when you are on holiday and you wake up on the beach with the sunlight on your face.

LOOKING PAST OUR SHORTCOMINGS

We were making progress, but I still felt that the ladies were too hard on themselves. There were physical aspects that we all wanted to improve; however, by giving into these flaws, we weren't appreciating the true beauty of ourselves—what was inside of us. My hope was to get these ladies to see their inner beauty just as much as their outer beauty.

For this, I went back to the Lord Ganesha mantras; after all, this god was plump and had the head of an elephant, yet looking at him, you just see a belly full of joy and we can all gain from his good spirits.

Om Sumukhaya Namah- meaning 'the constant beauty in soul, spirit, in face, in everything'

Again, I wasn't expecting us to meet a week later and to be filled with confidence about our perfect bodies and beautiful souls. Yet, as with more balance between the positivity and negativity, I was hoping that to start with, for every negative the ladies came up with, they were able to think of a positive. This, for me, would be a sign of progress.

We practised the new mantras morning and evening and once a week together for fifteen minutes. What I also loved about our group was the freedom to practise our mantra in a way that we felt comfortable. Even when we were in a group, some sat, some lay down. It was very easy for us to get into the rhythm of the sounds, and it wasn't necessary for all of us to be chanting together. In fact, there were some weeks when we were all in silence.

The thing that amazed me even more was the energy that I felt as we repeated our mantras. This energy followed me, and I could even sense it when I was at home, repeating them alone. It wasn't an energy that I had taken from the others and therefore was depriving them of. When we discussed this feeling, the other ladies agreed.

The other feeling that we shared was that although these were chants to worship some of the most important deities in Hinduism, we still didn't feel like it was the same as sitting in church and praying to God. We respected the religion, but perhaps because our focus was on the Sanskrit and the sounds, the mantras felt like a chant rather than a prayer.

This was a very important matter for me. In the beginning, I felt like I was taking advantage of the Hindu traditions. I imagined the deities watching over me thinking, "look at this cheeky one using our language but not praying to us". Learning more and more about these rich Eastern philosophies, I know this is not the case, as they are traditions based on passing on wisdom.

And this is what our group did. We took steps to clear our minds in preparation for the next stages of our journeys. We did so with respect and a genuine passion for what we were doing. We shared what we learnt and saw the benefits of these powerful mantras.

On a personal note, I found that working with this fantastic group of ladies emphasised that I was now on the right path in my life. I had discovered that thanks to mantras, I was able to help people. Now it was time for me to step out of this comfort zone and find some men to join in my groups!

MANTRAS FOR EMOTIONAL HEALING

After the success of my first little group, I was on cloud nine. My learning had allowed me to really identify which areas of my life I wanted to change, and I could see the commitment starting to reap its rewards. Physically, I felt stronger. I was motivated to start swimming and the freshness of the water along with my heart pumping that little bit faster felt like I was cleansing myself.

I felt as if my family respected my role as a housewife more. Having more things that I wanted to achieve forced them to contribute and I no longer felt like I was the maid picking up after them. I didn't just leave them to fend for themselves, but it no longer defined who I was.

Another benefit I saw was my social life. For the first time since, I think, my teenage years, I had friends who were my friends—not Emily or Joshua's mum, not Simon's wife—but Verda's friends. Meeting new people gave me the opportunity to talk about my passion and I was pleased with the positive response to mantras and spiritualism. At first, I thought they were just polite responses, but when my new friends came back with questions, I felt like people really did acknowledge my expertise on the subject.

Nerves overcame me as I began to prepare for my next project, nevertheless, I knew in my heart that it was important to push forward, and I continued to alter the use of my mantras for the situations I was facing.

I decided it was time to promote my service. I didn't want people thinking that I was in this for the money, and so as not to turn my passion into something commercial, I chose to set up a donation system, where instead of a payment, people could choose from one of three charities to donate to. This was a great way for me to help others in need and I also hoped it would reflect on my karma.

The next group I wanted to create was dedicated to emotional healing. Again, as a new project, I had no expectation, but was delighted when the phone started to ring. I was even more delighted when I answered a call from a man! Then there were a few more male callers and I could tell that they were all still a little hesitant, so this led me to start a separate group for those who preferred a male-only environment. Those who were having doubts then came around to the idea. Perhaps it was one thing to try this rather "out there" idea but another to share their feelings with women they didn't know. Either way, I had four men who wanted to meet on a weekly basis to gain a better understanding of their feelings, and I ran another group alongside this, which was predominantly female. I want to share with you want we discovered.

A MANTRA TO WELCOME CHANGE AND NEW THINGS

I could see that there were some people who were still sceptical, and I could understand this. It made sense, and amused my group, that we should start with a mantra for being open to change and to try new things. After all, if they were not willing to try, it would be challenging to see the benefits of other mantras.

I felt the need for an English mantra and a shorter, simple Sanskrit mantra that wasn't specific to one of the deities, something that the whole group could benefit from. Our English mantra was "I am stepping into the unknown. I am welcoming change".

This was a powerful mantra and it was easy to control our breathing, inhaling on the first sentence and exhaling on the second. For our Sanskrit mantra, we began with one word, repeated twice and pronounced as it was read:

Neti Neti- meaning 'not this, not this'

We used this mantra to accept the fact that there were things in our lives that we wanted to change. This was an excellent place to start, because we learnt the importance of focusing on the sounds and vibrations, rather than the actual 'this' that we wanted to change. The group felt that it was important to appreciate the need for change before working on ways to make them happen.

OVERCOMING OUR BIGGEST EMOTIONAL FEAR

We began one session talking about our fears. The most common came up—not being able to care for the family, becoming ill—while one person said heights and another said birds. It wasn't until David (not his real name) admitted to fearing death that the others all agreed. This is a fear that can wake people up with a jolt in the middle of the night, or it can alter the way they live their lives, because they fear the consequences.

If you are able to overcome your fear of death, you will probably be able to overcome your fear of flying, as the fear of flying normally comes from the fear of a plane accident and death.

Lord Shiva has a thousand names—1,008 to be precise. But it is the lord of death and destruction that we require. Many misinterpret this as the "angry god", but his power enables him to destroy negativity as well as death. After the destruction, we experience creation and so Lord Shiva is also worshipped for his reproductive power. The mantra is called the Maha Mrityunjaya mantra:

Aum Trayambakam Yajaamahe Sungandhim Pushtivardhanam
Urvaarukamive Bandhanaat

We worship the three-eyed One who is fragrant and who nourishes all beings; may He liberate me from my death, for the sale of immortality, even as the cucumber is severed from its bondage of the creeper.

I was a little dubious about delving straight into the gods so early on. I chose to ask the group if they were interested in learning about the meaning behind the mantra and I was pleasantly surprised when they said "yes", reaffirming that Hindu traditions are meant to be shared, not forced upon others.

Sometimes, to overcome our fears, we just need a better understanding of the situation. So, I followed up with one of the Vishnu mantras, which are widely used to overcome fears:

Om Shri Vishnave Cha Vidmahe Vasudevaya Dhimahi
Tanno Vishnuh Prachodayat

Om, let me meditate on Lord Vishnu, Oh Lord Vasudeva, give me
higher intellect,
And Lord Vishnu, illuminate my mind

I didn't feel that the group was quite ready to learn about our healing energies just yet, and so we went on with mantras that we could all appreciate.

THE WIRING OF A MAN'S BRAIN AND A WOMAN'S BRAIN AND COPING WITH STRESS

Years ago, I watched the most hilarious video about how men and women have different ways to cope with stress. The Nothing Box from Mark Gungor was an amusing way to generalize how our brains differ. In the video, Mark suggests that men have the ability to think about absolutely nothing—to go into the 'nothing box'—

while women can never switch off in such a way. You can still find it on YouTube. Again, generally speaking, men have just as much stress as women do, but they tend to handle it differently. For example, a man might not feel comfortable discussing the emotions that arise when he is stressed. For this reason, I went onto a mantra that is intended to be used to handle stress and deal with negativity, in the hope that it would open up the minds of this group to make them more aware of their feelings, instead of going to the metaphorical 'nothing box'.

Om Gajakarnakaya Namah

Salutations to the one who has the ears of an elephant

Though it seems quite vague, it actually means that because Lord Ganesha has the head of an elephant, he is able to hear a lot, but like him, you should only choose to use the positive things, so that negativity doesn't cause further stress.

Regardless of gender, there are more ways that someone can suffer than just stress. So together, we also worked on the Devi Stuti mantra, another for the worship of Maa Durga:

Ya Devi Sarva Bhuteshu, Shanti Rupena Sangsthita
Ya Devi Sarva Bhuteshu, Shakti Rupena Sangsthita
Ya Devi Sarva Bhuteshu, Matri Rupena Sangsthita
Yaa Devi Sarva Bhuteshu, Buddhi Rupena Sangsthita
Namastasyai, Namastasyai, Namastasyai, Namo Namaha

The goddess who is omnipresent as the personification of the universal mother

The goddess who is omnipresent as the embodiment of the
power
The goddess who is omnipresent as the symbol of peace
Oh, goddess who resides everywhere in all living beings as
intelligence and beauty.
I bow to her, I bow to her, I bow to her again and again.

As well as blocking out negativity, this mantra builds inner strength and helps people to create more meaningful relationships with those they love.

The weeks went by and the males in the group did start to open up more. They were more aware of the actions throughout the day that led to stress and with this awareness, they were able to find the best times of the day to chant the mantra. Some found it was useful after lunch to help them during the afternoon, while another mentioned the benefits of chanting before meetings.

LETTING GO OF THE GUILT YOU FEEL

Shaun had had a life of wrong decisions and a few situations that he wished he could reverse. As he had grown out of his 20s, he had come a long way in improving his life, but his past still haunted him. He felt a lot of guilt about what he had put his family through and noticed that this was still having an effect on their relationship today.

The feeling of guilt was one that so many people felt. The most common, especially for the women in the group, was the guilt of not being there for their children, because they had to work.

The problem with guilt is that regardless of whether it is something in our past or in our present, the emotion eats away at us and prevents us from enjoying the great things we have in our lives. So, we used this mantra:

Om Vishwani Deva Savitar Duritani Parasuva
Yad Bhadram Tanna Asuva

Oh Lord! The Creator of the Universe, remove all forms of vice and
sorrow from us.
Give us those qualities that are ennobling

I loved how this mantra helped Shaun to let go of his past and get rid of his huge sense of guilt. On top of that, he began to live life with more dignity: he seemed to hold his head a little higher than in our first meeting.

ONE MAN'S FIGHT AGAINST LONELINESS AND DEPRESSION

Richard's divorce was finalised a year before our meetings, but the pain was still quite real for him. He was unable to move forward with creating a new life, and though he struggled to admit it at the time, he was depressed.

One of the core Buddhist concepts is that essentially, we are never alone, and we are all connected to everything. When a plant converts carbon dioxide into oxygen, we all breathe the oxygen. This way, we are connected to the plants, animals, and other people and therefore, are never alone.

Richard would benefit from a mantra from the Isha Upanishad that focuses on learning more about yourself. It emphasizes the idea that we are not alone:

Purnam Adah Purnam Idam
Purnat Purnam Udachyate
Purnasya Purnam Adaya
Purnam Evavashishyate

That is whole. This is whole
The whole arises from the whole
Having taken the whole from the whole,
Only whole remains

I also suggested that David practised the Green Tara Mantra. Green Tara is considered to be the Mother of all Buddhas and is associated with enlightened activity and prosperity. When worshipping Green Tara, we are asking for freedom from our sadness, from the mental strain that prevents us from experiencing freedom.

Om Tare Tuttare Ture Soha

I prostrate to the Liberator, mother of all the victorious ones

Interestingly, when asked for advice with regards to the Coronavirus crisis, His Holiness the Dalai Lama suggested that chanting the Green Tara mantra could be helpful.

DISCOVERING INNER PEACE AND A CONNECTION TO THE WORLD

From each group, there was a person who shared the same traits. Paul and Denisa both bit their nails and they both had one leg that constantly shook. There was a nervousness about them, and I could get a sense that neither of them felt grounded.

In times like this, nervous chaos needs to be removed so that a person is able to gain more control over their lives. Lord Brahma is the creator of all life forms, time, and dimensions. The Brahma mantra is ideal if a person needs to combat inner and outer conflicts that arise.

Both Paul and Denisa were determined to make the changes they needed to make and didn't shy away when I told them that the Brahma mantra needed to be repeated 108 times before sunrise.

Om Eim Hrīm Shrīm Klīm Sauh Satchid Ekam Brahma

This is one of the more difficult mantras to translate. You will recognize some of the seed sounds that we have already covered, then there are four words that can be translated separately:

- Sat- truth
- Chid- the spiritual mind
- Ekan- one, without a second
- Brahm- the entire universe

While essentially worshipping Lord Brahma, Paul and Denisa also had to pay close attention to the seed sounds and the vibrations that they created.

The Brahma mantra requires long-term commitment and to see the true results, you need to practice for a year. That's not to say that we didn't see improvements. Watching them chant this mantra, I could see the physical symptoms of their nerves slowing down, the speed of the leg shaking slowed down and they were calmer in their conversations. It was amazing to see the same effects in two different groups.

THE TIME TO INTRODUCE HEALING ENERGIES

The atmosphere in both of the groups was optimistic. Nobody had questioned or doubted the power of the mantras we had been using; on the contrary, everyone was hungry to learn more. I felt it was the right time to introduce how our energies had the ability to heal both the mind and the body.

As I began explaining the benefits of Kundalini yoga, everybody eagerly sat in the right position. Now, for many mantras, it is more important that you are comfortable and focus on the sounds. In Kundalini yoga, our goal is to activate the energy that sits at the bottom of the spine, so the person's position is as important as the sounds.

Ra Ma Da Sa Sa Say So hung

Sun, Moon, Earth, Infinity, all that is in infinity, I am thee

This is the Siri Gaitri mantra and is used when you are sat down, your elbows are close to your rib cage, and your forearms are at a 90º angle to your body with the palms facing up.

Along with the right position, it is necessary to be sat upright and to breath slowly, creating a visual image of the energy moving up through your body.

The opportunity to work with men and woman provided fascinating outcomes. I had seen that mantras were not limited to age, beliefs, culture, or gender. The use of mantras showed us that we were all human and that even though we express our emotions differently depending on our personal problems, there are solutions that will help any type of person.

Both the men and the women felt a sense of relief after a few months of using mantras daily. It was almost like they had a clean slate and were ready to move on to the next stage. They had discovered their emotional triggers and developed their own mantras to master their unique triggers. Those around them felt a greater sense of stability, with fewer emotional outbursts. The men and women of the group had begun their journey to a more peaceful life.

MANTRAS AND RELATIONSHIPS

One of the first things people ask me when we start talking about mantras is if there is a mantra to find Mr. or Mrs. Right. A wise woman once told me that you have to kiss a lot of frogs to find your prince or princess. I have to remind people that mantras aren't a quick fix to find solutions, but they are a tool that will help us to achieve what we desire in life.

Those who have had their heart broken feel like it is impossible to find love again. Some people feel like they will never have sex again—a desperate thought in itself! The mantras in this chapter are going to help us to discover love. If you have been in a relationship for a long time, you might feel that you need to rediscover the love for your partner. This is perfectly normal, especially if you are unhappy with other aspects of your life. And yes, we will look at ways to recapture the lust we felt in the honeymoon phase and look at mantras that will help us to increase our sexual energy and to increase our confidence when exploring our sexuality.

At the same time, it is important to remember that relationships are not limited to our romantic partners. They can be with family, friends, co-workers and each type of relationship is susceptible to ups and downs, miscommunications and challenges. Before we investigate mantras for romantic relationships, I want to talk about how we can enhance all of our relationships.

OVERCOMING OBSTACLES IN OUR RELATIONSHIPS

I didn't have obstacles with my daughter in her teenage years: she *was* the obstacle. Obviously, I didn't want to remove her from my life, but I certainly needed help overcoming the problems we were having. The colleague at work who never refills the coffee pot, the mother who fusses, the friend who belittles you in public—I'm sure you can relate with your own personal experiences. I think it is impossible to go through life without some problems in relationships.

Om Vighnanashaya Namah- meaning 'obstacles' (vighna) and 'one who removes' (nashnay)

I really like using this mantra and teaching it to everyone who is looking to improve their relationships. For me, I found it was a good place to start, to remove the problems that I was having with people, so that I was then ready to work on making a difference. It goes back to having a clean slate or a fresh canvas to work with.

UNDERSTANDING YOURSELF BEFORE TRYING TO FIX RELATIONSHIPS

My husband and I went through a "phase" where things were more than just rocky. It seemed that he could never see things from my point of view and that I was always the one making concessions. Reading a book on relationships might provide you with the knowledge, but it's only with experience in relationships that you gain wisdom.

Wisdom enables better communication and with better communication, you are able to get your point across without having to become angry or irritated. It isn't about backing down or proving that you are right. It is about learning to walk in other people's shoes. The Ganesha Gayatri mantra will help you improve your modesty and righteousness, as well as providing you with the wisdom to deal with other people:

Aum Ekadantaya Viddhamahe
Vakratundaya Dhimahi
Tanno Danti Prachodayat

We pray to the single-tusked elephant who is omnipresent.
We meditate upon and pray for the greater intellect of the Lord with the curved, elephant-shaped trunk.
We bow before the one with the single-tusked elephant tooth to illuminate our minds with wisdom"

I often use this mantra to show people that it isn't always easier to say the English translation! Lord Ganesha has one broken tusk, which symbolises the importance of having more faith than intelligence. I also find that by visualizing Lord Ganesha while chanting this mantra, I am reminded of his large ears (to listen more) and small mouth (to talk less).

GETTING IN TOUCH WITH YOUR VARIOUS SIDES

There is no scientific research or psychological study behind this theory. It's just how I like to view myself and the idea helps me get a better sense of myself as one whole being.

I find that I have a masculine side and a feminine side in the traditional sense of the words. I love tearing down walls, fixing the fridge when it breaks and taking care of my own car maintenance. The downside to my sometimes-dominating masculine side is that I am stubborn and won't ask for help.

On the other hand. I love to bake cupcakes with sprinkles and little hearts, I like painting my nails, and I can't resist crying at almost anything on TV. The downside is that I am not good at talking about how I feel, and I am infuriated when my husband goes into his nothing box (if you can remember from the last chapter).

This is why I was over the moon when I came across three mantras that I felt would help me create a balance between the masculine and feminine sides and allow me to appreciate a deeper sense of myself.

Om Aim Hreem Shreem -to call upon the divine feminine

This mantra is a combination of bija sounds Aim, Hrīm and Klīm, the female deities and feminine forces of the universe,

Maha Saraswathi, Maha Lakshmi and Maha Kali, respectively. It is best to use a mala for this mantra at both dusk and dawn.

Hare Krishna- to call upon the divine masculine

Lord Krishna is a compassionate god who can help eliminate the struggles in our lives as well as allowing us an abundance of positivity and luxury. The time of day is not as relevant as the time you spend on this chant. You should repeat it until you start to feel completely relaxed and happy; this will be at least 108 times.

Om Namah Shivayah- to call upon the deity of all deities

Lord Shiva is the supreme deity responsible for creation, preservation and destruction. This is the perfect mantra to become at one with your inner self and to take your inner self to a higher level. You can practise this mantra throughout the day whenever you feel the need, but try to make it part of your morning and evening routine in order to appreciate the deepest connection with yourself.

I have shared my theory and these three mantras with plenty of groups in the past and we all noticed that life no longer felt like Lego bricks that we were trying to stick together. When our masculine and feminine energies were not in battle with each other, but rather in harmony, the various aspects of our lives fit together better.

Now we will turn our attention more to romantic relationships, but that doesn't mean that with the right intention, they can't be used for other partnerships.

WHEN YOU ARE LOOKING FOR LOVE

Traditional advice when we can't find a partner is that we are not looking in the right place, or we are going after the wrong type of person, we need to make a bit more effort, or we need a little patience. None of it really helps, but the advice offers us a glimmer of hope for our love life.

A more productive approach would be to use a mantra to allow yourself to love. Instead of looking to change the circumstances, you can change yourself. More often than not, when we have had bad experiences in the past, we build a wall up around ourselves as a form of protection. It is a subconscious act: our heart wants to love but our mind is cautious.

Om Lambodaraya Namah- meaning 'salutations to the god who has a big belly'

Lord Ganesha has twenty-one names, which include names meaning 'the one with the beautiful face', 'the one who bestows success', 'the destroyer of obstacles'. Repeating this mantra can break down your wall of protection, or your obstacle, and it can allow you to see your true beauty.

It is far more sensible to start with this mantra before you begin your quest for love. Similar to when we prepare ourselves before moving onto emotional healing, you need to prepare yourself for love. It can take thirty days to see the full benefits of a mantra. It is possible that you will see improvements earlier on but there is no rush. This experience should be exciting and enjoyable, not just a case of "let's get it over with".

THE BUZZ AND BUTTERFLIES OF A NEW ROMANCE

Why on Earth would you need a mantra now, when this is the best part? You are at the stage when you are discovering things about each other, you are laughing at each other's jokes, meeting friends and family. Life is good at this point. Your new romance makes the working day easier; you sleep with a smile, and you exercise with vigour.

It is also a massive learning curve and you may not like everything you learn. When I saw this mantra that I am about to share, I immediately remembered the relationship between Hindu teachers and students, one that is built on offering wisdom, rather than forcing it on someone. It reminded me of when my husband cooked something and kept saying "try it, just try it" (it felt like 108 times!) rather than offering a taste.

Om Sahana Vavatu
Saha Nau Bhunaktu
Saha Viiryam Karavaavahai
Tejasvi Nau Adhitam Astu
Maa Vidvissaavahai
Om Shanti Shanti Shanti

Om, may the Divine protect both teacher and student
Let us be nourished and protected
May we work together with great energy
May our studies be effective
May we never hate or fight one another
Om Peace, Peace, Peace

Sometimes in a relationship, you will play the role of the teacher and other times the student. Whichever role you are playing at the time, it should be with love and joy and without conflict. While this mantra was traditionally used for students and teachers, I felt a deep connection with the words and those first stages of a new relationship.

AWAKENING YOUR SEXUAL ENERGY

If you are blushing at the mere thought, I strongly recommend this mantra! I hate to generalize, and I am not a feminist, but in most Western cultures, it is still seen as "unladylike" for a woman to talk about sex. Society still doesn't see that women have primal needs just as much as men do. The "I have a headache" joke is just far too outdated for the twenty-first century.

It is time for woman and men to get more in touch with their sexual energy and to enjoy sex. Each person in the relationship should feel comfortable exploring their sexual energy and instigating sex when they want to.

To awaken our sexual energy, we need to go back to the Sanskrit sounds and seed mantras that open our chakras.

Sat Nam- meaning 'I am truth'

Because it is used in Kundalini yoga, it is important that you are sat in the correct position with your elbows tucked in and your forearms facing forward with your palms up. To really impulse the energy that is at the base of your spine up to your head, the

Sat sound should be thirty-five times longer than the Nam and for at least three minutes a day.

HOLDING BACK THE GREEN-EYED MONSTER

Without wanting to talk about me too much, my husband called me jealous once after a night out drinking. He assumed that I was jealous because he had been socializing with other women, and this is a very common emotion to experience. However, what he couldn't see was that I was jealous that he had been out, talking to adults rather than at home cleaning up after the kids and following the usual mundane routine.

Jealousy presents itself for so many reasons. Many men I have spoken to become jealous of their wives when there is sudden career advancement, or even jealous of the bond that mothers have with their children. What is worse is that nobody enjoys feeling this way, so it is necessary to alleviate yourself from possessiveness and jealousy.

Such a powerful emotion requires a powerful mantra:

Om Mani Padme Hum- Hail the Jewel in the Lotus

When used with the intention to overcome jealousy, I like to break the sounds down and see them as a story or a journey along a path.

- *Om*- bringing harmony and aligning energy
- *Ma*- taking away your physical needs and opening the door to spirituality

- **Ni**- freeing you from your desires, replacing them with peace
- **Pad**- liberating you from ignorance and bias so that love remains
- **Me**- letting go of possessiveness and learning to accept
- **Hum**- releasing the hatred within you

Tibetan Buddhists use this to reach the highest state of compassion and this popular mantra can be used for so many reasons. Don't forget the importance of intention and your personal goals when you chant this.

WHEN YOUR MOUTH IS WORKING FASTER THAN YOUR BRAIN

In the heat of the moment, we say things that we don't mean. Even before the other person has had a chance to react, we know that we shouldn't have said it. We have seen the mantra Neti Neti in the section where we wanted to change. Perhaps it is a situation you want to change, or words you wish you hadn't said that you want to quash—"not this, not this" is a wonderful way to stimulate change.

On a similar note, there will be times where you have to recognise that you made a mistake and while you need to ask for forgiveness from your partner, you may find help by using a mantra. This particular mantra produces immense power through vibrations which help to protect you from negativity or evil. It is also a little longer, so I practise the sounds and pronunciation with people before we begin to chant. You may want to save a video of the Shiv Dhyan mantra so that you can listen a few times.

Karcharankritan Vaa Kaayjam Vaa
Shravannayanjam Vaa Maansam Vaa Paradham
Vihitam Vihita, Vaa Sarv Metat Kshamasva Jay Jay
Karunaabdhe Shree Mahadev Shambho

Supreme One to cleanse the body, mind, and soul of all the stress, rejection, failure, depression, and other negative forces that one faces.

If you have ever made a health juice in order to detox, this is like an equivalent in terms of mantras. Many people I work with feel a sense of relief after a time practising this mantra and it helps to find forgiveness from Lord Shiva for the mistakes we have made.

LETTING GO AND MOVING ON AFTER A BREAKUP

You don't wish it on anyone but at the same time, a breakup is almost a rite of passage, a memorable experience that leads onto the next stage of our lives. We often compare it to the five stages of grieving or a series of emotions that need to be processed. Clinging onto the past will only delay the process; speeding it up may unnaturally force it.

Whether the relationship has been for two months or twenty years, during that time, you will have created a bond that is difficult just to break. You will need time and space to discover how you overcome the pain and suffering you feel when a relationship ends. There are so many factors to consider; it is wrong to say it is time to chant a mantra and move on.

Because each breakup is different, I think it is important for people to create a mantra of their own to help them through suffering. You could be feeling sad, desperate, lonely, angry, bitter, or even guilty because you feel relieved.

In conjunction with your own mantra, I recommend the Purana mantra on Vishnu:

*Om Apavitrah Pavitro Vaa Sarva-Avasthaam Gato- [A]pi Vaa
Yah Smaret-Punnddariikaakssam Sa Baahya-Abhyantarah Shucih*

*Om, if one is impure or pure, or even in all other conditions,
He who remembers Pundarikaksha, he becomes pure outwardly as
well as inwardly*

Pundarikaksha- meaning lotus-like eyes

Be careful of people who say that this is a mantra to bring love back. If a relationship is over, there is a good reason for it. Thinking that love will come back is a form of clinging to the past. This mantra allows us to free ourselves from the mistakes we have made, but also to free ourselves from the ties that keep us locked to our past.

Relationships are a tricky business that we can often take for granted. We assume that once we have one it is set for life. But we forget that as we move through life, we change. The things that once seemed important are now replaced with more important goals. If your new goals aren't aligned with your partner's (whose will also change over time), then you will soon discover that you are on different paths.

In some cases, the goals are too different to come to an agreement and the best solution for both is to part ways. That being said, if you are able to start using mantras from the very beginning of your search for love, you may well discover that you are more open to love and the love you receive from others, you can enjoy a fruitful sex life for longer than the honeymoon phase, and you can learn to grow together, accomplishing individual and common goals.

MANTRAS FOR PHYSICAL HEALING

Which came first, the chicken or the egg? Was it your chronic headaches that led to your depression, because you couldn't do what you loved in life, or the depression that weighed so heavy on you that couldn't shift the pain in your head?

Relieving our physical aches and pains will help us when it comes to emotional healing just like you may have already seen your physical self improving after dedicating time to your emotional healing. The body and the mind may be two different things, but they are living in the same vessel.

The last chapter of this journey will look at specific mantras that can help to reduce the symptoms of illnesses and diseases.

I have said it before, but is so crucial that I will repeat it. Mantras are not a magic cure. They shouldn't be used instead of prescribed medication from a medical practitioner. When it comes to our emotions, it is easier to explore alternative approaches, because of the complexities of the mind. Mantras for physical healing are best used alongside medical recommendations.

Imagine you have a cold. The best thing is probably paracetamol, but you know that if you increase your vitamin C, you will help your body fight the symptoms. The mantras in this chapter are like an extra boost of vitamin C!

A QUICK REVIEW OF THE CHAKRAS

There are seven chakras in our body, starting at the base of the spine with the last at the very top of our head. Each chakra is like a spinning wheel, whereby energy enters one and then is driven up to the next, activating each one in turn.

There are seven bija sounds or seeds that with deep concentration and a focus on the sounds and vibrations that are created, can help to unblock the chakras and allow energy to flow throughout the body.

- Root Chakra – Lam
- Sacral Chakra – Vam
- Solar Plexus Chakra – Rum
- Heart Chakra – Yam
- Throat Chakra – Ham
- Third Eye Chakra – U
- Crown Chakra – Om

The Root Chakra is where our energy sits. The Crown Chakra is right at the top of our head, the closest point to a higher self and also the deities. It makes sense that the bija sound is Om.

Aside from these seven principal sounds, there are also marmas, a sound that relates to various parts of the body, or marma. There are fifty in total, divided into the head, joints and limbs, abdominal area, and tissues and organs. The marmas are incredibly specific to regions of the body and one sound will alleviate symptoms in the left nostril, while another will help free you from suffering in your right toes.

Mantras that activate the chakras and aim at healing certain parts of the body are only short sounds compared with some of the longer mantras we have now seen. Nevertheless, when you concentrate on the vibrations and direct those vibrations to the intended part of the body, there is great physical healing to be had.

A MANTRA TO PROTECT YOU FROM ALL DANGERS

Regardless of your culture and belief, most will agree that prevention is better than cure. For this, we turn to Lord Hanuman, who has many names, but you can see from his appearance why he is also called the monkey god. Despite his looks, there is nothing cheeky about him. He is considered by many as an incarnation of Lord Shiva and for this, is worshipped for numerous reasons.

One of the Hanuman mantras is intended for the protection against all dangers as well as to provide you with additional strength, stamina, devotion, and wisdom. The Hanuman

Gayatri mantra can also lead to more courage and help eliminate your doubts:

*Om Anjaneyaya Vidmahe Vayuputraya Dhimahi
Tanno Hanumat Prachodayat*

*We pray to the son of Anjana and the son of the wind go Vayu
May the Lord lead our intellect towards intelligence and knowing*

I wasn't the only one to appreciate the benefits. I used it from early September through to early January, as I had always been prone to the winter bugs. Whether the group members were using it for just a few months or all year round, there were definitely fewer sniffles and coughs and the long dark days of winter were met with more strength and motivation.

A MANTRA FOR THE FATHER OF AYURVEDA MEDICINE

This is another excellent mantra that can be used to help get rid of various illnesses and suffering when used in the right way. Lord Dhanvantri is one of the manifestations of Lord Vishnu and is the ultimate healer. As well as alleviating the suffering from illnesses and diseases, he can help to remove our fear of suffering and replace it with happiness.

The Lord Dhanvantri mantra is slightly different from the others we have seen, because the success depends on a belief in the powers of this deity. Each time you chant it, a touch of his healing power reaches you. If a person doesn't believe in his ability to heal, they won't be blessed with his power. The more often you repeat this mantra, the more divine power will reach you.

It is also necessary for you to positively prepare your mind before chanting the Lord Dhanvantri mantra. I begin with a short English mantra to draw my focus and reinforce my determination to rid myself of the pain. You can choose your own words; just make sure they are in the present tense and they are positive. "I am getting better" when said with conviction, can enable this mantra to really ease any type of suffering.

Om Nano Bhagavate Vasudevaaya Dhanvantaraye Amrita-Kalasha Hastaaya Sarva-Amaya Vinashaaya Trailokya Naathaya Dhanvantri Maha-Vishnave Namha

I bow down to the Lord Dhanvantri, the Lord with four hands carrying a conch, a discus, a leech and a pot of immortal nectar. In his heart shines a pleasing and brilliant blaze of light. The light is also seen shining around his head and beautiful lotus eyes. His divine play destroys all diseases like a blazing fire.

You would normally start with this mantra the full 108 times and then increase in multiples, so 216, 324, etc. It is also best to start before sunrise and continue as it rises. Many believe that with acts of kindness like donating to the poor, and using a crystal mala, you will see further benefits.

These benefits can include freedom from physical and emotional suffering, long-term illness, and even help for others who are sick. Some have also noticed relief from symptoms when they have exhausted all medical options.

A TIBETAN MANTRA TO PURIFY THE BODY AND MIND

If you are looking for a shorter mantra that will help to unblock physical and mental obstacles and clear away the negative thoughts and feelings you may have, this mantra will allow you to rid yourself of negativity and improve your overall strength.

Om Ah Hum Soha

The sounds will help to free ourselves from the guilt and shame of our negative actions (Om), from our negative words (Ah) and from our negative thought (Hum), and Soha is Tibetan for "so be it".

When we chant this mantra, it is important to visualise specific colours in parts of your body. On the Om sound, imagine a bright white light in your brain. When you repeat Ah, see the colour red around your throat area. For the Hum, see blue around your heart. The Soha isn't a colour word but it should help you to feel in the moment, letting things be as they are.

MY FORTUNATE MEETING WITH AN INCREDIBLE DOCTOR

As much as I wanted to visit patients in hospitals and introduce patients to healing mantras, I never felt that it was appropriate. It was like crossing a line that wasn't quite ready to be crossed. That is why I was ecstatic when a friend of a friend introduced me to a very open-minded doctor who was always looking for alternative ways to improve the quality of life of his patients.

He was a strong believer that taking pets in to see patients helped with faster recovery and was keen to see if mantras could make a difference.

Together, we looked at charts and discussed patients who were willing to try mantras alongside the treatment they were already receiving.

Incurable Diseases

When in Delhi, I met a pharmacist, so it was great to get an opinion from a medical practitioner. He introduced me to the Mhamirtunjya mantra of Lord Shiva and explained how it was one of the best mantras for those suffering from incurable diseases.

Om Haum Jum Sah- meaning 'Lord Shiva, give me life, fill me with life'

Along with this mantra, you need a glass of water with two tulsi leaves, a drop of ganga water and a teaspoon of turmeric powder. When chanting, the water absorbs the vibrations of the sound and is then drunk.

We worked with various cancer patients; some were in the middle of chemotherapy, others had tried all that science could offer. The outcomes were inspiring. The patients suffered from less pain, they had an increased appetite and overall, regained a lot of their lost strength. Many of the patients who I still talk to have continued using the Mhamirtunjya mantra, years after our original meeting.

More assistance from Lord Hanuman

My doctor friend and I spent time in the clinic too, offering mantras for aches and pains, migraines, even for pregnant women who wanted to improve their health and prepare for childbirth.

One case that caught my eye was a woman who had the flu literally every six to eight weeks. She had changed her diet, increased her vitamins and tried to be more physically active when she could, but nothing was making a difference. She was being tested for underlying medical conditions, but at the same time, we worked together on a Hanuman mantra.

On Namo Bhagvate Aanjaneyaay Mahaabalayy Swaahaa

I bow down and surrender to Lord Hanuman, he who is the son of the powerful Anjana.

I actually encouraged many patients to use this mantra because it is good for not only infectious diseases but also diseases in general. In the Hindu epic, Ramayana, the god Hanuman aided in the rescue of the Goddess Sita after she was abducted, so I felt this lady would gain from Hanuman's restorative powers as well as his courage, which would help her continue with her healing. As a mantra that helps to remove disturbances we face in life, we also felt that it would help clear her mind in case this was impacting her immune system.

Two years later, after maintaining a healthy lifestyle and practising this mantra daily, she was free from her continuous bouts of the flu.

THE HEART MANTRA

This is a popular Buddhist sutra. Also known as the Great Heart of Wisdom Sutra, or just the Heart Sutra, essentially, it refers to form as emptiness, explaining that all phenomena are fundamentally empty of essence and ultimate truth is beyond comprehension.

There are various translations of the heart mantra and it can be used in different ways, but our intention was to help people alleviate the symptoms of heart disease.

Gate Gate Pāragate Pārasaṃgate Bodhi Svāhā

Gone, Gone, everyone gone to the other shore, awakening, so be it

The mantra requires the visualisation of the person moving to the shore, but not actually leaving themselves. We worked together on images of the heart disease being taken to the shore and leaving behind what was essentially an empty heart, one not riddled with disease.

This mantra required great dedication and focus, so we also used an English mantra beforehand so that we could concentrate our hearts and minds. We started with deep breathing exercises and repeated "My heart is pure".

Those in our group were not the only ones to experience significant improvements. Many studies have proven a link between anxiety and depression, and chronic heart disease. One study included 41 people with acute coronary syndrome. Over 6 to 18 months, the impact of a 4-day spiritual retreat (which included meditation) was assessed on those who had various degrees of depression. Everyone was less depressed at the end of the study, but those who suffered from the highest levels of depression saw the greatest results.

When you feel like only a miracle will help

My stepfather was in the special forces, a lifetime ago, as he would say, but this gives you an idea of his physical strength. I always saw him as untouchable: nothing could stop him. Still, we started to notice him getting wobbly on his legs and shooting pains going down both sides. Doctors did all of the tests and discovered a pocket of fluid on his lower spine. He went ahead and had the surgery, but unfortunately, after three months of physical therapy, there was no improvement.

He was not going to go in for chanting, but he agreed that if I really wanted to try, I could. I knew it would have to be a mantra that saw fast results if I was going to sway him. I went for this:

Hang Hanumate Rudraatmakaay Hung Phatt

We bow to the highest principle, to Hanuman, the manifestation of the Reliever of suffering. Cut the ego! Purify! I am one with the god.

I was chuffed to bits when I got a phone call just a week later. His symptoms had almost disappeared. There was still the occasional jolt of pain, but he was back doing his DIY and even driving. I knew this mantra would provide him with the power he needed, and it was a relief to see this man so strong again.

A FINAL MANTRA FOR LONGEVITY

The Mahamrityunjaya mantra is one of the most powerful mantras to worship Lord Shiva. The vibrations can keep evil at bay and help restore wellbeing. They can help to overcome negative emotions like jealousy and greed. If you chant this mantra before going to sleep, it may even help prevent nightmares.

Most significantly, it can help rejuvenate your body and promote longevity, warding off death. With a profound belief in its powers and used in the right way, the Mahamrityunjaya mantra can bring your mind and body into one.

You should chant this mantra with your palm completely covering a glass of water. The number 108 is essential, 1 representing self, 0 for nothing, and 8, the symbol of infinity. There are other purported reasons that 108 is of spiritual importance, as we discussed earlier in the book. Once you have repeated it 108 times, you can drink the water or even use it as a spray for yourself or your home.

Aum Tryambakam Yajaamahe Sugandim Pushtivadhanam
Urvaarukamiva Bandhanaan-Mrityormuksheeya Maamritaat

We worship the three-eyed one, who is fragrant and who nourishes all
Like the fruit falls off from the bondage of the stem, we will be
liberated from death and mortality

While there is no possible way to prevent death, this mantra will help to prevent untimely death and the fear we have of dying.

It wasn't just the patients who benefited from the Mahamrityunjaya mantra: the families were also relieved of their suffering. It is extremely painful watching someone you love suffer, and this can often bring about an imbalance in emotions as well as physical problems. Most of the family members also felt rejuvenated, refreshed, and more positive after using this mantra.

Really, there are is an unlimited amount of power that can be unlocked when using mantras for physical healing. It is important that the user of each mantra is convinced that it is going to relieve them from suffering, whether that is for their own symptoms or somebody else's.

From skin disorders to broken bones, from cancer to heartburn, I have seen first-hand how mantras can help an array of people. It's not magic, but watching someone who had no hope of becoming stronger, to see them smile again and to start to enjoy life as they should, the only word to describe the feeling is magical!

CONCLUSION

We have reached the end of this particular journey together. Regardless of where you started, the challenges you faced, your beliefs, your age, or gender, you will now be able to take the knowledge from this book and begin to see the amazing benefits of healing mantras.

The importance of appreciating Hindu culture can't be stressed enough. It is such a pity that a culture and philosophy that has so much wisdom isn't more widely used or is used in the wrong way. The language and traditions are so meaningful that with a true understanding of the power a single sound has, people are able to turn their lives around. Though English mantras can also have healing abilities, it's the sound and vibrations produced in Sanskrit that encourage the most healing and a higher connection to your inner self and the deities, if you so choose.

One of the most significant things to bear in mind is that regardless of your situation, there will be a mantra, but before you randomly select one that you like the sound of or is a little bit easier to roll off the tongue, it is crucial that you strip back all of the layers of stress, pain, obstacles, and worries that you have in your life. You need to discover who you are in the present, not someone's mum or another person's assistant, just you.

From now on, there should be no more vague goals or desires. In order to choose the mantras that will lead to an improved life, you need to know exactly what your intentions are and where you want to go, moving forward. Every person is an individual, so take the time to find out what makes you unique.

Remember the main goals of life according to Vedic thought: Dharna, Artha, Kama, and Moksha, and how important it is that your goals are aligned with the gunas: Sattva, Tamas, and Rajas. When you know what you want to achieve based on your goals and intentions, you will be able to find the most relevant mantras for you.

The how, when, and where you practice your mantras will never be imposed on you. You can't make a mistake by sitting in the wrong position and enrage the gods or feed your negative karma. Most of the time, it is more important that you are comfortable so that you can concentrate. The Kundalini mantras require you to be sat up straight so that the energy at your spine can flow freely up to your mind. In an ideal world, you will be in a peaceful setting, but if that's not possible, as you continue to practise the mantras, your concentration will improve, and you will find it easier to block out the distractions of the world.

Most mantras are more effective when practised before sunrise, as it's the perfect way to clear your mind, align your energies, and start the day with a positive outlook. If you aren't keen on rising as early as the sun, try to incorporate mantras into your morning routine, before the stresses of the day begin. It is also recommended to repeat the mantras before going to bed to encourage a sound night's sleep.

Malas are a wonderful tool that can help you count the number of times you are repeating a mantra and this allows you to focus the mind on the sounds, vibrations, and in some cases, like the Shakti mantras, the area of the body that requires healing.

The glass of water is another amazing tool that will increase the power of the mantras. Don't forget that sound waves travel through water faster than air, so being in front of a glass of water or even covering one with your hand will transfer the sound vibrations to the water.

With regards to both emotional and physical healing, I do recommend using one or even a few of the mantras that prepare the body and mind. Diving straight into a mantra to heal a broken heart won't be as effective if you haven't prepared yourself to begin healing. Think of it as a warmup before going for a run.

I was so fortunate to watch people from my groups and patients in the hospital turn their lives around. The stories are based on real cases, but naturally the names were changed. Though not religious, I can only say that sharing their experiences was a blessing and something I will always be grateful for. Following the journey of people like Shaun, Emma, and Sophie as they freed themselves from everything holding them back showed me that anyone who is willing can learn how to control their emotions, overcome anxiety and go after the things they want in life.

'Flu lady', my stepfather, and the hundreds of patients who were willing to try, despite previous bad experiences or being sceptical, were able to get back on their feet. They were able to go back to the life they thought they would never experience again, but this time, stronger and more determined.

You will notice that many mantras can be used for a variety of reasons and at first, you might struggle to see how the same set of words can achieve two completely different results. This again relates back to your intention of the mantra. Even after years of practice, make sure you are clear with your intentions and adjust your goals before finding a mantra so that the right powers and energies are produced.

You will also find that there may be different translations for the same mantra. Don't worry about this. Have you ever played the game 'whisper down the lane' where you whisper a word to a person, and they have to whisper it back until it reaches the last person? Look at mantras as a game of whisper down the lane that has lasted for around three thousand years and you will see how the concept and meaning are there, but different teachers have translated it in different ways, depending on their regional dialect.

Finally, it has been a great privilege to share my learnings and experiences with you. So many years ago, I had no direction or motivation and I couldn't see my purpose in life. Without healing mantras, I could never have imagined finding the strength, confidence and passion to write a book like this. I hope you have enjoyed reading this book. For further insight you can read my other books on chakras and tarot cards. I truly hope that you to will be able to change your life for the better.

REFERENCES

Dudeja, Jai. (2017). Scientific Analysis of Mantra-Based Meditation and its Beneficial Effects: An Overview. International Journal of Advanced Scientific Technologies in Engineering and Management Sciences. 3. 21. 10.22413/ijastems/2017/v3/i6/49101.

7 Simple Mantras for Healing and Transformation. (2019, October 2). Retrieved from https://chopra.com/articles/7-simple-mantras-for- healing-and-transformation

A. (n.d.). 18 Ways to Create Good Karma. Retrieved from https://chantamantra.com/index.php/ articles/38-18-ways-to-create-good-karma

A. (2017, February 6). Practice the 12-Minute Yoga Meditation Exercise. Retrieved from https://alzheimersprevention.org/ research/kirtan-kriya-yoga-exercise/

A. (2020a, April 24). 10 Powerful Mantras for Meditation - Dhyan Mantras. Retrieved from https://vedicfeed.com/powerful-meditation-mantras/

A. (2020b, July 21). 15 Powerful Ganesh Mantras To Remove Obstacles & For Success. Retrieved from https://vedicfeed.com/powerful-ganesh-mantras/

Alpert, Y. M. (2017, June 26). 13 Major Yoga Mantras to Memorize. Retrieved from https://www.yogajournal.com/ yoga-101/13-major-mantras-memorize #gid=ci020756a3b0142620&pid=majormantra9

Ashley-Farrand, T. (1999). Healing Mantras. Retrieved from https://books.google.es/books?id =zbKv3Jk-3YQC&pg= PA123&lpg=PA123&dq= how+long+does+it+take+for+ healing+mantras+to+work &source=bl&ots=GcKMeCxiDO&sig =ACfU3U2jCoNIy7VUb_0M1qtlsRyytOKfIQ&hl =en&sa=X&ved=2ahUKEwjEj- _Tu7bqAhXcA2MBHdqGBX0 Q6AEwAHoECAkQAQ #v=onepage&q= how%20long%20-does%20it%2 0take%20for%20healing%20 mantras%20to%20-work&f=true

Astrology, T. (2019, August 5). Here's Why The Mahamrityunjaya Mantra Is Chanted 108 Times For Lord Shiva. Retrieved from https://timesofindia.indiatimes.com/astrology/hindu-mythology/ heres-why-the-mahamrityunjaya-mantra-is-chanted-108-times-for-lord-shiva/articleshow/70530345.cms

Ayurveda 101: The Three Doshas- Vata, Pitta, Kapha. (2014). Retrieved from http://www.eattasteheal.com/ ayurveda101/eth_ bodytypes.htm

Ayurvedic Medicine and Therapies and Sunshine Coast. (n.d.). Retrieved from https://yuktibotanicals.vendecommerce.com/pages/the-four-goals-of-life-according-to-ayurveda-purushartha

Cañete, T., Borras, G., Ramos, S., & Khalsa, D. S. (2019). Emotional and Cognitive Improvement with Kirtan Kriya Meditation: A Pilot Study for Mild Cognitive Impairment Patients in a Catalan Community. Mindrxiv. https://doi.org/10.31231/osf.io/y6fku

Castro, J. (2013, November 22). What Is Karma? Retrieved from https://www.livescience.com /41462-what-is-karma.html

Construction of the Vedas - VedicGranth.Org. (n.d.). Retrieved from https://sites.google.com/a/vedicgranth.org/www/what_are_vedic_granth/ the-four-veda/interpretation-and-more/construction-of-the-vedas?mobile=true-

Cowan, J.P. (2016) The Effects of Sound on People. John Wiley and Sons.

Crowley, J. (2017, January 8). 3 Sanskrit Mantras to Boost Your Meditation Practice. Retrieved from https://www.yogiapproved.com /om/3-sanskrit-mantras-boost-meditation-practice/

Desk, F. W. (2019, August 18). Eka Vimshati Namavali of Ganpati: 21 names of Lord Ganesha with meaning and mantras. Retrieved from https://www.freepressjournal.in/webspecial/eka- vimshati-namavali-of-ganpati-21-names-of-lord-ganesha- with-meaning-and-mantras

Digital, T. N. (2020, May 17). The Sun is an eternal source of energy; check out the benefits of chanting the Surya Mantras every morning. Retrieved from https://www.timesnownews. com/spiritual/religion/article/the-sun-is-an-eternal-source-of-energy-   check-out-the-benefits-of-chanting-the-surya-mantras -every-morning/592967

Espada, J. (2020, March 24). Buddhist healing: strengthening health, helping others — downloadable text from Jason Espada: A Collection of Buddhist Methods for Healing. Retrieved from https://buddhaweekly.com/science-mantras-mantras-work-without-   faith-research-supports-effectiveness-sanskrit-mantra- healing-even-environmental-transformation/

Frawley, D. (2010). Mantra Yoga and the Primal Sound. Retrieved   from   https://books.google.es/books?id= a1An08EBHCgC&pg=PA35&lpg=PA35&dq=how+can+ mantras+be+used+for+good+gunas&source=bl&ots= WYcl8cZnzG&sig= ACfU3U3ypcr_YV31mALnu3ifJmc9UchhgQ&hl=en&sa=X& ved= 2ahUKEwii5fukusXqAhULKBoKHVHKBjoQ6AEwCnoECAU QAQ#v=onepage&q=how%20can%20-mantras%20be%20used%20for%20good%20gunas&f=true

Guru Shakti. (2019, October 10). Retrieved from https://www. gurushakti.org.in/672/sadhna   /success-in-life/brahma-mantra-

Hayter, S. W., & Jenny, H. (1977). Cymatics, Vol. II. *Leonardo*, *10*(4), 334. Retrieved from https://monoskop.org/ images/7/78/Jenny_Hans_Cymatics_A_ Study_of_Wave_Phe-nomena_and_Vibration.pdf

https://www.sivasakti.com/tantra/other-hindu-deities/shiva-the-god-of-destruction/. (n.d.). Retrieved from https://www.sivasakti.com/tantra/other-hindu-deities/shiva-the-god-of-destruction/

Iyendo, T.O. (2016). Exploring the effect of sound and music on health in hospital settings: A narrative review. Int J Nurs Stud 63 pp. 82-100

Dudeja, J. P. (2017) Scientific Analysis of Mantra-Based Meditation and Its Beneficial Effects: An Overview. International Journal of Advanced Scientific Technologies in Engineering and Management Sciences 3 (6) pp. 21-26

Luenendonk, M. (2019, September 25). These are the 10 Most Exciting Mantras for Meditation. Retrieved from https://www.cleverism.com/mantras-for-meditation/

Lynch, J., et al. (2018). Mantra meditation for mental health in the general population: A systematic review. European Journal of Integrative Medicine 23 pp. 101-108.

Majumder, S. (2014, August 13). Why is Sanskrit so controversial? Retrieved from https://www.bbc.com/news/world-asia-28755509

mala beads. (2016, October 29). Retrieved from http://www.religionfacts.com/mala-beads

Mantra - New World Encyclopedia. (n.d.). Retrieved from https://www.newworldencyclopedia.org/entry/Mantra

Mark Gungor - The Nothing Box - Part 1. (2013, July 14). [Video file]. Retrieved from https://www.youtube.com/watch?v=SWiBRL-bxiA

Mark, J. J. (2020, July 22). The Vedas. Retrieved from https://www.ancient.eu/The_Vedas/

mindbodygreen. (2020a, January 30). The Transformative Powers of "Bija Mantra" Meditation. Retrieved from https://www.mindbodygreen.com/ 0-5930/The-Transformative-Powers-of-Bija-Mantra- Meditation.html

mindbodygreen. (2020b, April 23). ROYGBIV: Your Guide To The 7 Chakra Colors & How To Use Them. Retrieved from https://www.mindbodygreen.com/articles /7-chakra-colors-what-they-mean-and-why-they-matter

N. (2020c, July 1). 10 Powerful Vishnu Mantras You Should Chant. Retrieved from https://vedicfeed.com/powerful-vishnu-mantra-to-chant/

Nidich S., O'Connor T., Rutledge T., et al. (2016). Reduced trauma symptoms and perceived stress in male prison inmates through the transcendental meditation program: a randomized controlled trial. The Permanente Journal 20 pp. 43-47

NursingAnswers.net. (2020, February 11). Mantra, Music and Reaction Times: Its Applied Aspects. Retrieved from https://nursinganswers.net/essays/ mantra-music-reaction-times-study-applied-9478.php

Ochsner, J. (2014). Meditation and Coronary Heart Disease: A Review of the Current Clinical Evidence. Retrieved from https://www.ncbi.nlm.nih.gov/pmc/articles/PMC4295748/

OM AH HUM Meditation. (2018, June 29). Retrieved from https://www.lamayeshe.com/ article/om-ah-hum-meditation

Om Apavitrah Pavitro Va - In sanskrit with meaning. (n.d.). Retrieved from https://greenmesg.org/stotras/vishnu/om_apavitrah _pavitro_va.php

Prabhu, M. U. (2018, August 10). Mantra Yoga & Shakti Mantras. Retrieved from https://www.vedanet.com/mantra-yoga-primal-sound/

Pradīpaka, G. (n.d.). Learning Sanskrit - Sacred Mantras - Hrim - Sanskrit & Trika Shaivism. Retrieved from https://www. sanskrit-trikashaivism.com   /en/learning-sanskrit-sacred-mantra-s-hrim/476-

Purushartha: The 4 Aims of Human Life. (2019, December 10). Retrieved from https://chopra.com/articles/purushartha-the-4-aims-of-human-life

ReShel, A. (2018, June 12). The Power of Nāda Yoga. Retrieved from https://upliftconnect.com /the-power-of-nada-yoga/

Sakhare, P. (2020, April 14). Green Tara Mantra: Om Tare Tuttare Ture Soha - Learn How to Say It. Retrieved from https://www.yowangdu.com/tibetan-   buddhism/green-tara-mantra.html

Sankar, G. (2015, November 25). Spirituality: Chant Dhanvantri Mantra for healing, good health. Retrieved from https://zeenews.india.com/entertainment/   and-more/spirituality-chant-dhanvantri-mantra-   for-healing-good-health_1826074.html

Search Results for "Gayatri pronunciation" –. (n.d.). Retrieved from https://neensnotes.com/?s=Gayatri+pronunciation&submit=Search

User, S. (n.d.). Daily Vedic Family Prayer. Retrieved from https://aryasamajhouston.org/resources /articals/daily-vedic-family-prayer

Vilhauer, J. (2019, June 29). Mantra: A Powerful Way to Improve Well Being. Retrieved from https://www. psychologytoday.com/us/blog   /living-forward/201906/mantra-powerful-way-improve-   your-well-being

What are Affirmations? (n.d.). Retrieved from http://power-thoughtsmeditationclub.com/what-are-affirmations/

What is the meaning of the mantra Om haum joom sah? How does it work? - Quora. (n.d.). Retrieved from https://www. quora.com/What-is-the-   meaning-of-the-mantra-Om-haum-joom-sah-How- does-it-work%20/

Wikipedia contributors. (2020, June 25). Karma in Hinduism. Retrieved from https://en.wikipedia.org/wiki/Karma_in_ Hinduism

Wray, A. (2014, November 20). Mantra 101 – How to Choose a Mantra. Retrieved from https://www.malacollective.com/ blogs/mala-   collective/15766480-mantra-101-how   -to-choose-a-mantra

MODERN CHAKRA

UNLOCK THE DORMANT HEALING POWERS
WITHIN YOU, AND RESTORE YOUR
CONNECTION WITH THE ENERGETIC WORLD...

INTRODUCTION

It seems like a lifetime ago now, but towards my late twenties, I fell into a bit of a slump that I couldn't get out of. It shouldn't have been that way, because life was good, but there was something out of place that I couldn't label or identify.

If you have read my book *Healing Mantras*, you will remember my rather individual friend who passionately threw herself into spiritualism. She was somewhat misguided and felt the need to keep putting her crystals on various parts of my body while she chanted. I didn't feel like I was being healed at all, in fact, I felt quite uncomfortable really.

I couldn't tell her this. She was completely convinced that she had become a spiritual healer. I thought I should find some proof that she was being conned. And so, my research began. The first book I read on chakras and their healing potential was like listening to the juiciest piece of gossip. Talking to myself, I filled the room with "No Way?", "Really?", and endless "Serious-ly?"s. I learnt that although my friend's methods were wrong, understanding chakras could provide me with the help I needed.

"When you touch the celestial in your heart, you will realise that the beauty of your soul is so pure, so vast and so devastating that you have no option but to merge with it. You have no other option but to feel the rhythm of the universe in the rhythm of your heart."

– Amit Ray, author and spiritual teacher

I came across this quotation and I felt it made great sense. Each and every one of us has so much power and potential, but it is rare that we are able to use it.

We can't reach our potential, because, on the one hand, we are lost by what this is. We might focus on our potential with regard to our day-to-day responsibilities, whether at work or at home. We can see our potential in a hobby or a sport. But what about our potential to be a good human being? What of our potential to pick up someone else's trash, or to spend some time with the elderly neighbour, because she has no family?

On the other hand, there is already so much weight on our shoulders, can we really take on anymore? Feeling the true beauty of your heart is so impactful and awakening that we may fear this. There is too much to cope with already and we can't pull ourselves away from what society tells us is important.

In today's world, it is impossible to escape stress. We live under so much pressure to be the best at everything we do and to be successful that we spend almost all of our time reaching for success, but when we get there, we always want more. For some, it is just impossible to break free from the pressure they are under to accomplish even the smallest of things.

This has massive health impacts, both physically and mentally. Chronic stress can lead to negative behaviours, like alcohol abuse and overeating, for example. Emotionally, we feel anxious and even depressed.

Others may have suffered traumatic times in their past—perhaps an abusive partner, divorce, or the loss of someone close to them. Such events are incredibly difficult to move on from and sometimes, without help, people can never start appreciating life again.

At the same time, your life could be going relatively well, but you could still feel like something is out of place, that there is an imbalance in your life and that if you knew how to correct this, you feel that you would be able to find some inner peace, perhaps even enjoy the beauty in the world, rather than letting the negatives overpower you.

Your initial interest in chakras might be similar to mine—pure curiosity. You might have a physical or mental illness that you feel will benefit from unblocking your chakras, or perhaps you are desperately looking for a way to find some mental peace. Even if you want to learn about chakras so that you can help others, we are going to delve deep into the world of chakras and how they can be used in our modern world.

Together, we will work through techniques for unblocking your chakras so that you can take advantage of the energy that is kept within us. It is important for me to provide as many tools as possible, so that you can experiment and see which methods best suit you, so feel free to use the ideas that, to an extent, get you excited and motivated. The aim is not to make this a lecture with daily homework.

The results can be life-changing, and I don't want to sound dramatic here. Since studying chakras, how they are used, and their specific benefits, I have not only seen improvements in my life, but also in all of those that I have worked with—even the complete sceptics.

We have learnt how to take care of ourselves so that we are better able to help others. We have found more motivation to do things that we often put off, whether that's the spring cleaning or the cruise we always dreamed of. By unblocking our chakras, we have been able to find happiness in our lives and to really feel the rhythm of our hearts.

I changed my life from one of going through the motions to one of significance. I knew I didn't want just to be someone's wife or someone's mum. I wanted to continue with my roles, but to define myself as more. By creating balance in my life, I found the confidence not only to meet like-minded people, but also to share my learnings and my zest with others.

My journey started with doubt and I admit I was dubious of this Eastern philosophy. The more I discovered, the hungrier I became for the subject. I collaborated with medical practitioners, physiotherapists, and psychologists as well as spiritual experts, in order to gain an extensive understanding of chakras. I became so passionate about chakras that I wanted to know everything there was to know, starting with the foundations of chakras.

PART I

THE WHAT, WHERE AND WHY OF CHAKRAS

In the first part of this book, we are going to gain a fundamental knowledge of what our chakras actually are and why it is important to learn how to create balance among them. We will explore the universal energies and how such energies can be found in everything. As well as energy, we will appreciate how vibrational frequencies play a role in our healing.

You might be able to learn enough about chakras from a blog or two, but then you may come back asking why there hasn't been the result you had expected, or why you feel like your emotions have moved to the other extreme, rather than finding a balance.

This is why I always begin a book with plenty of detail and history, so that you can get a complete feel for the concepts. Here, we will learn about the direction and strength of the energy that flows through us, and most importantly, we are going to look at safe practices. Before we work on techniques to awaken our chakras and find balance, we have to learn exactly what a blocked chakra feels like and identify exactly what it is we hope to gain.

CHAKRAS 101

The very first thing I wanted to do during my research phase was to meet someone who had benefited from unblocking their chakras. I didn't want to talk to a healer, or even have a chakra-cleansing session. I wanted an honest conversation over a cup of coffee with an everyday person. This is when I met Helen.

Helen worked as an administrator in a hospital. She was grateful to have a job, but there were a lot of negative things about it. She saw horrible cases, witnessed people suffering and had to cope with the tense emotions of patients and families on a daily basis. She was single and her family lived in another state. Her social life involved her pet dog. She was quiet, timid, sweet, and you could tell that she would never say "no" to doing something for others, even if it meant great sacrifices for herself.

She rarely cooked for herself and admitted to not having the best diet. She constantly had colds and sore throats and didn't have the energy or the inclination to exercise. She didn't want to meet new friends and go out, because she didn't feel emotionally strong enough.

After meeting with a chakra expert, Helen told me how her life had changed. The most significant shift was seen in her job. She felt more energetic at work. Each patient that came through the doors was no longer a problem for her. She saw herself as their solution. Her attitude had changed, and this allowed her to appreciate her role in their care. Being more emotionally aware, Helen became better at helping the patients and this resulted in the patients being nicer.

At the end of her day, she didn't feel so burdened by her awful day at work, and felt she wanted to start doing things. Her experience with the chakra expert had been a positive one and so she joined a yoga class to continue learning more. Here, she met new people and she made plans with them. She met a lovely man and though she was still a little shy when talking about her feelings, the happiness radiated from her.

I knew at this point I had only spoken to one person, but I also knew that Helen had no reason to exaggerate her experience. It lit a spark. If Helen could unblock her chakras and notice such a difference, what other possibilities could be achieved?

So, how can our chakras be used to make the changes we want? Let's begin by looking at what chakras are exactly.

WHAT ARE CHAKRAS?

In the simplest terms, chakras are understood to be energy wheels that are positioned along the length of our spine. It is a very intricate subject, as each chakra is linked to certain areas of the body. Each of the chakras are said to have individual traits, and in modern usage, they are often also related to a specific colour. All of these points are important to know in order to gain the most benefit.

Chakra- meaning 'wheel' (pronounced /sha-kra/)

For a clearer mind and a healthier body, energy needs to flow through our bodies. When we experience an imbalance, it often means that one or all of our chakras are blocked, and this prevents energy from flowing. In the most widely-studied modern system, there are seven principal chakras, the first at the base of our spine and the final one at the crown of our head. Historically, the concept of chakras has played a role in both Hindu and Buddhist traditions. Buddhist texts typically refer to five principal chakras, whereas Hindu works mention six or seven. In this book, we work with the seven chakra system that has become the most popular framework in the West. This is based on an eleventh century Hindu text that was translated and popularised—with modern additions, including the use of colour—in the twentieth century.

Imagine each of your chakras as a water wheel. When the first water wheel spins correctly, it will pour water into the next, and allow that one to start spinning, and so on. When someone throws a stick into the first water wheel, none of the others will receive any water. Our energy can be sat at the base of our spine, around the first chakra, but only when we remove the metaphorical stick, will our energy start to flow.

For now, we will just touch on the main functions of each chakra, as each one has a dedicated chapter later on. In some spiritual teachings, you will see twelve, twenty-two, or even more chakras. The core seven chakras are related to the body; the additional ones are related to spirituality. By way of introduction, we will talk about twelve, but for the rest of the book, the focus will be on the seven that we can work on through physical practice. Even though the association of each chakra with a particular colour is a modern addition, I personally find it helpful in visualising these different energy centres and bringing to mind their functional attributes, so I have included the colours here.

Root Chakra (associated colour-red)

This is this first chakra and is found at the base of your spine. It is connected to your tailbone, legs, feet, bladder and large intestine. The Root Chakra is related to power and when blocked, you may feel that you don't have the power you need to get yourself out of a situation.

Sacral Chakra (associated colour-orange)

As it is close to the reproductive organs, the Sacral Chakra is about sex and fertility. It can also impact your spleen, gallbladder, and kidneys. There is a strong relationship with honesty, and in particular, an honest sex life, in which you take responsibility for your sexual activities.

Solar Plexus Chakra (associated colour- yellow)

You can detect your Solar Plexus Chakra in your chest area. It points to your pride and confidence and if it is blocked, you may struggle to feel good about your achievements. If you have problems with your digestive system, small intestine, or pancreas, you might need some healing in this area.

Heart Chakra (associated colour- green)

As it is located close to your heart, unblocking this chakra can have wonderful results on your relationships and the love you feel. However, when blocked, you may experience heartbreak or issues with your lungs, shoulders, arms, hands, and/or the thymus gland (the creator of cells that help our immune system).

Throat Chakra (associated colour- blue)

The Throat Chakra sits just over your vocal cords and is essential for communication. If blocked, you might feel like nobody seems to understand your point of view, or that they just aren't listening. It can also impact your mouth, including the tongue and gums, your neck, glands, and even perspiration.

Third Eye Chakra (associated colour- indigo)

Sitting between your eyes, just on the forehead, the Third Eye Chakra not only relates to good vision but the ability to foresee the circumstances in your life. The energy in this wheel can help improve your instincts and alleviate problems with your ears, nose, throat and brain.

Crown Chakra (associated colour- purple)

At the highest point of our physical body, the Crown Chakra is our closest connection with the divine. It is often linked to positive karma. Some do not consider this as a true chakra, but simply a centre for the other chakras. In line with the seven chakra system, I count it as a seventh chakra. Scriptural sources also vary regarding its location: some place it at the top of the head, while others regard it as beyond the physical body. For religious people, prayer can help to develop your divine connection; for the non-religious, we can practise meditation. It can affect our nervous system and the pituitary gland (the master gland that secretes hormones into our bloodstream).

Picturing my colourful chakras running up my spine always made me think of the multicoloured ice poles and my legs were the stick. The colours continue for the additional five chakras:

- 8th chakra- seafoam green, it activates our spiritual skills
- 9th chakra- blue-green, the skills we have learnt from our life experiences
- 10th chakra- pearl white, awakening the divine creativity
- 11th chakra- pink-orange, advanced spiritual skills such as telekinesis
- 12th chakra- gold, the connection with the cosmos

As we are concerned with physical and emotional healing, it won't be necessary for us to talk about the eighth to twelfth chakras, however, it is still a very interesting area if you want to learn more.

THE HISTORY OF CHAKRAS

Like so many things in the world, the West tends to take credit for things that have been around for years. In this case, when chakras reached the West around a hundred years ago, we didn't claim to invent the idea of chakras, but we did blend together various traditions and add our own western spin.

The term 'chakra' originates in the vedas, the ancient scriptures that underpin Hinduism. However, David Gordon White, a scholar of Indian cultures and religions, argues that chakras, in the sense that we now understand them—as inner energy centres—were introduced in Buddhist texts in the eighth century of the Common Era. Similar notions of 'energy centres' are also found in Jewish and Christian texts.

As with many of the traditional Indian spiritual teachings, the knowledge and wisdom were not passed down through writing, but orally. When the concepts reached the West, we began to create books about chakras.

Because of the age of the chakra teachings and the traditional methods of teaching, the main concept may have remained essentially the same, but many interpretations have developed along the way. This is most noticeable when talking about the number of chakras. I have already explained that there are differing interpretations of the number of key chakras—typically five, six or seven—but the additional energy wheels also cause debate, with some even believing there are a hundred or more.

Over time, the precise location of the chakras has also been debated. This is because they aren't organs or sets of tissues and bones. The Heart Chakra is associated with the heart, but it isn't over the heart. Some believe that it is in the centre of the chest, while others feel it is to the left, above the heart.

Yoga is mentioned in the Rigveda and the Upanishads, important Hindu scriptures, but some believe it predates these. However, scholar of religious studies, Geoffrey Samuel, suggests that yoga was likely not developed as a systematic study until the fifth or sixth century before the Common Era. Yoga is both a philosophy and a broad set of practices, but in the West, we typically use the term in a narrower sense to refer to hatha yoga practices, consisting mainly of a set of postures, or asanas. Hatha yoga has origins in Tantra, esoteric Hindu and Buddhist traditions, and its texts date from between the ninth and eleventh centuries. Needless to say, the practices of yoga have seen a great number of changes, both over many centuries of cultural practice in the Indian subcontinent and through the course of their introduction to the West. As yoga and chakra healing has matured to meet the ever-evolving needs of humanity, we begin to see how the original teachings, which already varied from region to region, have adapted to cultural influences.

HOW CULTURAL CHANGES HAVE INFLUENCED THE DIRECTION OF OUR ENERGETIC FLOW

It fascinates me how even those with higher spiritual awareness can still disagree on which way our energy flows. Does it pass up through our body, or does it flow down? Previously, we focused on the energy that flowed from our Root Chakra up to our Crown Chakra. This was because of the importance of attaining a higher state of consciousness and your energy needed to be driven upwards towards the divine. It was a case of mind over matter. The elevated levels of stress we suffer from today mean that we should be trying to ground our energies. This helps us to remain connected with our physical self and enables us to calm down, even to reduce the stress and anxiety we feel.

Who are we to argue with the great Hindu teachers? These teachers shared their wisdom and allowed their students to create their own processes based on their experiences. I try to follow their example, particularly when deciding if our energy flows up or down.

Visualisation of your energy is an essential part of chakra healing. I try not to focus on whether my energy is flowing up or down. After all, I am a little greedy and I want to gain a better understanding of my higher consciousness and at the same time I want to reduce my stress. I like to visualise my energy spreading throughout my body, touching the areas that need it the most.

As you experiment with the techniques, you may find that in certain circumstances, you will benefit more from imagining your energy flowing up out of your body and towards the divine. I found this helped when I needed inspiration and to find creative ways to solve problems.

Other times I felt that parts of my body required a greater flow of energy, so I concentrated on opening the flow of energy and directing it to where it was most needed, whether that was up, down, or all around. The more you practise, the more aware you will become of the directional flow of your energy and it is important that, with regards to healing, we are all looking for different outcomes.

HOW DO CHAKRAS WORK?

Everything in the world has energy. It is something we tend not to think about, as we don't have time to stop and look around. Every cell in our body releases energy. The kind of energy and how much depends on the functions of the cells. Up to here, science and spirituality can agree.

However, there is no evidence for the existence of chakras. Practitioners may argue that this is because the kind of energy we are harnessing is not detectable by means currently available to scientists. We cannot prove the existence of chakras, so this requires a leap of faith for those who prefer to follow the facts. I tend to compare chakras to love. You know what it feels like, even if you can't see it or touch it.

Chakras can spin either clockwise or anticlockwise. When spinning clockwise, energy is pushed out of our body into a field around you.

Anticlockwise chakras draw energy from the world around you and pull it into your body. These powerful wheels of energy can be open or blocked. They can even be overactive or underactive.

It is believed that the chakras use the endocrine system and the nervous system to interact with the physical and energetic body. Each one is located near and works with one of the endocrine glands or a plexus (a group of nerves). This is how working to unblock a particular chakra can help to heal certain parts of the body related to a particular endocrine gland or plexus.

We can use chakras to heal parts of our consciousness too. Your senses, perception of reality and the various states of awareness are divided into seven groups and each is associated with a chakra. When a certain part of your consciousness is stressed or suffering, you will likely feel the tension on or around that chakra. The physical symptoms are a sign of our consciousness telling us of a problem within that chakra. Your legs will probably stop shaking once the nervous situation is over, but if a problem like a heartache, anxiety, or depression are not dealt with, the connected chakra will continue to present physical symptoms of the suffering.

If we go through a negative experience that produces low-frequency energy, the chakra that it is linked to may close as a form of protection. The chakra can also close when we avoid handling our negative emotions. This is how I was able to understand my problems. I knew that something was wrong, but I couldn't physically put my finger on the problem. It was the tension across my body that I felt, like a form of immense pressure.

WHAT INFLUENCES THE BALANCE OF OUR CHAKRAS?

Our daily lives are full of experiences, both good and bad, that can impact the balance of our chakras. The hug of a loved one or the smile of your child stimulates your body and influences the way you feel. Watching the news causes us to feel sorrow and shame for those worse off than we are. Even stubbing your little toe can adjust the energy you have within you. While at a physical level, these interactions register as neural activity and hormone responses, I believe that each action is also registered in one of the seven chakras, depending on the physical part of the body or the emotions we feel.

Different cultural environments can play a role in the balance of our chakras. For example, in western cultures, we place emphasis on mental abilities and scientific theories. This leads to the third chakra dominating over the others. Mediterranean countries can arguably experience a stronger second chakra, because of their mores sensual and expressive cultures.

Our body tries to maintain a balance within the chakras, but with so much going on, it is a challenging mission. When one chakra is underactive, another one will work overtime. This draws energy away from other parts of your body. Despite trying to fix the wrong, we tend to feel more imbalance.

Our lifestyle will also determine the flow of our energy and potential imbalance. A balanced diet is essential, in order to feed each chakra with the right type of fuel. Again, we will talk more of this when we go into the details of each chakra. There is a massive difference between working at a desk all day and being able to get out and experience the smells and colours of the natural world.

Knowing exactly what chakras are and how they function is the first step to exploring the relationship between our energy centres and how we can look to unblock them. There is no end of unit tests and I know that you might not remember all of the names and exact characteristics just yet—that's ok. For now, it is great that you are aware of the seven chakras running along your spine and you are ready to learn how to unblock them.

POWERFUL HEALING CENTRES

As we work together through this chapter, I will provide examples of potential signs and symptoms so that you can relate to the concepts more easily. Be careful though, our brains have a way of tricking us into thinking that this is the exact same problem that we have. Going through the different understandings, take a moment to see how this relates to you and your chakras. Hopefully, by the end of this chapter, you will have a list of the chakras that you feel are blocked or overactive.

HOW DO BLOCKED CHAKRAS AFFECT YOUR HEALTH?

Each of our chakras will contain an element of Prana, the ultimate, pure, healing energy. When chakras are blocked, you might notice a range of symptoms, because it's this healing energy which keeps us happy and healthy.

Though we have touched on how each chakra can impact the body, let's take a closer look at what you could experience when the chakras are blocked.

Root Chakra

The Root Chakra is like the foundations of your body and will provide you with support. It is closely related to our survival instincts, the need for food, shelter, and security. Because of the stress we feel when our basic needs are not met, a blocked Root Chakra can lead to anxiety disorders and our fears taking control of our lives. With excessive nervousness, we may experience problems with our bladders, like when you go to the toilet five times before an exam. There could also be issues with the lower back and limbs.

Sacral Chakra

When this chakra is blocked, you may have a problem expressing your sexual pleasure, as well as lacking that sense of completeness when we are happy. It can also point to how you express your creativity. When blocked, you may have ideas but be unable to find the right way to go about turning them into a reality. In terms of physical health, you might have problems with your reproductive system, sexual dysfunctions or a lack of sexual appetite.

Solar Plexus Chakra

We rely on the Solar Plexus Chakra for our determination and commitment. It is the control we have over ourselves and the unique power that we possess. A lack of confidence may be noticed when this chakra is blocked. You might also find it more difficult to make the right decision and you might spend a lot of time procrastinating. These negative emotions you feel about yourself can lead to bursts of anger. Due to the location, it is most often associated with digestive problems.

Heart Chakra

As well as the logical connection to the heart and how we give and receive love, the Heart Chakra being blocked can make it more difficult to forgive and make us feel less compassionate. A blocked Heart Chakra can bring about some very powerful negative emotions, including jealousy, hatred, and grief. You might find it impossible to forgive others and move on. If you are not in a relationship, a blocked Heart Chakra can make it far more difficult to find love. Physically, you might have a low immune system, heart or lung problem, high or low blood pressure or poor circulation.

Throat Chakra

This chakra is the ruler of your communication. You might think you have expressed yourself well, but others don't seem to follow what you are saying. You might struggle to find the words for the right situation. I realised I might have a problem with a blocked Throat Chakra when I met with the vicar to plan my grandad's funeral. The first thing I said when I opened the door was "Good God, you're tall", followed by "Jesus, sorry", and I just couldn't shut up. When blocked, you may also find it difficult to listen, which is equally important in successful communication. There might be thyroid issues and tension across your shoulders up to your neck through to your head.

Third Eye Chakra

As well as your intuition, many believe that the Third Eye Chakra is the link between your physical self and the world around you. It is critical to unblock this chakra if you want to be able to clear the cloudiness around situations and see things for how they really are. I found this necessary when planning practical goals that I knew I had the skills to obtain. A judgemental attitude, depression, and/or anxiety may be accompanied by headaches, dizzy spells, and other potential health issues related to the brain, such as memory problems.

Crown Chakra

When open and balanced, you can benefit from being fully aware of who you are in relation to the rest of the universe. For some, this is about gaining a spiritual connection, but for others, it is about feeling your normal self, well and positive. When it is blocked, you can feel as if you don't know what your purpose is, or that you are not connected to anything. Without connections, you can feel as if you are very much alone in the world and this can be extremely distressing. A blocked Crown Chakra can be associated with neurological disorders, nerve pain, recurring migraines, insomnia, and depression.

WHAT MIGHT YOU EXPERIENCE IF YOUR CHAKRAS ARE OVERACTIVE?

The above physical and emotional symptoms are what you can expect to feel when one or more of the chakras are blocked. When they are underactive, it is quite possible that you will experience milder symptoms. So, if you are experiencing headaches, it could be that your Crown Chakra is underactive, rather than blocked, which could lead to migraines.

When your chakras are overactive, you might experience some of the following emotions:

Root Chakra- you might be nervous, especially when it comes to change. You may also be overly obsessed with material objects, possibly greedy.

Sacral Chakra- it is possible that you are too quick to form relationships. You might be too sensitive, causing you to be moody. You might like the drama in life and have a habit of crossing boundaries.

Solar Plexus Chakra- you may feel the need to dominate others and you can come across as aggressive. You might expect perfection from yourself and others.

Heart Chakra- your love could be too much for some and you appear to be clingy in relationships. You may not have enough boundaries and tend to say "yes" just to please others.

Throat Chakra- it is likely that you talk too much and you fail to listen to others. This could be to the extent that you are verbally abusive and criticise others.

Third Eye Chakra- you may struggle to concentrate, often slipping into daydreams or even hallucinations. As you aren't in touch with reality, it might be hard for you to use your good judgement.

Crown Chakra- your focus on spirituality may lead you to abandon your bodily needs. It might be hard for you to control your feelings.

WHAT TO EXPECT WHEN YOU TAKE THE TIME TO AWAKEN, BALANCE, AND GRADUALLY OPEN YOUR CHAKRAS

When the chakras are all functioning in the right way, the flow of energy within your body will be corrected and you will gain an overall sense of balance in yourself and your life.

This will be achieved when you become aware of certain properties of chakras, including:

- The different qualities of energies within a chakra and their frequencies
- The correct level of intensity, not being overactive or underactive
- If they should be flowing clockwise or anticlockwise
- The polarity—if the energy flows inward or outward.

The experiences we have been through in life will not only affect one chakra. The seven chakras are interlinked. While we will focus our healing efforts on one or maybe two chakras, there will be a positive impact on all of them.

Most significantly, you will notice a balance between your spiritual side and your physical self. The lower chakras include the Root Chakra, the Sacral Chakra, and the Solar Plexus Chakra. These lower chakras generally reflect your physical self, how you view yourself and the emotions you feel. They flow up to the Heart Chakra. The higher chakras—the Throat Chakra, Third Eye Chakra and the Crown Chakra—are generally concentrated on your spirituality and higher consciousness.

These connect to the lower energy wheels via the Heart Chakra.

We will strive to gain a balance between your physical and spiritual self. This will allow you to experience a better body, whether you want to strengthen a certain part of you or overcome an illness. With this, you can view yourself in a positive light and see an improvement in the feelings you have for yourself. But we will also work on the spiritual side to make sure you feel complete. This doesn't imply that you will all of a sudden discover your religious beliefs: it is about being more conscious of who you truly are.

HOW WILL YOU KNOW IF YOUR CHAKRAS ARE BALANCED?

Similarly to the precise location of the chakras, it is difficult to put a finger on what it is like when the lower and higher chakras are all balanced. It's that moment when you realise that life is good or when you wake up one morning and you suddenly appreciate that you don't have the weight of the world on your shoulders. You are happy and you genuinely feel great and optimistic. It's hard to imagine, because, for many of us, we have put up with years of just trying to survive; we can't remember what this feeling is actually like.

For me, it was the sensation of the sea covering my feet—the contrast of the warm sand below and the cool water above. You know the feeling of working hard on a hot summer's day, completing your entire to-do list and sitting down with a cold beer to take in your success. Or waking up on a Sunday with the whole day just for you. It's freedom from the life you wanted to leave behind you.

You will sense the balance of your chakras when you are aware of how each of the seven energy wheels is functioning. You will see great changes in so many areas of your life, as if the puzzle pieces are finally fitting together.

Why We Don't Want to Open Our Chakras

Our goal in this book is to balance our chakras. Just as one problem in your life can affect a number of other areas, one imbalanced chakra can cause the others to become out of balance, interrupting the complete flow of the energy in your body.

When your chakras are balanced, you will notice that it is easier to heal, both physically and mentally. You will have a greater sense of who you are and what you and your body need. You are more aware of the world around you and you can learn how to use what the world offers to your advantage. Because of heightened awareness of your own emotions and those of others, you will be better at communicating and creating more meaningful relationships.

With that in mind, I want to quickly mention the reason why we want to balance our chakras and not open them. Opening chakras before you are ready can be dangerous, as you aren't prepared for the amount of openness you can receive. Your true nature can become more powerful; this initially seems like a good thing, but you must learn how to cope with negativity and pain. Otherwise, you may end up adjusting to this negativity and even projecting it onto others around you.

If we haven't had enough time to learn about our chakras, opening them could lead to a rush of emotions that we cannot protect ourselves from, even feelings that aren't our own and that could be coming from those around us. If you take on the negative emotions of others, you will be overwhelmed, and this could lead to anxiety and depression. Ironically, you could find yourself in a worse situation than you are currently in.

Before jumping into opening chakras, it is critical that you learn how to cleanse and slowly awaken them, so that you can better control your emotions and the potential outcomes. You do not want to open your chakras and find yourself in a realm that you can't handle.

I have witnessed first-hand what happens when people try to force open their chakras. They feel like they are in a desperate situation and this requires drastic actions. Highly sensitive people have rushed the process instead of taking the time to awaken and then balance chakras. I have seen the strength of other people's negativity consuming them and causing them to do all sorts of extreme things. In some cases, it was incredibly hard to come back from.

The point is not to scare you, but just to say that there is a logical, safe process to working with chakras and learning how to balance them. This is the process that we will work on throughout the book.

WHICH TO TACKLE FIRST—BALANCING CHAKRAS OR HEALING EMOTIONS?

So, here is the chicken and egg conundrum of chakras and our emotions—which do we tackle first? By the time your body sends the right signals to let you know you are thirsty, you are already dehydrated; the same goes for chakras. By the time your body tells you that there is an imbalance in your chakras, the emotional damage has already been caused. Do you start by working to understand and overcome your emotions so that you can balance your chakras, or do you focus on balancing your chakras to help your emotions?

Changing one thing can often negatively impact something else, albeit briefly. If you have ever had a massage, you might feel sensational straight after, but the massage has caused a release of chemicals in your body, and this can cause you to feel achy or groggy the following day.

For this reason, we might have to use other methods alongside the balancing of chakras, in order to successfully release one symptom without allowing the consequences to take their toll. I am a huge fan of yoga and meditation. Both have been used in Hinduism and other religions together with chakra healing. Mantras are another tool that enabled me to really see some amazing changes in my life. Let's take a look at how you too can benefit from some of the other life-changing techniques from the Eastern teachings.

PART II

UNDERSTANDING THE TECHNIQUES USED TO BALANCE CHAKRAS

It's pretty fascinating stuff when you dig a little deeper than the top layer. For me, it was almost like just understanding that these spinning wheels existed enabled me to become more aware of my flow of energy and the impact of this slightest thing that can, in turn, have an impact on other chakras.

Part 2 is all about how we can begin to create a balance. We will cover a wide range of techniques that aren't only associated with Hinduism. If you have ever wanted to explore the healing benefits of reiki and reflexology, it's time to get comfortable and read on.

If you never understood why a certain smell calms you down in an instant, we will talk about some of the key essential oils that are used in aromatherapy. A book about balancing the chakras just wouldn't be complete without exploring yoga and meditation. And you will be able to discover ways of combining various techniques to find the best healing methods for you.

Part 2 touches on some of the ideas, let's call it the appetisers, before the main course, which is coming up in Part 3!

MANTRAS AND MEDITATION, THE KEYS TO THE HEALING KINGDOM

I had already dabbled in a little yoga, but I was far from an expert in my early days. It is not essential that you have practised yoga to enjoy the benefits of meditation, nor vice versa. At the same time, you don't need to be able to speak Sanskrit or believe in the deities to appreciate the effects of mantras.

This chapter is going to explain the difference between affirmations and mantras and how both of these tools can be used to further create balance in our lives. Then we will move onto meditation, an area that I personally found extremely challenging, but I am so glad I was determined enough to stick at it.

WHAT IS A MANTRA?

Mantras are words or sentences that focus on sounds rather than the actual meaning. Most traditional mantras were originally prayers or songs that were used to speak to the gods and gain a higher conscious connection to the spiritual world. Like chakras, mantras were first mentioned in the Upanishads and are a key part of the Hindu teachings that have been passed down orally over thousands of years.

Whether meditating or just chanting mantras, the repetition of the sounds is a tool that allows your mind to focus, to stop working overtime regarding your chaotic life and to simply be in the moment. Each sound in the mantra has a specific vibration that it is believed can encourage immense healing in the body.

Mantras are usually repeated 108 times and people will often hold a mala to help them keep track of the number of repetitions. A mala is a set of 108 beads, and you slide your finger over each one in turn as you say your mantra. This is another tool that will help you to remain focused on your healing, rather than the number of times you have said your mantra.

When chanting, or even repeating a mantra silently, certain parts of the brain are activated so that we feel less stress and more relaxed. The positive vibrations help to reduce the negativity we feel.

Western science has even taken an interest in the healing benefits of mantras. To date, a number of scientific studies have been carried out, with very mixed outcomes. This is partly because the conditions of the experiments are very difficult to control. For example, it is tricky to account for preconceptions that participants have about mantras and to rule out other factors that may also be at play during the experiment.

Medical researchers conducted a systematic review of mantras in 2018, collating the findings of over two thousand sets of study data, but found that ninety percent of those studies were of 'weak quality'. The researchers concluded that 'there is some evidence that mantra meditation can improve mental health and negative affectivity [experience of negative emotions] in non-clinical populations, however poor study quality may hinder the extent to which one can be certain about the accuracy of these findings.' My advice in this book is simply to suggest that you try out mantras, be open to possibilities, and see if they work for you. I personally feel that they can be very powerful and have found them highly useful in my own life.

To gain the most from mantras, it is recommended to chant them for ten to fifteen minutes in the morning and evening. More specifically, many of the mantras should be chanted before or during sunrise; however, I found that starting my day with my mantras was a great way to begin with a positive outlook. Last thing at night is a good time to calm the mind before falling asleep.

There are probably hundreds of thousands of mantras, all with various purposes and intentions. If you want to learn more about mantras, you can find my book *Healing Mantras*. It takes a closer look at the history of mantras and how they have a positive impact on healing. There are hundreds of examples and even pronunciation tips. The group that we are going to look at are bija mantras.

WHAT IS A BIJA MANTRA?

Everything we say produces sound waves, which transmit at certain vibrational frequencies. Bija mantras are also known as seed mantras; these monosyllabic seed sounds have no literal translation, but it is believed that the vibrations they create can lead to incredible physical and emotional healing.

More specifically, bija mantras were created with the intention to create a balance between the body and mind and even the soul. This is done by tapping into the unique rhythms and pulses the different parts of our body have.

The healing benefits of sound waves have gained more credibility in the last half a century or so, due to the study of psychoacoustics, the neuroscience of music and music psychology. What some would once call sound energy for healing, others would today call sound therapy.

I'm still fascinated by how such small words, even sounds, could stimulate all of my senses and allow me to become more aware of everything around me. The bija mantras for chakras can really help you to concentrate on your body and its needs at the time.

BIJA MANTRAS FOR CHAKRAS

There is one bija mantra for each chakra. It is most beneficial if you are sitting down in a cross-legged position, if you are comfortable to do so. Grab a cushion or a yoga mat if it helps. It is important that you are sat up straight and if possible, in a calm environment.

- Root Chakra- Lam
- Sacral Chakra- Vam
- Solar Plexus Chakra- Ram
- Heart Chakra- Yam
- Throat Chakra- Ham
- Third Eye Chakra- U or Aum
- Crown Chakra- Om or Aum

In each of these seeds or syllables, the a is pronounced as u, so you produce a more throaty, deeper sound. Lam is pronounced lum, the same sound as plum. The exception is the Third Eye Chakra, which is pronounced like the U in uber.

Chanting one of the bija mantras to awaken your chakra requires a focus on the area you are aiming to heal and create balance in. Let's look at some examples of how to use these mantras.

Sandra had pulled a muscle in her calf and needed to allow for more energy in her Sacral Chakra. She repeated "Vam" 432 times. This was 4 sets of 108. She did this in the morning and evening but also before she went for her daily walk.

Charlie had recently separated from his wife. He felt a tightness in his chest and was in complete despair. He chanted "Yam" 108 times in four sessions throughout the day.

Carol felt that she was slightly overweight. She also suffered from frequent headaches and had problems sleeping. In this case, we needed to work on two of her chakras—the Root Chakra and the Third Eye Chakra. In order to concentrate fully on the area that needs healing, you should complete one set of the bija mantra and then a second set for a different chakra.

Carol chanted "Lam" 108 times followed by "U" 108 times. She did this twice a day, but when she began to feel a headache coming on, she also stopped what she was doing and repeated "U", the Third Eye Chakra, 108 times.

It is also recommended that all mantras are repeated for a minimum period of thirty days. You may also find it helpful to focus on the colour that is associated with the particular chakra you are working on.

Finally, don't forget your breathing. It must be slow, deep, and controlled. Maintaining a steady rhythm with your breathing will help you not to rush through the process. Visualisation and breathing are so important when using bija mantras for chakra healing; we will touch on both in more detail towards the end of this chapter.

WHAT ARE AFFIRMATIONS?

The mind is both incredibly powerful and incredibly busy! It is estimated that we have over 6000 individual thoughts per day. Even imagining that we have this many thoughts is exhausting. We then have to realise how many of these thoughts are negative. One study found that sixty to seventy percent of participants' spontaneously occurring thoughts were negative, despite the fact that most of them considered themselves to be positive people.

"There is nothing either good or bad, but thinking makes it so."

— WILLIAM SHAKESPEARE

This quote from Shakespeare makes a lot of sense. Realistically, we all have to do the grocery shopping. This is neither good nor bad until we relate an emotion to it. Yet, if I think that the supermarket is going to be packed and on top of that, I have a huge shopping list, shopping becomes a negative thought. On the other hand, if I am thinking that if I buy those ingredients, I can try that new recipe I have been meaning to make, shopping becomes a positive thought.

The problem is that today's society is a rather negative one. There is not a great deal of positive news on TV or in the papers. It's easier to complain about life than it is to see the positive. But this is incredibly draining on our mind and it's not necessary. The trick is learning how to start thinking more positively. This is where affirmations can help us.

An affirmation is a short sentence that is simple and has great power to the user. Repeating an affirmation changes the way we think and behave and when repeated enough times, with the right conviction, will allow a person to become more positive. When you have chosen the appropriate affirmation for you, you can make the necessary changes even by just thinking about it.

Affirmations are used to create motivation, which can help you achieve the goals you have set. You may also find it easier to reach your goals, because by positively altering your subconscious, it becomes easier to meet new people. They can enable you to activate your inner energies and help you bring about the changes that you want to make.

HOW TO USE AFFIRMATIONS TO CREATE A MORE POSITIVE YOU

In the first place, you need to make sure your affirmation is relevant to you and has meaning. It must fit with your intentions. Here are some excellent affirmations that I have used for myself as well as people I have helped:

- I am fearless
- I can do this
- I choose what I become
- I wink at a challenge
- I am successful
- I am healthy
- I am happy
- My life is full of fun
- I believe in myself
- Life is good

If you choose the affirmation "I can do this", you need to know exactly what it is you want to achieve and as you repeat the words, create an image in your mind of what it is you can do. If you want to improve your health, you have to visualise yourself as a healthy person as you say the words.

As with the bija mantras, you should repeat your affirmation at least twice—first thing in the morning and last thing at night. I always use mine throughout the day when I need to believe in myself a little more. Again, commit to at least thirty days of using your affirmations.

It is possible that you need an affirmation that is more specific to you and in this case, you can create your own. When you do, there are a few things that you should remember:

1. Your affirmation must ring true to you, something that you feel is relevant for the situation you face. Keep it short and simple.
2. Your affirmation must be positive. In order to create positivity, your words need to be positive.
3. Your affirmation must be in the present tense. Your subconscious is only concerned with the present, not the past or the future. You need to tell your subconscious how you want to be now.

I have always found it helpful to keep a note of the changes I feel over the thirty days. This will help you to be aware of your emotions and when your affirmation is making an impact. It is highly likely that if you are determined and consistent, you see positive changes sooner.

VISUALISATION, BREATHING, AND MEDITATION

Ok, so breathing is probably not the challenging aspect here, although not everyone has the ability to completely focus on their breathing without their minds wandering off. Visualisation and meditation require great concentration and focus, and this certainly doesn't come easily to everyone. Let's tackle them separately.

VISUALISATION

Visualisation involves using your imagination to focus on behaviours or situations that you wish to happen in your life. This could be getting a promotion, finding love, or overcoming certain illnesses or physical problems, and so on. Visualisation is not just about seeing yourself in this position, but engaging all of your senses, imagining the smells and sounds of what you want to achieve.

This doesn't mean that if you imagine yourself how you want to be, the next day it will simply occur. The mind and the body are linked, but it takes repeated visualisation for the mind to communicate the changes to the body and for the body to start making these subtle changes. It's a work in progress.

I will admit that the concept was difficult for me to get my head around in the beginning. Surely, if it was that simple, we would all be doing it and we would all be happier. I needed something a little more solid before I tried visualisation, because, in order for it to work, you have to truly believe it will.

Depending on who you talk to, visualisation will have different names. Some people call it guided imagery or mental imagery. In the world of sports, it is often called sports visualisation.

Many athletes will use sports visualisation to see themselves winning their race or game. One person who caught my attention was Michael Phelps. Most famous for being the most decorated Olympian of all time, few people know that he suffers from Marfan Syndrome, which can affect the bones, muscles, ligaments, and the aorta. Phelps created a mental videotape of each step of his race, from the starting block to winning the race. He repeated his "tape" before going to bed and when he woke up. He also used the technique during training sessions.

I was starting to believe.

Then I came across a study related to chronic pain and fibromyalgia. Chronic pain is defined as an ongoing pain that lasts for at least three months. Shockingly, around 10 to 40 percent of the population suffer from chronic pain, which has a massive knock-on effect on the economy. People who suffer from fibromyalgia experience chronic pain and fatigue. A 2018 study found that fibromyalgia patients who engaged in visualisation of their 'best possible self' experienced improved pain management and reduced incidence of depression.

A 2014 study found that visualising a safe space can help to reduce the pain of having an operation. There were plenty more studies I found about the positive effects on the immune system as well as on stress and anxiety, and this is when I felt more convinced that I could also benefit.

HOW TO USE VISUALISATION FOR HEALING

It all begins with finding a comfortable position and relaxing your breathing. Start by focusing on the muscles in your feet and making sure they are completely relaxed, then work your way up through your body until every muscle is relaxed. You can go from head to toe if you prefer.

Start to imagine what it is you want to achieve. If you have a cold that you want to get rid of, you might imagine your body fighting the virus. If you want to quit smoking you could imagine your lungs breathing in the clean, fresh air. Then start to concentrate on stimulating your senses. What exactly does that clean air smell like, fresh-cut grass, pine? What can you hear, the birds, the wind in the leaves? Can you feel that breeze on your face? Once you have created the complete image in your mind, repeat it. Every time you practise your visualisation, replay the image you created.

Sometimes, people need a little help, especially when they first begin. You might want to consider joining a group or asking for someone to help you talk you through your image until you feel you can do it alone. You could also look for some online visualisation tools.

When we use the visualisation technique to awaken our chakras, we completely focus on the chakra that we want to heal. Begin again with breathing and relaxing all of your muscles, then start to imagine the wheel spinning and the energy beginning to flow, sense the power of this energy and the positive impact you want it to make on your body. Imagine the colour of the chakra.

Have you ever seen a fiery eye in a firework display? When I use visualisation for healing chakras, I like to imagine the chakra as the fiery eye. It's the firework that gives off often bright, intense lights that spin around. Picturing this, for me, was the perfect way to imagine the chakra full of positive healing energy.

BREATHING AND MEDITATION

Meditation was another slight struggle for me, but for a different reason. I felt that the visualisation required a belief that it would work. Meditation, for me, required emptying of the mind, and this is what I found hard. Even though I was determined, things kept pushing into my brain and distracting me—tasks that needed to be done, feelings, the shopping list. In the beginning, I had to keep restarting over and over and I almost felt frustrated. I wanted to experience the benefits of meditation and gain some inner peace and clarity.

At this point, I learnt why breathing is so important. By concentrating on your breathing, your brain is kept busy and this helps to prevent it from being distracted by other thoughts. But when you think about it, breathing is quite boring and you might wonder how much can you really think about this involuntary action. Surprisingly, quite a lot. Before you begin meditating, consider these things about a simple breath:

- Your breath is probably the simplest yet most powerful thing you have. All it does is go in and go out; it can't change direction and we can't speed it up to get it out of the way and do something more interesting. On the other hand, without it, we cannot survive.
- Concentrating on your breathing allows you to focus on something that occurs in your body rather than your mind. Most of us are so overwhelmed by our own thinking that we don't concentrate on our bodies. When you imagine your breath passing through your

body and the oxygen moving through every inch of it, you begin to create a closer connection between the body and the mind, and you can enjoy the moment.

- Each breath is different. We can change the depth, and the duration, we can speed it up and slow it down at will. The curious thing about breathing is that it is something that we have complete control over, yet it is one of the few things that nobody tells us how to do.
- Breathing allows our body a chance to regain balance after a fight-or-flight situation. Today, fight-or-flight can be anything from the stress of work to traffic or the kids fighting. When man came face to face with a predator, his breath would speed up and there would be tension in all of his muscles. After, man would have time to relax and find balance. We often don't give ourselves a chance to breathe after the stress we deal with. Mindfulness breathing or concentrating on your breathing is a chance for your body to relax and find balance again.

"When you own your breath, nobody can steal your peace."

— ANONYMOUS

Once you begin to really think about the process of breathing, its significance and the fact that if you are breathing, you have something to celebrate, and you will find that there is actually quite a lot to consider. This will really help you when you begin using mindful breathing to help with healing.

FIVE WAYS TO USE MINDFUL BREATHING FOR HEALING

- Enlightenment

Meditating while mindfully breathing opens your mind to deep insights that you may otherwise miss. It can awaken your mind and who you really are, and with enough practice, some are able to achieve enlightenment.

- Relaxation

Breathing and meditation bring about a tranquillity that is rare in our everyday lives. It can help you to clear your mind so you can really relax. Even focusing on breathing in and out for a few minutes can help you to relax during moments of stress throughout the day.

- Freeing yourself from negative thoughts

We have already seen just how much negativity passes through our minds in a single hour. It is useless trying to block out this negativity, as it will just come back at another time. Instead, mindful breathing can enable you to identify the negativity and let it flow out with every breath, stopping it from becoming attached to you.

- Finding Inner Peace

Finding inner peace lets you free yourself from the stress and anxiety that are constantly present. It gives our mind and body a chance to experience calm. It's a moment of happiness that provides us with more power to face our problems later.

- Understanding More About Your Body

When I was pregnant, I was intrigued by the idea of a contraction being the muscles in your body that are calling out for more oxygen and that is why breathing is so essential to help with pain management. Learning how your body reacts to your breathing can provide important information about who you are within your body and what your body needs.

The goal of meditation may be different for some, but the principal reason for practising meditation and mindful breathing is to create a stronger connection between your mind and your body, to find peace, and balance, to be able to relax and deal with your negative thoughts so that you can enjoy a happier life. Achieving a higher awareness of yourself through meditation is easier when you learn how to focus on your breathing. This pulls you into the here and now and is a great way to appreciate that life is probably better than you tend to think.

Mantras, affirmations, visualisation, and meditation are simply phenomenal tools and when used the right way, can bring about the changes you need to start enjoying life more. These can be physical or emotional or a combination of both. These ancient Eastern techniques are unique to the individual and you should allow time to experiment with them and learn exactly how they can be used with the specific chakras that you want to awaken.

Another practical tool that can help create a balance within our chakras is chakra astrology. The next stage of our journey will concern the connection between chakras and the planets.

CHAKRA ASTROLOGY

When we start talking about astrology and the planets, my mind rushes straight back to geography classes in school. I remember the teacher repeating the mnemonic "My Very Educated Mother Just Served Nine Pizzas" because Pluto was still considered a planet then. As a child, you start to wonder why you need to remember such information.

I now wonder if the point of learning about the planets and the solar system was to simply remind us that we are part of something much larger and that universal balance is equally as important as our internal balance. I also think that as we become adults, we become so wrapped up in the craziness of our own lives that we are unable to see the bigger picture.

The planets have an important role in who we are. I think it was probably in the 90s that astrology started to be the latest fashion. Can you remember Mystic Meg? Rushing out to buy the latest edition of Cosmopolitan to read your stars? What we did to the concept of astrology might have put some people off, but I promise, when you take away all the glitter and jazz, there is a great sense to how the planets affect our bodies and who we are.

Practitioners of vedic astrology believe that the first breath we take after we are born is etched into our cells. A birth chart is an astrological tool that tells a person more about the planets at the time they took their first breath. Our birth chart describes our spiritual, physical and mental aspects.

Understanding the position and different aspects of the planets at the time of our birth can help us to appreciate the part we play in the universe and how we can ensure there is balance within ourselves.

We have already learnt of the immense amount of energy and power our chakras can have. Now consider the energy and power of the entire solar system. Each of our chakras is associated with a planet and tend to mimic the nature and characteristics of that planet. You might say that each of us is our own mini solar system within the solar system we studied at school.

Loka- meaning 'planet'

Loka also means the degree of level, and it is the level of our vital energies that are connected to the planets. Being in tune with the planets is another form of meditation that can help us to balance our chakras. Let's look at each of the chakras again, but now in relation to the planets.

THE CONNECTION BETWEEN OUR CHAKRAS AND THE PLANETS

It is not known precisely how old the Hindu system of astrology (Jyotisha) dates back, but the oldest surviving text that refers to it is over two thousand years old. It may have been influenced by the Hellenistic astrology of ancient Greece. In the form that survives today, Jyotisha is based around the movements of five planets, plus the Sun and the Moon, and the influence that these movements and the relative positions of the celestial bodies has on life here on Earth. The outer planets are excluded, as they were not known at the time the system was developed.

Since the twentieth century, some have identified a link between the location of the planets and experiences with the seven chakras. They believe that when the celestial bodies move, the effects can be seen on things like our creativity, activity, and even the conflicts we have. Although a modern, western interpretation, some consider the involvement of chakras with Hindu astrology to be a useful facet of modern chakra practice. Let's take a brief look at the key astrological associations.

The Root Chakra: Mars

This chakra is related to the expression "I am" and has close ties to our ability to survive and the need for stability. When we are fully aware of our reality, we are able to leave our past behind us and live in the moment. This provides us with motivation. When the energies of Mars are agitated, we can notice feelings of guilt, fear, insecurity and even anger.

The Sacral Chakra: Venus

The expression "I feel" is related to our sensuality and tenderness. As Venus is the planet of worldly pleasures, when all is balanced and well with Venus, we can enjoy the pleasures of the world. More specifically, we can do this with spontaneity and without becoming attached to these pleasures. We are comfortable with who we are in all senses, physically, emotionally, and sexually.

The Solar Plexus Chakra: The Sun

We all know how much better we feel when the Sun is present, and the expression "I do" is seen in the increased determination to get things done on those bright days. We are more optimistic and confident about life. The Sun allows us to feel recharged and to take advantage of the skills and talents we have to achieve things. When all is right, our ego doesn't get in the way.

The Heart Chakra: The Moon

The Moon signifies the mother in astrology and the two words are "I love". The Moon gives us support and nourishment, and it can aid us with our boundaries. When everything flows correctly, there is a genuine sense of peace and joy. You are able to love and embrace love completely.

The Throat Chakra: Mercury

As the throat is tied to our speech, the expression is "I speak". If Mercury is in balance and functioning, we will find it easier to express ourselves, not only with our words, but also with our creativity.

The Third Eye Chakra: Saturn

"I see"—when Saturn enables us to think with great clarity, you will have the insights to comprehend the consequences of your actions. If Saturn is considered to be well-positioned, the laws of karma, time, and life are understood.

The Crown Chakra: Jupiter

When Jupiter is well, we are able to receive wisdom on all levels. The expression "I understand" allows us to expand and to be generous. The power that Jupiter can give us when well-placed is the ability to understand the practicalities of life, people, as well as higher concepts

So now we know what the impact of various planets, the Sun and the Moon can have on our chakras, but we still haven't answered the question of how. For this, you will need some creative imagination!

Imagine yourself sitting crossed-legged and the chakras running in a vertical line from the base of the spine to the crown of your head. Now picture a circle around your body. From the top of the circle, there will be segments, six to the left and six to the right. The outer segments are projected at a thirty-degree angle and this represents the Root Chakra. Each segment from here is split into thirty degrees and represents the next chakra, each having a segment to the left and the right.

When a planet is in a projection area of one of the chakras, it will impact that chakra according to its nature and characteristics. Notice that there is no segment dedicated to the Crown Chakra. This is because the Crown Chakra relates to the higher connection to the spiritual world and connects us to the divine.

The influence is also dependent on whether the planet is in the section of the chakra to the left or the right. The segments that are on the left of the circle will play a role in the receptive part, or the energy that is received. On the contrary, those that are to the right are influenced by the emissive side, or the energy that is controlled.

Now let's look at the different chakras again with a focus on the receptive (left) and emissive (right) side when the planet is in line with the projected segment of the related chakra.

The Root Chakra

The receptive side points to material energy and physical action. There is plenty of activity on this level. It also shows that you have courageous friends in your corner.

When Mars falls to the emissive side, you will notice greater stability. The energy you feel will be more controlled, yet there will still be plenty of action and more so, the courage may be coming from you.

The Sacral Chakra

Still related to sexual energy, on the receptive side, it indicates our sexual potential. Still, there is more to it than merely sex. The alignment allows you to meet people and be able to support them on a psychological level. It will enable you to find a passion for your interests and hobbies.

When Venus is in line with the emissive side of the Sacral Chakra, you will feel more seductive and appreciate the power of seduction. You might even find that you will be able to use these feelings to take back more control of your sexual power.

The Solar Plexus Chakra

You will feel more confident when the Sun is in the receptive side of your Solar Plexus Chakra. This is probably helped by the high-quality energy that you naturally feel and that radiates from those around you.

When the Sun is in your emissive side, you will feel like you have more charisma. More significantly, you will have more willpower and determination and greater control over these emotions.

The Heart Chakra

To the left, you will receive love and the things you enjoy in life and be more respective. You will find it easy to soak up the energies around you and take information in from others or from the natural world.

Love will beam from you when the Moon appears on your right side; your feelings will be profound, and you will gain an inner perspective that is clearer when regarding the energies of this level.

The Throat Chakra

The receptive side relates to our passive intuition and you will be more receptive. You will see that it is easy to find your energy and you absorb it, soak it all in. You will also notice that you are intrigued by any information that others tell you, both spoken and written.

On the emissive side, your intuition is active, with a greater connection to other worlds. You have become a master of your understanding and mental control.

The Third Eye Chakra

On the one hand, your mental interests will be heightened, and you may feel the need to analyse things more. The memory will be better too. On the other hand, Saturn on the receptive side might point to a lack of resources and energy.

When Saturn falls to the emissive side, there will be mental creativity, but there will also be a practical side to this. You find benefits to high levels of control and planning, and this could be truer with regards to your finances.

MEDITATION AND CHAKRA ASTROLOGY

You have probably picked up on my love for spiritualism by now, but I have so much respect for it, because of the variety of ways that one can learn more about oneself and unlock one's potential so that they one lead a more fulfilling life. One of these techniques is meditation. Meditation can have numerous forms, from walking to even the mundane jobs we have, like doing the laundry. It's all about your state of mind.

When we start to reveal the concepts of astrology and chakras, they open the door to appreciating that though we are here and living our own lives, we are also observers, watching how the world changes around us. I feel like I am a weathervane placed in a field. While I remain still, I can see, experience and appreciate the changing weather. Standing in the peacefulness of the field, I am able to meditate on these changes and the effects on my life. I can witness all extremes, from the storms to the sun.

HOW TO USE ASTROLOGY AND MEDITATION TO BENEFIT YOUR CHAKRAS

We begin by visualising the chakra that you wish to create more balance and focus on its location in the body. Concentrate on the energy and that each planet (or the Sun/Moon) is related to, focus on your breathing and imagine your body beginning filled with this energy.

Rather than look at each chakra again, let's round this chapter up with a look at what you should concentrate on when visualising each of the celestial bodies during meditation.

The Sun- imagine your conscious identity, how you are when you feel most alive. Meditate on your creativity and your attitude towards yourself. Imagine the pure energy and light from the Sun filling your body and flowing towards the chakra you are visualising.

The Moon- when you focus your attention on the Moon during meditation, you should think about your emotions and how they are forever changing. It is a chance to understand your dominant-state feeling, the feeling that most often creeps up. It is a chance to understand your inner needs.

Mercury- Mercury relates to the mind, your perceptions and looking for fresh knowledge. You will learn how to communicate better, whether that's your ideas, your feelings, or your wishes.

Venus- this planet is linked to our hearts' desires and our ability to give and receive love. You should be able to visualise this love filling you and those you care about. This will also bring forward our tastes and what we find pleasure from in life.

Mars- the root energy from Mars enables us to release energy and fulfil our most primal needs. We can meditate in order to express ourselves without inhibitions, to find our pure energy and motivation.

Jupiter- there is a level of understanding that allows us to appreciate the meaning of life. With Jupiter in our minds when we meditate, we can appreciate the opportunities that are given to us in life. We aim to improve our knowledge and wisdom.

Saturn- Saturn is associated with time and to some extent, how insignificant time is on the larger scale of things. Meditation will allow you to appreciate that the problems you suffer from now will not impact your life in five or ten years' time, unless you allow them too.

There is a lot of information to consider and it does require a certain level of knowledge regarding the chakras, the planets (or Sun/Moon) and their different positions. You might be tempted to study all of what we have mentioned, but that is a lot to digest, particularly as we still have plenty more to go.

My advice would be to look at your birth chart, understand when the celestial bodies fall into the segments of your chakras and focus on the chakra for which you would like to see an improvement. There is definitely time to work on all of your chakras, but if you try to look at them all at the same time, you may discover it is difficult to visualise the specific chakra and meditate on the associated planet.

The next chapter is going to take a fascinating look at chakra massage and aromatherapy. We will also look at other techniques that can help balance our chakras, including one in particular that has gained popularity in recent years.

CHAKRA MASSAGE AND
AROMATHERAPY

Even the words massage and aromatherapy are enough to bring a wave of calm over me and I have always felt that aromatherapy is never given the credit it deserves. We learnt about the importance of engaging all of our senses when we practice visualisation. Now, we are going to continue with this as we understand the significance of touch and smell while we work to balance our chakras.

CHAKRA MASSAGE

We have already looked at a few ways to unblock and create balance in our chakras, from meditation to mantras and affirmations. Massage is another useful technique, especially for anyone who is new to chakra healing. Because the technique is relatively simple, you can do it yourself.

If you choose to go and see a massage therapist, I would strongly advise you to make sure they specialise in chakra massage and are well-recommended. I worry so much that there are people giving our passion a bad name and trying to earn a quick buck, so I prefer to massage my own chakra areas.

Remember in the beginning how we said that a chakra isn't an organ or something we can see. We can't put our hands on a specific part of our body to start to awaken that chakra. Chakra massage involves movements and massage in areas of the body that are associated with the chakra. This massage carefully and correctly begins to awaken the chakra, allowing the wheel to start spinning and the energy to flow.

For example, by massaging the muscles in your neck up towards the base of your skull and in a clockwise direction, you can begin to release energy in your Throat Chakra. When we dedicate a chapter each to the different chakras, I will go into much more detail about massage techniques.

REFLEXOLOGY

Reflexology is an ancient Chinese healing technique based on the concept of a person's vital energy of qi (pronounced 'chee'). The Chinese believe that balance in this flow of energy is essential to help us stay free from disease and illnesses. Instead of focusing on the seven chakras, reflexology refers to pressure points on the feet, hands, and ears.

That being said, there are correlations between the sole of the foot and the seven chakras. This is because there are pressure points along the sole of the foot that stimulate specific nerves or glands. Now, I could go into all of the medical names for the parts of the body and you could look it up online, but where would the fun be in that? Why not take a piece of paper, draw around your left foot and then draw a vertical and horizontal line so that you have a cross right in the middle?

Slightly to the top of your cross and on the left-hand side, is the adrenal gland. Then, across the middle of your heel, there is a strip that is associated with the sciatic nerve. These two pressure points are related to the Root Chakra. Go on, you know you want to get your pens out and colour it red!!

For the Sacral Chakra, we need to move away from the sole of the foot temporarily. On the inside of your left foot, below and about one finger back, you will find the pressure point that is tied to the uterus or the prostate. On the outside of your right foot, in the same position below the ankle, there is the ovary or testicle pressure point. You could make a little note in orange.

Back to the sole for the Solar Plexus Chakra, and there are two pressure points. The first is just above the cross you drew, known as the solar plexus. The second starts on the inside of your left foot, just above the vertical line and spreads across almost to the horizontal line. These pressure points will be yellow.

Just next to the solar plexus pressure point, slightly higher and to the left, there is the heart pressure point. It is a larger area than the others, probably the size of your thumbprint. A little more to the left is the thymus gland. Dark green would be good, but failing that, green is fine.

Moving up the sole of the foot, you will find the thyroid gland. This is located right under the joint of your big toe. You can colour this area blue.

Literally above the thyroid gland, there is a strip across the bottom of the big toe that is associated with the pituitary gland. This is linked to the Third Eye Chakra and should be coloured purple.

Finally, across the top of your big toe, there is the pressure point for the Crown Chakra. It is associated with the pineal gland. Imagine it like a painted tip of a toenail (but on the opposite side of the toe) and a lighter purple.

All of these pressure points have a mirror image when looking at your right foot. This is except for the Sacral Chakra, which has specific left and right foot areas, and the thumb-sized heart pressure point, which is only found on the sole of the left foot.

I confess I am terrible with lefts and rights, which is why I found it easier to draw my own feet and mark the different pressure points, and if you use colours, it makes it easier to remember which nerve or gland is associated with each chakra. Again, I grabbed the first colours I could find. If you want to be more specific, you can pop back to chapter one.

Once you have identified the pressure point you would like to work with, you can apply pressure with your thumb for between one to five seconds and then release for one to five seconds. You can repeat this for up to fifteen minutes. There are other techniques where the pressure is slowly increased and lasts for up to sixty seconds. This is usually only continued for up to five minutes.

There are plenty of alleged benefits to reflexology. There is some evidence that it can help to lower stress levels, alleviate pain and improve your mood. Some people also think it can help with digestion issues, infertility, nerve and arthritis pain and that it can provide a boost to the immune system, but there is insufficient clinical evidence to date to support these claims.

I consider myself to be a responsible spiritual healer and so I must warn you that if you have certain health concerns, you should consult your doctor first. This includes circulatory problems in your feet, blood clots or inflammation in your legs, open wounds, foot ulcers or infections, thyroid problems or epilepsy. Also, consult a professional if you are pregnant. These pressure points may induce contractions.

REIKI

From Japan, reiki is an alternative healing technique that encompasses higher power and life force energy to get a spiritually guided life force energy. This energy is known as ki, the Japanese version of the Chinese qi. It is simple and, as with the other methods we have looked at, it doesn't require any form of religious belief.

While you don't need to be religious in any way, you do need to be dedicated to seeing improvements in yourself. You also need to commit yourself to a virtuous life, so one that is respectful, honest, and kind. This type of lifestyle is the last link in completing the system and gaining the most healing value.

Healing from reiki involves placing hands on parts of the body to increase the life force energy within you. The mechanisms of reiki have not been scientifically demonstrated, and its alleged benefits have not been reproduced reliably in controlled settings, so it is widely considered a pseudoscience. However, when carried out correctly, I believe that the benefits are amazing. You may notice improvements throughout your whole body from your emotions to your body, mind and spirit. It is incredibly relaxing, and the sense of peace is blissful.

With regards to our chakras, a reiki master, or at least someone who has been trained by a reiki master, will place their hands on parts of the body that are associated with a particular chakra to help adjust the imbalances. Try to find someone who comes recommended, as 'reiki master' is not a protected term, so anyone can claim the title!

Many of these body parts we have already talked about, but it is well worth a recap.

- **The Root Chakra**- adrenal glands, kidneys, spine, leg bones
- **The Sacral Chakra**- reproductive systems, spleen, bladder
- **The Solar Plexus Chakra**- pancreas, liver, stomach, spleen, lower digestive tract, gallbladder, autonomic nervous system
- **The Heart Chakra**- thymus gland, heart, circulatory system, lower lungs, hands, skin
- **The Throat Chakra**- thyroid gland, throat, jaw, upper lungs, vocal cords, upper digestive tract
- **Third Eye Chakra**- pituitary gland, lower brain, central nervous system, left eye, ears, nose
- **Crown Chakra**- pineal gland, upper brain, right eye

So, the only potential downside is that depending on your location, you may find it difficult to find a professional reiki practitioner. However, reiki education is becoming easier to find. In America, for example, reiki education is offered in over 800 hospitals for free.

On the upside, it is a simpler form of healing from your point of view, as it is down to the expert to understand the exact locations of the healing areas. Perhaps the hardest part in today's world is living a virtuous life.

As well as an overall improvement in wellbeing, reiki healing is believed to help alleviate pain, increase relaxation, reduce stress and anxiety and improve cognition in the elderly.

AROMATHERAPY

Am I the only one who smells the fabric softener and cleaning products in the supermarket before buying them? I love walking past the Body Shop, the smell of fresh-cut grass, puppies and bakeries. All of these smells have an effect on me that makes me smile. I close my eyes and breathe it all in!

Aromatherapy is the use of essential oils for healing, or at least to aid other healing techniques. Essential oils are (or at least should be) natural and are plant extracts taken from flowers, bark, leaves, or fruit. Various parts are steamed or pressed and then bottled.

When essential oils are breathed in, the olfactory system sends signals to the brain. In the brain, certain smells will stimulate activity in the amygdala, the part of the brain where we experience our emotions. This is why the smell of a

Sunday roast can fill you with memories of happy family meals, and so on.

Aromatherapy might not work for everyone, as each person reacts differently to different smells. The air freshener in my husband's car makes me feel sick, whereas freshly cut grass makes him sneeze. When used in the correct way, they are perfectly safe and worth trying to see what benefit they have for you. Some studies have shown that they can help with anxiety, depression, insomnia, and nausea. If you are the type of person who is happier just from smelling coffee, it is likely that you will see some improvements in your mood alone.

Surprisingly, there are no regulations when it comes to labelling a bottle of essential oil, and so, because you can't be sure exactly what is in the bottle, and also because some are poisonous, essential oils should never be ingested. A few drops of peppermint essential oil in hot water doesn't make a peppermint tea.

Instead, an ideal way to gain from aromatherapy is to use wearable objects that are made of absorbent materials. I have a set of wooden mala beads that I use for mantras. It is perfect for rubbing in some essential oils and I can also use it as a bracelet or necklace. This may sound a bit girly, but the leather or rope wristbands will also work well. There are also traditional burners and more modern diffusers for filling a room with scent.

Body oils are a combination of essential oils and types of cream. These are wonderful for massages and, as you can imagine, the perfect complement for chakra massage. You shouldn't use pure essential oils, because they are concentrated, and you might find that the strength will irritate the skin. On that note, be careful of allergic reactions. Some people are allergic to cinnamon, so can't eat it, but it is probable that they are allergic to cinnamon bark oil too; obviously, this is just one example. It is a good idea to do a patch test on a small area of skin before using a new skin product for the first time, to check for any adverse reaction.

When choosing essential oils, it is best not to go cheap—and this is coming from someone who loves a bargain! The cheaper brands may be mixed with other chemicals, so try to find labels that state '100% essential oil'. It is also worth buying dark glass bottles, because this helps to retain the quality of the plant extracts.

Some of the most common essential oils are peppermint, tea tree and lavender. I bought a small wooden box, because I knew I was going to end up with a good collection of bottles. Getting two birds with one stone, I also rub the essential oils into the box.

You may have guessed what I am about to say next! I believe that each of our chakras responds to certain essential oils, helping us to find a better sense of balance. The use of essential oils with chakras does not originate from the vedas, although those ancient texts do mention certain plants that have been used in traditional medicine. Rather, this is another modern component of chakra practice that I find helpful. One oil that I had never heard of before was lime essential oil. It works wonders on helping you see the truth and straightening out the differences between fantasy and reality; therefore, it helps to create balance in your Crown Chakra. For the other chakras, I will explain more about specific essential oils in the following chapters.

Isn't it just amazing how many options you have? This is what is just so brilliant about chakras and alternative healing methods. You have so much potential to explore reflexology, massage, reiki, and aromatherapy. If you feel that something doesn't suit you, it doesn't mean that you won't be able to create balance within your chakras: it just means you can experiment with other options.

I have tried everything that we have talked about so far. I'm not going to tell you my favourites, because I don't want to influence you, and to be honest, over the years, I have discovered that certain options work better for certain situations. Mantras and affirmations, including the two-word expressions relating to the chakras, are best when used on a continuous basis. I like massage and reflexology when I feel that I need to destress, and aromatherapy works very well with both. Any opportunity that arises where I can learn from a reiki master, I am there! But there is no doubt that our senses can provide wonderful healing opportunities.

There are two more techniques of chakra healing that we are still going to talk about before an in-depth look at each chakra. One is more common, and you might even say socially accepted. The other may seem a little far out there for some, but, as with so many of the alternative healing approaches, I was captivated by the power of healing crystals.

CRYSTALS FOR BETTER INNER VIBRATIONS

When I first began writing books, I was told that I should try to leave myself out of it, because really, the idea is to help you. But I strongly disagreed and went my own stubborn way. With a topic like spiritualism, I find it helps to include my side of things, especially considering that I started as a non-believer.

My first experience with crystals was way back in the nineties, when I was close to finishing high school. A few of the cool kids started going on about how crystals were making them better people. First of all, in high school, our definition of a better person was somewhat mistaken and secondly, they had no idea of how they worked. Not wanting to go against the crowd, I carried a few around and as soon as the year was over, I vowed never to fall for "that rubbish" again.

The second time someone insisted I try the powers of crystals, I still lacked the confidence to say "no, thank you", and I remained cynical throughout.

Once I started to explore the Eastern philosophies, I did recognise that I was becoming more open to trying new concepts; however, there was still something about crystals that I couldn't get my head around.

During my travels around India, I started to come around. In many parts of India, people can't afford modern medicine and therefore stick to the traditional healing methods, one of which was the use of crystals. Perhaps it was seeing them used in one of their original settings that made me feel like I could also learn how to use them to help with the balancing of my chakras.

HOW DO CRYSTALS HELP BALANCE YOUR CHAKRAS?

When someone first told me that each crystal has a vibrational frequency, I was certainly not any more convinced. But it did start to make sense. Everything is still composed of energy; it is just the form and strength of energy that is different. The vibration frequency of crystals will depend on the material, thickness and, needless to say, their colour.

To an extent, the thinking behind crystals and healing is all about understanding the vibration frequencies of each stone and how this will help with particular chakras. Thankfully, crystal healing has also been around for thousands of years, and so the trial and error has been done for us. Because of this, so many people have been able to benefit from gemstones and crystals when awakening and balancing their chakras.

You know by now that crystals and gemstones of a certain colour are going to be associated with each of the chakras. I should note that this is another modern addition, and these associations are not based on the vedas. However, the vedas do mention certain gems for use in spiritual practice. While you might be tempted to choose a crystal that you relate to your chakras—like a particular tone of red, crystals that have the same shades will also work well. What is more important is to look at the particular attributes and energetic qualities, as well as feeling a connection to that crystal or gemstone.

Take, for example, clear quartz. It's like the "Om" of crystal healing, the master that can often be paired with other crystals to enhance their healing benefits. It can increase energy levels, and even help to store energy and release it when necessary. It is perfect for creating balance across the whole body and may even help with concentration. I have clear, raw quartz in my crystal cluster, but it's not one of my personal go-to crystals. I prefer those that are smoother, have been polished and have elements of colour. I still believe in its qualities and use it when the time is right, but you need to be drawn to the crystals you choose.

A bit like our essential oils, there are a few crystals that are great to include at the beginning of your collection, and I wanted to quickly look at these before we focus on our chakras.

Blue lace agate- part of the quartz family, this is a light blue stone with soft darker blue bands across it. It can help lower your levels of anxiety and enable you to absorb its calming energy.

Selenite- this is a crystallised form of Gypsum and is very powerful in spiritual healing. It can assist in clearing your energy field and especially useful if you have to deal with other people's negativity.

Pyrite- also known as Fool's Gold because of its colour, pyrite is also used in Feng Shui for attracting wealth. For healing, it can help to remind you of how full your life is.

Shungite- this a lustrous black stone that is believed to absorb negative energy.

Black tourmaline- it can be quite rough or beautifully smooth when polished. Black tourmaline can be used for an overall layer of spiritual protection. It can help to ground your energies as well as to protect them.

Just to give you a little taster of the different crystals, you can find one for each of the associated chakras, but I don't recommend buying this one straight away. When we focus on the chakras individually, we will look at more crystals and gemstones that you might prefer.

- Root Chakra- Fire Agate
- Sacral Chakra- Coral
- Solar Plexus Chakra- Topaz
- Heart Chakra- Jade
- Throat Chakra- Aquamarine
- Third Eye Chakra- Amethyst
- Crown Chakra- Clear Quartz

USING CRYSTALS TO BALANCE YOUR CHAKRAS

Crystals and gemstones are ready to be used, but if you want to gain the most from their energies, they need to be programmed with your needs and intentions. It's like when you buy a new phone: you have all of the hardware there ready, but you need to download the right apps for you. The phone will still work without your favourite apps, but with them, you will get more out of the phone.

To program your crystals, you need to know exactly how you want them to work. If you have a fire agate, you will want to hold your crystal in your hands, close your eyes and relax. Focus your attention on your crystal and the Root Chakra. Then you need to say aloud or in your head a sentence that shows a commitment to your stone. Examples of these sentences may include:

- I will work with this crystal to create balance in my Root Chakra
- I will work with this crystal to take more control over my life
- I will feel the vibrations of my crystal and find more peace

Finish off with a meaningful "thank you". You will need to do the same for each of your crystals, repeating a sentence that is appropriate for the intentions and goals of that stone. Now that each of your crystals is programmed, you can explore some of the best ways to use them. Don't forget that you don't have to stick to just one use: feel free to combine them as you see fit and in a way that can be incorporated into your daily lives.

1. Wear your crystals

The more contact you can have with your crystal, the more energy you will be able to absorb from it. The popularity of crystals has encouraged a whole new fashion where crystals are part of the clothing design. You can also wear jewellery with your crystal. Because I was still a little dubious at first, I found an ideal solution was to search for rings with my crystal and program it before wearing it.

This might all sound a bit girly, but there are plenty of more masculine solutions for jewellery that contain crystals and gemstones. An alternative option is to make your own.

1. Keep them in a purse or pocket

They may be out of sight, but not out of mind. Knowing that your crystals are still close to you throughout the day means you can still hold them at regular intervals. Pockets are great, especially if you have a habit of keeping your hands in them.

1. Hold them while you meditate

Meditation is a way to feel a closer connection with your spiritual energy and with yourself. Holding a crystal while you meditate will further strengthen this connection. For added benefit, you can program your crystal to match the intention of your meditation.

1. Create a crystal layout

Once you have a crystal for each of your chakras, you can lay down and place each one on your chakra, so you would start by placing your fire agate on your Root Chakra and continue up along your spine. This is perfect for gaining a complete sensation of energy. Rest there for five minutes while you focus on your breathing.

1. Add them to the tub with your favourite bubble bath

The bath is a great way to combine crystal with aromatherapy for complete relaxation along with the combined intention of your crystal. Make sure that your crystal is one that is suitable for use in water.

1. Include them in your decor

The crystals you have should be those that you are attracted to, so it makes sense that you place them around your home. You can admire their beauty and cleanse the energy in your home. This is logically the best option for the larger crystals that may look a bit stupid sticking out of your pocket or hanging around your neck.

1. Sleep near your crystals

Whether on the bedside table or under your pillow, you can gain from the energy of the crystal while you are asleep. Hold your crystal while you lay in bed, take a few deep breaths and imagine the energies of your crystal.

THE THREE CS OF CRYSTAL CARE

Just like the phone we originally programmed, our crystals need to be taken care of. This requires cleansing, clearing, and charging them so that they continue to provide us with the energies, support, and healing that we are working towards.

Cleansing

Your crystal has already had its own journey before arriving in your hands. As we aren't sure what has happened to it along the way, we need to cleanse it to remove any possible negative energies. It is also worth mentioning that some gemstone mining has been associated with exploitative practices, so look for an ethical crystal supplier.

Before programming your crystals, run them under a tap with cool water. If you can, take them to a river or a source of naturally flowing water. Adding salt to the water will enhance the cleansing, so seawater is perfect. Some people like to burn sage too.

These physical acts are only one part of the cleansing. You need to mentally remove any negative energies, especially those coming from you. Replace any doubts you may have with respect for their abilities.

Clearing

Crystal energy works both ways. As we absorb the benefits of their energies, they also absorb the energies around them. It is important to clear your crystals, particularly if you are going through an incredibly stressful time, if you have had an argument with someone, or if you have been ill.

You can clear your crystals the same way as you cleansed them when you first got them. Either run them under the tap or wash them in a natural source of water, optionally using salt and smoke from sage to help remove the negative energies they might have absorbed. Don't forget that not all crystals can be submerged in water and for some, you can only use smoke.

Charging

Everything that requires energy requires charging, from our electrical devices to our own bodies. Here are some ways for you to charge your crystals:

The Moon- placing your crystals under the moonlight, especially a full moon, will recharge your crystals with feminine energy and can help us with our spiritual and emotional healing.

The Sun- we know how energised we feel when the Sun is out. Placing your crystals in direct sunlight allows them to take in the masculine solar energy, which may help you for those occasions that require a big effort on your part.

Earth- burying your crystal in the earth for up to twenty-four hours can recharge it with energies from nature and nearby plants.

Use other crystals- create a circle with your other crystals and place the crystal to be charged in the middle. Again, you should probably leave the crystal circle for at least twenty-four hours.

Use your own energy- If you feel that you are buzzing with positive energy, lay your crystals out in front of you and focus your energy on the crystals. I like to think of this as giving a little back!

CHOOSING THE RIGHT CRYSTALS FOR YOU

There are more than three hundred types of gemstone on our planet. Technically, not all gemstones are crystals, as the latter refers to a particular chemical structure, but here I use the two terms interchangeably. You may find that one crystal has specific attributes that you think will benefit you, then a website will tell you that it has other energetic powers. It may be that neither is wrong; in fact, one crystal may have different meanings associated with it.

With so many to choose from, it can feel a little overwhelming when you first begin, especially if you have walked into an alternative healing shop and seen all of the options. You can buy a set, but there is one big risk with this: you may fall in love with a few of them, but not all of them. Your crystals have to speak to you; you have to choose them and not accept what comes in a pack.

Don't get me wrong, some of the sets available are beautiful and are absolutely perfect; just be careful if you are buying them online.

Use your intuition. Rather than searching for crystals based on your chakras, choose ones that you like the feel of and the colours of which appeal to you. No crystal will be wrong for you or do you harm, because you are going to cleanse it and program it with your own intentions.

Also bear in mind that although crystals have great energy, they won't perform miracles. You won't wake up after twenty-four hours and feel like a completely new person. A good rule of thumb is to keep your crystal with you for thirty days. After this time, if you don't feel any different, you can try a different crystal, always remembering to cleanse, program and when necessary, clear and charge them.

Entire books are dedicated to crystal healing, so you can understand that one chapter really is just the introduction. As I keep promising, you will learn more about specific crystals for each chakra once we have looked into the amazing practice of yoga, the different kinds of yoga and how they can not only strengthen our body but also optimise the balancing process.

YOGA: YOUR ULTIMATE SELF

Oh, Yoga, how I love you! For myself, and so many others, yoga was the first introduction to the spiritual world, without even realising it. I started practising yoga before I ever found an interest in other spiritual practices. In my early days, I loved yoga for stretching and I felt myself getting physically stronger. I enjoyed the step away from the buzz of the outside world and a chance to take in the peace.

THE ORIGIN OF YOGA

Mantras were first mentioned in the ancient Hindu scriptures, the Upanishads, and we know that the teaching of mantras was predominantly oral, which has allowed for some differences in interpretations. Yoga also dates back to more than 5,000 years ago to the Indus-Saraswati civilisation in Northern India. The first mention of yoga was also in the Upanishads, but some believe the practice might be as old as 10,000 years.

I am going to assume that you don't know that yoga has four key historical periods and I will briefly mention them. Some may not be interested in the history of yoga and that is absolutely fine. I have always appreciated the research and knowledge so that I can have more respect for the Eastern philosophies and how they came about.

Pre-Classical Yoga

The Vedas, the sacred Hindu texts, were used by Vedic priests, or Brahmans, and Yoga was thought to have begun as a ritual sacrifice. Brahmans, along with Rishis (Indian spiritual masters) then developed the concept of yoga into a style of teaching that encouraged the sacrifice of the ego through karma yoga and jnana yoga, action and wisdom respectively. At this point, there was no clear definition of what yoga was: it was more of a combination of different beliefs and methods.

Classical Yoga

In the second century CE, yoga became more systematic, thanks to Patanjali's Yoga-Sutras. The Yoga-Sutras have a great influence on today's yoga practices and Patanjali's description of the path of Raja Yoga is still known as classical yoga.

Post-Classical Yoga

Skip ahead a few more centuries and yoga masters were beginning to create systems that were not related to Vedas, but instead, on ways to rejuvenate the body. In this period, the masters formed Tantra Yoga, based on the idea of cleansing the body and the mind. It was used to explore the connections we have between the spiritual and physical world, which led to what we know as Hatha Yoga.

Modern Yoga

This leads us to the yoga we practise today. From the late 1800s, yoga masters began travelling west. Books were written and yoga centres began popping up all over the world. The varieties of Hatha Yoga include yoga postures (asanas), yoga breathing (pranayama), internal cleansing (shatkarma), and life-force energy (prana). Most of today's yoga focuses on yoga postures.

There are two forms of yoga that can catch our attention when looking to balance our chakras—Chakra Yoga and Kundalini Yoga.

REACHING YOUR POTENTIAL WITH CHAKRA YOGA

Regardless of our previous yoga experience, we can all appreciate the benefits of a good stretch. First thing in the morning or after a few hours of sitting at the desk, a stretch helps us to loosen the muscles that have tightened after lack of activity. Stretching increases blood flow to our muscles.

Now when we combine the stretching we do with certain yoga poses with controlled breathing, we are able to increase the amount of oxygen that flows throughout our entire body. It is a successful method for cleansing the body and encouraging a balance among our chakras. The postures used in Chakra Yoga involve keeping your body aligned and specifically your spine straight, allowing the energy to flow more easily to each chakra.

Some people will incorporate meditation into Chakra Yoga. You can increase your focus and sharpen your mind at the same time as awakening your chakras. Let's take a brief look at a couple of yoga poses that will benefit each chakra.

The Root Chakra

Here, we are looking to create more power around the area that keeps us grounded, the pelvic floor muscles. The Warrior Pose stretches out our hips and the Chair Pose strengthens the hip flexors.

The Sacral Chakra

If you can see this chakra as the centre of your fluids, such as sweat, blood and tears, this chakra being awakened will encourage flow and fluidity in the rest of your body. It is also advised to work on hip-opening poses such as the bound and open-angle poses.

The Solar Plexus Chakra

This can be seen as the home of your potential power and vitality. Yoga poses that involve twists will help to experience the energy in this chakra. Some of the simpler poses include the Triangle Pose and the Half Lord of the Fishes Pose.

The Heart Chakra

As the Heart Chakra is the meeting of our lower and higher chakras, the poses should create harmony between the body and the spirit. Backbends awaken the Heart Chakra, allowing the energy to enhance our compassion and feel more secure about ourselves.

The Throat Chakra

The Plow and the Camel Yoga poses are good for stretching the back and shoulders. On top of this, the Camel pose expands the stomach area and encourages energy up towards the throat.

The Third Eye Chakra

The place where the body meets the mind, healing can include Nadi Shodhana, or alternate nostril breathing. In terms of yoga poses, the Cat-Cow pose strengthens the neck and the spine helps to reduce stress and can encourage emotional balance.

The Crown Chakra

The higher up the chakras, the more we work towards our spiritual connections. For this reason, meditation is one of the best ways to encourage energy to the Crown Chakra. You can also practise the Half Lotus pose, which goes nicely with meditation.

Another reason to love yoga is that you don't need anything. If you want to join a class to really master the techniques, there are classes available at all times of the day and for all different levels.

That being said, not everyone can squeeze a full class into their daily routine. Fitness games on consoles like the Wii and the Nintendo Switch have very sophisticated Yoga "games" that allow you to practice particular poses or even create your own routine, whether that's just for a couple of poses before you start your day or even fifteen to twenty minutes. There is plenty of flexibility in creating your own yoga routine.

A BLENDED APPROACH WITH KUNDALINI YOGA

Despite sounding like a type of pasta, Kundalini Yoga goes hand in hand with the balancing of chakras. The West was introduced to Kundalini Yoga in the late 1960s, as a blend of earlier yogic traditions.

Kundalini Yoga concentrates on the energy that sits at the base of our spine. Through breathing, movement, and sound, we are able to tap into this energy and encourage this energy to flow up through our seven chakras.

Kundalini Shakti- meaning 'serpent power'

The snake has powerful imagery, first as the inactive energy is seen as 'coiled energy' and second, the process of Kundalini Yoga is a transformation of oneself, just as a snake would shed its old skin.

There have been enough scientific studies to demonstrate the health benefits of Kundalini Yoga. A study in 2018 showed that it can help to reduce the symptoms of anxiety disorders, while another in 2017 showed a decrease in cortisol levels and perceived stress. Some of the other health benefits may include:

- Toned muscles
- A boost in your mood
- Lower blood pressure and heart rate
- Better focus
- Faster metabolism
- Improved digestion
- Relief from lower back pain
- Depression management

The good news is that we have already covered the three core aspects of Kundalini Yoga—breathing, mantras, and poses. The last thing for us to do before we probe into each individual chakra is to see how our breathing, mantras, and poses relate specifically to Kundalini Yoga.

Breathing

There are specific types of controlled breathing (pranayama) for each action performed in this type of yoga and each one is focused. Some are long deep breaths and others, like the favoured Breath of Fire, are short and fast. The Breath of Fire requires fast, equal breaths, gently in through the nose and forcefully out through the nose.

Pranayama has been shown in trials to reduce perceived stress and boost cognitive functions.

Mantras

Mantras use the power of specific sound vibrations to channel energy, either to specific chakras, or for all-over energy flow. These vibrations seem to have a way of making a person feel better by increasing positivity and lifting the mood.

In Chapter 3, we looked at the seven bija, or seed mantras, for each of the chakras and we will revise them in Part 3. I also want to look at some other popular mantras that are used for Kundalini Yoga in general:

"Har" but it can also be Hara or Hari- Creative infinity

"Hari Nam, Sat Nam Hari Nam, Hari.
Hari Nam, Sat Nam, Sat Name, Hari"- The name of God is the
True Name

"Ong So Hung"- Creator, I am Thou
"Hum Dum Har Har"- We the inverse, God, God"

Don't forget that you don't need to practice any religion to benefit from mantras. Although they are often considered types of prayers, it is the vibrations that we are gaining from. If you don't feel comfortable with these mantras, the bija mantras are only sounds, rather than having any religious vocabulary; it's a personal choice.

Poses

These yoga poses, when combined with breathing and mantras, are known as Kriyas. There are thousands of Kriyas and they are based on your intention. Here is an example of one of the basic ones:

The Ego Eradicator

Pose- Sit in the Easy Pose with legs crossed and spine straight, lift your arms straight out to a 60° angle, curl your fingertips in and raise your thumbs up. Close your eyes.

Breathing- Breath of Fire, short equal breaths through the nose

Mantra- "Ma" and keep your focus on the area above your head

You can do the Ego Eradicator for one to three minutes before you get up in the morning and if you feel it is necessary, you can extend it for up to six minutes. It is an ideal Kriya for opening your lungs, feeling more mentally alert, and uniting your magnetic field.

You should be clear on your healing intentions by name. Still, it is widely agreed that the primary goal of Kundalini Yoga is to push your life force energy up from its coiled position, through the chakras. Once it has reached the Crown Chakra, you are able to appreciate enlightenment.

Needless to say, this will take some dedication. If you are already comfortably using some mantras, you can incorporate these into your Kundalini Yoga. You can also combine this with aromatherapy and have your crystals nearby, if this is what you feel is right.

The power of the mind, focus, dedication, and a genuine belief in your chakra energy and balance are the key things that need to remain consistent. The rest are tools and techniques that you should enjoy exploring.

With so many different things to try, consider keeping a journal to make a note of the techniques you have tried and how you have felt afterwards. This will allow you to narrow down the best methods that work for you gradually. I love looking back at my journal and it inspires me to try things again to see the new impact after gaining more experience.

PART III

A STEP-BY-STEP GUIDE TO BALANCING
CHAKRAS

The time has finally come, and this part of the book needs little introduction! The next seven chapters will each cover one of the seven chakras. We will review what we have already learnt about them in terms of the associated body parts and emotions. We will delve deeper into what to expect in the process of awakening and balancing chakras.

The techniques we have been over have been quite general so far, but now is the moment that we work on choosing the precise crystals and essential oils, as well as massage techniques for the associated body parts.

There will be some new mantras and affirmations to try and a few other meditation tips. Finally, rather than naming yoga poses and Kriyas, I am going to use my creative side to describe how to perform these powerful actions.

Many people believe that Earth itself has its own chakras. To complete our understanding of chakras, I will tell you a little more about each of these. My goal in life is to visit them all, but the few that I have been to have allowed an incredible connection to the different chakras.

I am so excited to be taking this final step of the journey with you, so let's make it a memorable one.

AWAKENING THE ROOT CHAKRA

L et's begin by reviewing what we have covered so far in terms of the location of the Root Chakra and which symptoms may be experienced when it is blocked. Up to now, we have only used the English name, but it is also called the Muladhara Chakra. The first of the seven chakras is located at the base of our spine.

It's the closest chakra to earth and is tied to our sense of being grounded. It is the support and foundation for our lives. It is related to feeling safe and secure, as well as our basic needs such as food, sleep, and a place to live.

Red is the colour linked to the Root Chakra. Your Root Chakra is associated with your legs, feet, ankles, bladder, and the large intestine, adrenal glands.

Here is a quick guide to the physical and emotional symptoms associated with the Root Chakra:

- Physical symptoms when blocked: the inability to sit still, weakness in the legs, overweight, kidney stones, circulatory issues.
- Physical symptoms when overactive: bladder issues, constipation, fatigue, anaemia.
- Emotional symptoms when blocked: it is likely that you will feel insecure about life and even anger. I describe it as the feeling when you have itchy feet and can't find a way to settle yourself.
- An overactive Root Chakra: your basic needs aren't being met and this leads you to feel threatened, bringing about anxiety and fear.
- An underactive Root Chakra: you may live in a dreamland and be far from grounded. It could be that you have never had to worry about the basic things in life.

When your Root Chakra is balanced, you will feel happy and comfortable within yourself and your environment, like you belong. You are able to appreciate your body and your place in the world. Above all, you feel in control of your life.

HOW TO HEAL A BLOCKED ROOT CHAKRA

Healing Through Sound

The bija mantra, or seed mantra, for the Root Chakra is "Lam", a deep sound that will help to clear blockages and encourage energy to start flowing up to the other chakras. By chanting Lam 108 times, you should start to feel less worried and more grounded. The English version (not the translation) is "I am".

There are also several affirmations that can help to unblock and create balance in this chakra. While you can still make up your own affirmations, I wanted to give you a little inspiration with words that are related to a connection to the Earth:

- I am grounded
- I am standing with my feet firmly on the ground
- I am safe
- Like the trees and the stars, I have the right to be here
- I trust myself
- I feel the good in life

AWAKENING THE ROOT CHAKRA WITH VISUALISATION AND MEDITATION

In Northern California, you can find Mount Shasta. This active volcano has a breath-taking and spiritual presence, surrounded by natural beauty, forests and meadows. Many see Mount Shasta as the Root Chakra of Earth's energy and native Americans worship this volcano, believing it is the centre of the universe.

The connection between the planet Mars and the colour red is no coincidence. Meditating while visualising this planet will help to draw in its energies. It is wise to meditate outside, where you can be in closer contact with the earth. I like to lay down on the grass, but you might prefer to sit on the ground, or at least sit on a chair with your feet placed firmly on the ground to help you feel rooted.

Take long, slow, deep breaths and imagine the energy of Mars and your astrological sign filling each part of your body. You can visualise this energy as a light that passes into your lungs and spreads all the way down to your toes. If you are laying on the ground, you may feel the light in a complete circle around you, a link between your body and the ground.

Each breath should fill you with warmth and comfort, like you are being embraced, but it should also make you feel empowered, strong, and give you a sense of belonging.

Don't forget to express your gratitude to Mars before and after your meditation.

YOGA AND REIKI FOR YOUR ROOT CHAKRA

For our yoga poses, we should practice Sukhasana (Easy Pose), Malasana (Garland Pose) and Virabhadrasana II (Warrior II).

Easy Pose- Sitting down with crossed legs, tilt your pelvis forward slightly so that your spine is completely straight. As you sit on the ground, breathe in the energy from the Earth and breathe out any negativity or anxiety you may feel.

Garland Pose- The best way to describe this is like you are (a woman) taking a pee in the countryside! Squat down low with your feet pointed out at an angle. Tuck your elbows into your knees and keep your hands in the prayer position. This is another pose that keeps you close to the ground and can strengthen your lower back, hips, calves, and ankles.

Warrior II- Stand with your legs spread as far as possible while being comfortable. Keep one foot in the same position while you turn the other 90º clockwise with your knee facing in the same direction. Your arms are raised to a 90º angle with the tips of your fingers stretching in opposite directions in line with your body. Repeat the same in the opposite direction. Warrior II helps us with our flight-or-fight response and enables us to face our fears.

For reiki healing, lay down and feel the stretch in your spine, lay your hands over the very tops of your legs so that they are covering the lower pelvic area. Massaging your gluteus maximus, gluteus medius, and gluteus minimus (that's your bum and outer hip muscles to us laymen) will help to relieve tension around your Root Chakra. You can also massage and stretch all of the muscles in your legs.

AROMATHERAPY AND CRYSTAL HEALING

Frankincense has a fresh, clean smell and can help slow down the breathing when meditating. Patchouli offers clarity and allows you to enjoy the present moment by yourself, it may even help you to focus and reach your goals. Cedarwood is another one of my favourites because it has a very calming effect and a real scent of nature.

Red crystals, in general, are going to be of great help for creating balance in your Root Chakra, whether that's to keep them on you or for visualisation during meditation. Some others that I have used are:

- Black Tourmaline- this semi-precious black stone is used to help keep us grounded.
- Red Jasper- it is a deep earthy red colour and it reminds me of the power Mars has and it will help to cleanse and balance.

- Bloodstone- I love the dark green colour with the speckles of red. You can wear this to increase your self-esteem and protect yourself from negativity.
- Red Carnelian- the lighter red, almost orange appearance can give you strength and courage, particularly useful for the fight-or-flight instinct.

By using just one of these techniques, you will start to see a difference. Once you have explored different methods to awaken your Root Chakra and decided on the best choices for you, you will soon start to feel balance as your energy begins to flow up towards the Sacral Chakra.

AWAKENING THE SACRAL CHAKRA

You will also hear the Sacral Chakra being called Svadhisthana and it is the second chakra as we move up our spine. We associate the Sacral Chakra with the pleasure we are able to experience through our senses. It lets us feel the world around us and can create flexibility in our lives. It plays a significant role in our sex life, including the ability to express our sexual desires.

Orange is the colour that is tied to our Sacral Chakra, more specifically, an almost-transparent orange. Because of the association with water, the Sacral Chakra may take on a light blue colour.

The Sacral Chakra can impact our reproductive system, the ovaries, testes, and uterus. It might also cause problems with our kidneys when unbalanced. Let's revise some of the other symptoms associated with a blocked Sacral Chakra:

- **Physical symptoms when blocked:** Lower back pain and stiffness in this area is quite common. People may experience urinary problems, kidney pain and/or infections. Impotence or infertility may even be present.
- **Physical symptoms when overactive:** As well as the abovementioned, you might suffer from cysts and bladder issues. The excess energy in your Sacral Chakra can cause warmth in your lower abdomen area.
- **An overactive Sacral Chakra:** Emotions could be running high, you might experience mood swings or become overly sensitive, dependant, or obsessive.
- **An underactive Sacral Chakra:** You may fear pleasure and be generally insecure. The lack of energy can make you feel tired and without desire or inspiration.

When you start to bring balance to your Sacral Chakra, you will feel like you have complete control of your emotions. You will be confident and generous, and you will be fully aware of personal boundaries. As you can imagine, you will also be able to enjoy positively exploring your sexuality.

HEALING THROUGH SOUND

Focus on the area around three fingers below your navel. Repeat the bija mantra "Vam" in multiples of 108. In English, you can repeat the words "I feel", while concentrating on your various feelings and senses. Don't forget what you can hear and smell.

For affirmations to help awaken and balance the Sacral Chakra, you can choose one of the following or even combine them if you prefer. For added impact, start your Sacral Chakra affirmation with "I feel".

- I feel joy inside me
- My life is happy
- Creativity flows through my body
- I celebrate my sexuality
- I deserve pleasure and passion
- I have faith in my feelings

AWAKENING THE SACRAL CHAKRA WITH VISUALIZATION AND MEDITATION

It makes sense that a large body of water is the Sacral Chakra of the Earth. Lake Titicaca in Peru and Bolivia is home to 'Isla del Sol', Island of the Sun, and makes for a stunning image of orange and light blue.

Meditation is a wonderful way to become more attuned to your emotions and allow all of your feelings to flow. I like to imagine my emotions attaching themselves to the energy spinning in my Sacral Chakra and then passing around my body.

It is best to meditate while sitting down with your hips higher than your knees. Loosen the sacral area by tilting your pelvis back and forward a few times and then completely relax your lower back and hips.

Though Venus is the planet that is linked to our Sacral Chakra, many people will use the Sun as part of visualisation due to its bright orange appearance. Imagine the Sun setting over the ocean. Breath in as the waves roll in and out as they drift back. Take in the colour of the Sun and its rays reflecting on the water. Absorb its vibrancy and focus this energy on your Sacral Chakra. To stimulate your senses, you can play the sound of the ocean while you meditate.

YOGA AND REIKI FOR YOUR ROOT CHAKRA

The following poses can help to increase the energy in your Sacral Chakra, but they can also release any excess energy you may have, causing an overactive chakra. The Utkata Konasana (Goddess Pose), Prasarita Padottanasana C (Wide-Legged Forward Bend C), and Supta Baddha Konasana (Reclined Bound Angle Pose) work towards opening your hips and filling you with the confidence to experience a fulfilling life.

Goddess Pose- Stand like the New Zealand Rugby team do when they are about to perform the Haka—hips wide open, knees bent, feet turned outwards, and slowly sink down. Keep your spine straight and place your palms together in front of your heart.

Wide-Legged Forward Bend C- This is one of the best stretches for your body and I love it, but please take care not to lose your balance! While standing up, spread your legs as far as you can and keep your feet facing forward. Link your fingers behind your back and rest them on the base of your spine. Slowly roll your neck, then shoulders and spine down so you are looking through your legs. Push your hips forward as you gradually move your hands away from your spine towards the floor.

Reclined Bound Angle Pose- Lie down with your knees bent and your feet together flat on the floor. Let your knees fall to the ground as the soles of your feet touch. You can stretch the spine more by crossing your arms above your head, or you can practice reiki by placing your palms on your Sacral Chakra.

Like the Root Chakra, chakra massage is focused on those bum muscles again, but you can also concentrate on the iliopsoas muscles, those that run from the lower spine to the pelvis.

AROMATHERAPY AND CRYSTAL HEALING

I found that Clary Sage is perfect for giving yourself an emotional uplift and, as the name suggests, it will help to clarify how you are feeling. Orange oil can stimulate the liver as well as your creativity. To increase your sex drive, Ylang Ylang and its aphrodisiac qualities may help your relationship.

For the crystals, amber and citrine are good stones to keep for the visual aspect. Others closely related to Sacral Chakra healing include:

- Orange and coral calcite- This stone can be used for cleansing and it is also a good crystal for distance healing.
- Orange Carnelian- This stone can restore vitality and help to calm an overactive Sacral Chakra.
- Orange Aventurine- To unblock your Sacral Chakra and inspire your imagination and creativity, keep Orange Aventurine close by.
- Tiger's Eye- The stone of the mind can be dark and

golden to yellow. It can help you to understand your emotions and make clearer decisions.

Not having control over your emotions or experiencing extremes such as depression or isolation are very sad and difficult ways to live life. It is amazing what just a few minutes a day can do to change your outlook on life for the better. Whether it's wearing a crystal in a piece of jewellery or starting your day with a bija mantra, you too can start to see a change.

AWAKENING THE SOLAR PLEXUS CHAKRA

The Manipura, or Solar Plexus Chakra, is located above the Sacral Chakra, where your diaphragm is. It can influence the way we view ourselves in society and help us to find our path in life. The energy found in the Solar Plexus Chakra helps us to find momentum and action so that we can create ideas which then lead us to realise our dreams.

We have seen that the Solar Plexus Chakra is yellow, but as this Chakra's element is fire, it can often be a golden, firefly yellow, much like the Sun. It also connected to the heat and energy produced by the Sun.

Suppose you have noticed problems with your digestive system, whether that's the stomach or intestines. In that case, you may have a blocked Sacral Chakra. It is also associated with the central nervous system, the liver, pancreas, and the metabolic system.

Physical symptoms when blocked: You might experience ulcers, gas, nausea, eating disorders or even respiratory problems like asthma. Liver or kidney infections may be related to the Solar Plexus Chakra and even nerve pain or fibromyalgia.

Emotional symptoms when blocked: People often feel as though they lack purpose. They can obsess over the tiny details of life and can't see the whole picture. You may find it important to have complete control over everything or the other extreme is a sense of helplessness.

An overactive Solar Plexus Chakra: When overactive, you might come across as dominating to the point of aggression. It is easy to criticise yourself too much and those around you.

An underactive Solar Plexus Chakra: You will tend to be passive in most situations. It is hard for you to make choices and you will often be quite timid.

You will be able to assert yourself when your Solar Plexus Chakra is balanced. This helps you to get what you want without having to overexert yourself. The balance you experience spreads to your relationships.

HEALING THROUGH SOUND

The vibrations created with the bija mantra "Ram" should be drawn towards your Solar Plexus Chakra, imaging the energy flowing up your spine towards your diaphragm. Focus on the colour yellow filling your body.

The words "I do" can be very empowering. As a blocked Solar Plexus Chakra can impede our ability to create ideas and carry them out, I find that the words "I do" reminds me that I am able to develop ways to do what I want to do.

Some affirmations that you can use throughout the day or as part of your morning routine are:

- I am capable of achieving my dreams
- I am valuable
- I am confident I have the skills to succeed
- I know what is best for myself
- I do not need to control
- I use my power for good

AWAKENING THE SOLAR PLEXUS CHAKRA WITH VISUALIZATION AND MEDITATION

Some cultures see the Solar Plexus Chakra as the house of the soul. The Earth's Solar Plexus Chakra is believed to be two rocks about eighteen miles apart, Kata Tjuta and Uluru in Australia. Looking at these giant rocks, I get a sense of both security and power.

Nobody can deny the power of the Sun! When there is a break in those cold rainy days and the sky is lit with this ball of power, we walk with an extra bounce in our step, and we smile.

It's important to make the most of the Sun so we can meditate outside. Go for a short walk, or even just around your garden a few times to get the body moving. Sit down and face the Sun with your palms open towards it. Relax, breathe and feel the warmth surround you. Believing in the power of the Sun will enable you to do this indoors or during the darker, colder months. Visualise the sun and the warmth on your face, moving across your body towards your fingertips and all the way down to your toes.

Every now and again I like to go to a park or sit in the countryside early in the morning. No technology, no distractions, just peace. I sit down and watch the sunrise. I empty my mind of everything and literally just spend twenty minutes watching the Sun in admiration. The connection with nature and the tranquillity helps me to feel in control and more determined.

YOGA AND REIKI FOR YOUR ROOT CHAKRA

To increase the energy flow to our Solar Plexus Chakra, you can try Virabhadrasana I (Warrior I), Navasana (Boat Pose), and Parivrtta Anjaneyasana (Revolved Crescent Lunge.

Warrior I- Stand with your legs spread as wide as you can, turn to one side so your feet and body are pointing in the same direction. Lower the stretch as you bend your knee, placing more weight on this front leg. Reach your arms towards the sky.

Half Boat Pose- This requires a good level of balance. Begin by sitting down with your knees bent and feet flat on the floor. Keep your spine straight and raise your knees. There should be a straight line from your shoulder, through your arms, knees and down to your ankles. The full-boat pose requires your hands taking the tips of your toes as you sit in a V shape.

Revolved Crescent Lunge- from Warrior I, drop your chest towards your knees. Now, if your left knee is bent, take your right elbow and place it on the outside of the right knee. Keep your gaze forward as you put your hands together in the prayer position. Hold for five seconds and repeat on the other side.

Massaging the Solar Plexus is very simple to do yourself. Start by laying on the floor and place your hands on your diaphragm. Feel for warmth for a few minutes. In a clockwise direction rub ten circles over your stomach, don't feel the need to rush this and don't worry about those "softer" bits of belly. Don't tense your muscles just to try to hide a little fat.

AROMATHERAPY AND CRYSTAL HEALING

Geraniums are lovely flowers and the essential oil is like loveliness in a bottle; it can help lower anxiety. Juniper berry can be used internally to improve kidney function. Cypress oil has a lovely evergreen smell, as if you are walking through the woods, and it has been known to help with respiratory problems.

Some ideas for healing crystals could be:

Mookaite- this is a very special stone that is only found in Australia, so I love it for the connection to Uluru and Kata Tjuta. The golden, yellow, and tones of rich red have strong connections to the Earth's electromagnetic current.

Lemon Quartz- when you catch the light on lemon quartz, it can be compared to the rays of the Sun. It is known for its ability to promote optimism.

Yellow Tourmaline- it can look very similar to Lemon Quartz, but Yellow Tourmaline can be used to help cleanse and detoxify the body.

Yellow Jasper- aside for helping bring balance to the Solar Plexus, it can also offer you protection.

The Solar Plexus Chakra is the last of the three lower chakras, those that are related to our ego, our insecurities and our fears. The next chakra is the Heart Chakra, the connection between the lower and higher chakras or the body and the mind.

AWAKENING THE HEART CHAKRA

The connection between our higher and lower chakras, the Heart Chakra is essential for emotional development and unconditional love. Also known as the Anahata, the Heart Chakra sits in the middle of the chest, though some feel it is more to the left, just above the heart. As well as joining the higher and lower chakras, the body and the mind, it also links the Earth world to the spiritual.

Green is the central colour of the spectrum, so it makes sense that it is associated with our most central chakra. Green has strong ties to healing and obviously to nature. However, the Heart Chakra can also be represented as pink, because of the relationship with love.

The Heart Chakra is linked to the thymus gland and immune system. It can have an impact on our lungs, breasts, arms, and hands, and most logically, our heart.

Physical symptoms when blocked: You might experience heart problems, such as palpitations, or, in extreme cases, heart attacks. There may be links between high blood pressure and poor circulation. Some may experience respiratory problems while others can have stiff or painful joints in their hands.

Emotional symptoms when blocked: Heartbreak, extreme sadness, and even grief can be felt. Some people could be angry, jealous and feel hatred towards themselves and others.

An overactive Heart Chakra: People with an overactive Heart Chakra may be clinging in a relationship, they may not have set their own boundaries and have a tendency to try to please everyone.

An underactive Heart Chakra: It will be hard for you to be open about how you feel, and this can make you feel isolated from the world, even cold.

If your Heart Chakra is balanced, it will be easier for you to let go of the grudges you hold. Your emotions will flow freely, and you will not fear them but embrace them. It will be easier for you to trust people and form stronger relationships.

HEALING THROUGH SOUND

Mantras and affirmations will include the Bija mantra "Yam" and the English words "I love". Take the sounds and imagine pulling the energy up through your body. While I often like to imagine my chakras like the spinning firework wheel, in this case, as I chant, I like to see this energy as a river of love throughout me.

Suppose you want to practice some English affirmations. In that case, it is still important to imagine being filled with love, passion, and happiness.

- I am open to love
- I love myself unconditionally
- I am worthy of love
- I choose love
- I give love, I receive love
- My heart is filled with cheerfulness and joy

AWAKENING THE HEART CHAKRA WITH VISUALIZATION AND MEDITATION

When you hear "Glastonbury", your mind will go straight to music, but it is a town that represents the idea of love and is thought to be one of the Earth's Heart Chakras. As a dual chakra, the other location of the Heart Chakra is Shaftesbury (another town in the South of England. The towns fit together, with Glastonbury a town of love and Shaftesbury one of will. Some believe the Heart Chakra expands to Stonehenge.

Interestingly, others feel that the Heart Chakra is the Halekalá volcano in Hawaii.

If you feel like your Heart Chakra is blocked or underactive, your visualisation needs to include imagining love flowing into your body. On the other hand, if your Heart Chakra is overactive, it's time to visualise this love flowing out of your body and sending it to others who need it.

Breathing is a vital part of meditation and the Heart Chakra because your lungs are one of the associated organs. When meditating, maintain your attention on deep breaths of green light. Each breath you take in should be directed to a pink light in the centre of your chest. See how the green light meets the pink as they swirl together.

You can also try Hridaya mudra. Sit down and bring the tips of your ring and middle finger to your thumb. Place your hands on your knees and concentrate on your heart and chest area. Your middle and ring fingers are associated with the energy channels of the heart. By bringing them to your thumb, you are essentially closing the circuit. Hridaya mudra can help you release the emotions that you have kept bottled up.

YOGA AND REIKI FOR YOUR HEART CHAKRA

Rather than putting your hand on your heart for reiki, place it a little higher on your chest, between the Heart Chakra and the Throat Chakra. This is where your thymus gland is, and its job is to produce white blood cells that fight infections. Keep it there for a few minutes as your focus on your breathing.

The Marjaryasana/ Bitilasana (Cat/Cow Pose), Bhujangasana (Cobra Pose), and Ustrasana (Camel pose) are all lovely yoga poses that open the chest area to bring more energy to the Heart Chakra.

Cat/Cow pose- Position yourself on all fours. As you inhale, tuck your tummy right in and around your spine. On the exhale, you slowly roll your spine the other way so that you can feel your back dipping into the stretch. Repeat a few times with each inhale and exhale as deep as you can manage.

Cobra pose- Lie on your front, place your hands under your shoulders. Start by raising the crown of your head, then gradually elevate your upper body using your hands to support your body. Only lift up as far as it is comfortable.

Camel pose- Begin by kneeling on a mat and keep your hips in line with your knees. Reach behind you so that your shoulders drop and your chest opens. Hold your heels with your hands. If you struggle to hold both heels, start on your left side and then repeat with your left.

To encourage energy to the Heart Chakra through massage, you should focus on those muscles that are around the shoulders and very lightly on the pectoralis muscles, the large muscle across your chest. Remember, if you have any heart conditions, please consult a doctor first.

AROMATHERAPY AND CRYSTAL HEALING

Bergamot essential oil comes from the rind of the bergamot orange, which is actually green. It can help improve your mood and lower your cholesterol. Add fresh basil to your recipes to help lower the risk of heart disease, as well as cypress and eucalyptus essential oils.

There are lots of crystals that will help bring balance to your heart chakra. Emerald and green jade are the obvious choices for the colour but here are some of my other favourites:

Unakite Jasper- this lovely green crystal has soft touches of pink and one of nature's best crystals for the heart and the mind.

Pink Rhodochrosite- with its feminine energy, this crystal promotes commitment and caring. It can increase your feeling of self-worth and lift depression.

Rose Quartz- the crystal of universal love, unconditional love, self-love and friendships. It can bring about a sense of inner peace and help to restore trust in relationships.

Prehnite- this can be a lovely green colour and reminds me of grapes. It is another crystal associated with unconditional love and peace.

No one chakra is more important than the next, but personally, I noticed so many improvements in my life when I started creating balance in my Heart Chakra. It's about more than just feeling more love in a relationship. It's hard to see at times, but there is so much love around us and when we are able to see this, life becomes more positive. The smaller things that used to get you down no longer seem as relevant.

AWAKENING THE THROAT CHAKRA

Located in the neck, the Throat Chakra or Vishuddha is imperative for our communication. It is also important because it is the gateway for energy to flow up to our head. Not only this, but the throat is where sounds are based on the rest of the body in the form of vibrations. Without the throat, we wouldn't be able to benefit as much from our bija sound mantras.

We most often visualise the Throat Chakra as blue, specifically turquoise blue, but also aquamarine blue or even a cloudy purple.

The Throat Chakra is associated with the neck, the shoulders, ears and mouth. It can also impact the thyroid, a butterfly-shaped gland in front of the windpipe. It's what helps the body turn food into energy, our metabolism, as well as helping to regulate blood pressure and body temperature.

Physical symptoms when blocked: There may be a stiffness across your neck and shoulders. Sore throats can be expected or hoarseness. Some people suffer from laryngitis. When blocked, you may be susceptible to earaches and infections, problems with your teeth, or thyroid problems.

Emotional symptoms when blocked: People tend to be overly critical of themselves. There is a lot of fear when the Throat Chakra is blocked. But you might not be able to find the words to express this. It's quite normal also to feel insecure.

An overactive Throat Chakra: There is too much talking and not enough listening. Some people might become verbally abusive and look down on others.

An underactive Throat Chakra: You may feel overly shy. It could even be that you struggle to speak the truth and feel the need to lie.

You will be able to appreciate your wisdom when the Throat Chakra is balanced. You won't need to fear those moments when you know what you want to say, but can't find the words to explain yourself. You can actively listen to others as well as your inner voice. You can express your feelings, your needs, and your creativity.

HEALING THROUGH SOUND

Our bija mantra is "Ham", but because of the importance of sound and vibrations, you may also want to use other Sanskrit mantras. I like the Adi Mantra, "Ong Namo Guru Dev Namo" (pronounced ong naa moo groo day na mo). It means "I bow to the creative energy of the infinitive; I bow to the divine channel of wisdom".

English affirmations can be linked to the words "I speak", for example:

- I speak the truth and I speak it freely
- My words express my love
- I share my creativity and wisdom
- I speak and I listen
- I am safe and I trust
- I communicate my truth

AWAKENING THE THROAT CHAKRA WITH VISUALIZATION AND MEDITATION

The Throat Chakra has three earthly locations. Two locations are in Egypt—Mount Sinai and the Great Pyramid of Giza. The third is the Mount of Olives in Jerusalem. If you look at the three locations on a map, you will be able to make out the connections in the form of a right-angled triangle.

To attune to the planet Mercury and the energy of communication, close your eyes and breathe through your nose quickly for twenty seconds. Open your eyes and focus on one object while you maintain short rapid breaths. Close your eyes and repeat the process four or five times. This meditation is excellent for getting in touch with your creativity.

You can visualise a bright white light entering your body with each short breath, feel it pass down your throat and fill your lungs. This can be combined with a blue light passing in through your ears to help you listen. Each breath pulses the energy to your heart and into the blood to the rest of your body. Move your focus to the planet Mercury and visualise your ideas and dreams becoming a reality.

YOGA AND REIKI FOR YOUR THROAT CHAKRA

Naturally, you can massage your muscles that run the length of your neck to help release tension. If you want to have a little fun, try singing. The vibrations will spread throughout your body, and singing can help shy people find a bit of confidence. Sing wherever you feel comfortable doing so.

The same yoga poses we saw for the Heart Chakra can be used for the Throat Chakra. Once you are feeling more confident, balanced and stronger in your body, you can move on to the more advanced poses, such as the Salamba Sarvangasana (Supported Shoulder Stand), Halasana (Plow Pose), and Matsyasana (Fish Pose).

Supported Shoulder Stand- From lying flat on your back with your arms next to you, palms down, bring your knees up so that your feet are flat on the floor. Lift your hips off the floor and by using all of your core muscles, you will lift your knees towards your chest as your lower back comes up off the floor, followed by your mid-back. Use your hands to support your back. Straighten your legs so that your shoulders, hips and ankles are all in a straight line.

Plow Pose- Once you are balanced and breathing steadily in the shoulder stand, you can slowly bring one foot down to the floor behind your head. There should be no tension in your neck or shoulders. If this is comfortable, you can bring the other foot down. Don't be surprised if this takes a little practise.

Fish Pose- Lie down on the floor facing the ceiling. Tuck your hands under your bum and bring your index finger and thumbs together so that they form a diamond. You are going to gradually move your head so that the crown of your head is on the floor; you will be looking in the opposite direction of your feet. Open your chest towards the ceiling and take three or four slow deep breaths.

AROMATHERAPY AND CRYSTAL HEALING

Frankincense has a high spiritual frequency and has been shown to help with underactive thyroids. Geranium essential oil encourages communication with our inner selves and the sweetness of the citrus can also alleviate a sore throat. Peppermint is so refreshing—I love it for everything. The sharpness of the essential oil has a positive impact on the sharpness of your mind and can help with respiratory infections.

The crystals for the Throat Chakra are some of my favourites, because of the wide range of colours you can find. Rather than just looking at blue, explore the different shades of blue and those that have specks or streaks of white too.

Amazonite- It is more of a turquoise green and is good for creating emotional balance and to protect you from negativity.

Turquoise- depending on each stone, you might notice a stronger shade of blue. It's a good crystal to keep on you if you want to get better at expressing yourself clearly.

Lapis lazuli- It's a beautiful dark blue speckled stone. Along with improving clarity and creativity, it can not only help you to understand your inner truths but also express them.

Aquamarine- sometimes we need a little assistance being compassionate and understanding what others are telling us. Aquamarine can help us overcome fears while allowing us to be more tolerant.

Emotional intelligence is an incredibly important skill to have. Some of the smartest people I know are unable to explain some of their most basic emotions. Being able to communicate will allow us to experience more fulfilling lives, both personal and professional.

AWAKENING THE THIRD EYE CHAKRA

The Third Eye Chakra is the sixth chakra from the spine. It is located at the brow, above your nose and between your eyes. This chakra permits us to see the inner and outer worlds; more precisely, we can internalise the outer world and internalise the inner world. As it is located in the brain, when balanced, we can also experience a balance between the left and right hemispheres of the brain.

The Third Eye Chakra takes us one step closer to the spiritual world. Its energy can help us with our spiritual contemplation and self-reflection. Our eyes allow us to see the world and draw our own conclusions but the Third Eye lets us see the world from the point of view of an observer.

The Sanskrit name for the Third Eye Chakra is Ajna. It is associated with the colour blue, or a bluish-purple, even indigo. It can also be seen as translucent purple.

It is linked to the pituitary gland (the master gland), the eyes and the brow. This chakra is associated with the base of the skull and our biorhythms, the cycles that our body goes through, like sleep.

Physical symptoms when blocked: Some of the most frequent problems are with vision, dizziness and headaches. It is even possible to experience migraines. Insomnia and other sleep disorders may also be symptoms.

Emotional symptoms when blocked: Through related to sleep disorders, you may suffer from nightmares. You may feel sceptical of everything or even extremely paranoid. Vivid dreams and delusions are also symptoms.

An overactive Third Eye Chakra: It may be impossible for you to focus or your mind easily drifts off. It can also be difficult for you to stay in touch with reality and your good judgement.

An underactive Third Eye Chakra: You might be stuck in the past and be scared of what is ahead. It's quite normal to be stuck in your ways of thinking and not be willing to explore new ideas. It is also possible that rather than trusting your inner voice, you stick to the rules of authority.

Balance in your Third Eye Chakra gives you the wisdom and the ability to see problems from a different perspective. It takes you that little step closer to enlightenment, and even those who are sceptical of the spiritual world are more accepting of that which is beyond us. The sense of clarity that comes with a balanced Third Eye Chakra brings a whole new level of harmony to your world.

HEALING THROUGH SOUND

"Aum" is the bija mantra for the Third Eye Chakra, the source of all sound and the sound that will activate the energy in this chakra. The power of "Aum" is immense, so I often combine it with my English affirmations, which will be related to "I see".

Don't limit your affirmations to what you can physically see around you; it goes much deeper than that:

- I see each situation as an opportunity to grow
- I see and trust how my intuition guides me
- I am one with my higher power
- My third eye is all-seeing
- I welcome new experiences and new energy
- I believe in my imagination

AWAKENING THE THIRD EYE CHAKRA WITH VISUALIZATION AND MEDITATION

This chakra shifts locations with each new astrological age, approximately every 2,100 to 2,500 years. Astrologers also believe that the Third Eye Chakra coordinates with constellations. Now, we are in the Age of Aquarius and so the location once again is in England, Glastonbury, specifically Glastonbury Tor. When we move into the Age of Capricorn, the Third Eye Chakra will be found in Brazil.

Saturn, in Kundalini, showers people with wealth. Some like to see this as material wealth. When I use visualisation, I imagine myself surrounded by rings, like Saturn, though mine are blue and indigo. I feel the wealth of knowledge and the faith in myself spinning around me.

A blocked Third Eye Chakra can point to a restriction of your thought patterns. Regularly meditating will help to encourage your wisdom to flow and a stronger trust in your intuition. It is important to meditate with your eyes open. Only when your eyes are open can your third eye see your inner self. Imagine your consciousness looking through your eyes to the light inside your mind. Pressing the tip of your tongue to the roof of your mouth can stimulate the Third Eye Chakra from below. Breathe slowly through your nose.

YOGA AND REIKI FOR YOUR THIRD EYE CHAKRA

Massage can really help with headaches and migraines, particularly if you combine it with the right essential oils. Though you can massage your forehead, the bridge of your nose and around the ears, I like to work with a friend, as it is much easier for them to massage the pressure points at the base of the skull.

You can also use your index finger to apply pressure on your Third Eye Chakra for one minute. Firm pressure can help to reduce eye strain, alleviate sinus pressure and help with headaches.

For yoga, you can work on Balasana (Child's Pose), Uttanasana (Standing Forward Fold), and Catur Svanasana (Dolphin Pose).

Child's Pose- I always get a sense of comfort from this pose. Sit on your heels and stretch your fingers forward in front of you on the mat. Extend your body as you rest your forehead on the floor in front of your knees and pull your arms behind you so that your hands are on either side of your feet.

Standing Forward Fold- Inhale as you bring your arms up in a circle, so your hands are above your head. On the exhale, fold down at the hips and reach your hands to the calf muscles, closer to the ankles if you can. You might need to start with your knees slightly bent until you build up your flexibility.

Dolphin Pose- Start on all fours, straighten your legs as you keep your forearms and palms flat on the ground. Keep your forearms flat and gently push your shoulder blades down. You should try to keep an even amount of weight on your feet and arms.

AROMATHERAPY AND CRYSTAL HEALING

I do always try to use each plant to the maximum. Bay laurel is great to throw whole leaves into soups and stews. As an essential oil, it can increase your awareness and perception. It can stimulate both the left and right hemispheres of the brain. Palo Santo is often burned and used for cleansing. It's a lovely, sweet smell and can enhance your spiritual awareness. Lavender is the right colour for the Third Eye Chakra and its ability to help you relax will assist with meditation.

As with mantras, it is your intention that is most important with healing crystals. The following are well known for their ability to help balance your Third Eye Chakra, but you can use others.

Amethyst- you can find this crystal in dark to light shades of purple. It is used to stimulate the chakra and create balance. It can offer you wisdom and protection from harm.

Black Obsidian- as well as emotional balance, black obsidian can remove negativity.

Purple Fluorite- some call this crystal the dream crystal and can help those who suffer from nightmares and spiritual discomfort. It can make decision making easier and improve our confidence.

Clear Quartz- with a focus on the Third Eye Chakra, the powerful vibrational energy of clear quartz can help transmit your thoughts to the rest of the universe.

Our chakra learning will soon be coming to an end, but if you are the type of person who loves to learn and explore, it certainly doesn't mean that chakra healing is almost over. The final chapter will look at the Crown Chakra.

AWAKENING THE CROWN CHAKRA

The name comes from the idea that the Crown Chakra sits on the top of our head. Even though it is furthest from our Root Chakra, it has strong ties with it, because they are both extremes. The Root Chakra keeps us grounded, whereas the Crown Chakra is associated with an awareness of our higher consciousness. In Sanskrit, it is called Sahasrara.

As the location suggests, this chakra is the closest link to the divine. For those who are religious, they will be able to appreciate a closer connection to their god. For those who aren't, they will still gain from the uttermost clarity. Unblocking and finding balance in your Crown Chakra releases you from your limitations, in space and time.

We associate the Crown Chakra with the colour purple or violet. That being said, the sheer power of the Crown Chakra can also have ties to gold, white, and a clear bright light.

With regards to our body, the Crown Chakra is linked to our pituitary and pineal glands and the central nervous system. With regards to our brain, it can be associated with the hypothalamus and cerebral cortex.

Physical symptoms of a blocked Crown Chakra: Mental fog and confusion are often seen with a blocked Crown Chakra. There could be neurological disorders or mental disorders like schizophrenia. Some may experience nerve pain.

Emotional symptoms of a blocked Crown Chakra: You may be feeling particularly lonely with no direction in your life. It's not just that you don't have spiritual guidance, you might feel like you don't deserve it. Some people become overly attached to material objects.

An overactive Crown Chakra: there is such a thing as an addiction to spirituality or reckless behaviour when it comes to your bodily needs. It could be difficult for you to control your feelings.

An underactive Crown Chakra: If you find setting goals and reaching them a challenge, your Crown Chakra could be underactive. It's also likely that you aren't open to the concept of spirituality.

When you start to recognise your spiritual side and open your mind to all that is sacred, you will know that your Crown Chakra is starting to become balanced. The best way to describe a Crown Chakra that is flowing with the right energy is a state of bliss, ecstasy and pure happiness.

HEALING THROUGH SOUND

"Om" refers to Atman and Braham, the soul and the entirety of the universe or the supreme spirit respectively. It can be used alone or as part of longer mantras, for example, "Om Santi, Santi Om".

In English, we use the words "I am", which leaves you a great deal of freedom to create your own meaningful affirmations. Here is some inspiration:

- I am at peace
- I am light
- I am divine
- I go beyond my limiting beliefs
- I am infinite
- I am complete

AWAKENING THE CROWN CHAKRA WITH VISUALISATION AND MEDITATION

You might assume that Mount Everest would be the Earth's Crown Chakra, due to its height. In fact, while still in the Himalayas, it is Mount Kailash that is dubbed as the "roof of the world". Though approximately 7,000 ft higher, Everest doesn't have the same sacredness as Mount Kailash. The latter is considered the most sacred mountain in Tibet and many consider it offensive to climb it, due to it being so holy.

Jupiter is the planet associated with the Crown Chakra. It is one of the most effective in the birth charts and is highly spiritual. In astrology, Jupiter is the teacher of the science of light and the ruler of the Sun and the Moon. The planet Jupiter is the fourth brightest object in the sky. This brightness can help us with our visualisation. Such light and brightness can be drawn in and absorbed, the power of the light reaching every inch of us.

When we meditate, it is helpful to relax our head and face, even imagine your head as a floating lotus surrounded by water. With each breath you take, imagine the lotus opening just that little bit more. The purple light that radiates from your head should be seen growing in a beam towards the sky. At the end of your meditation, be thankful, whether that is to the divine or your higher self.

YOGA AND REIKI FOR YOUR CROWN CHAKRA

For reiki healing by yourself, you should aim to place the palms of your hands on the back of your head with your wrists covering the crown of your head. Massages general focus on the scalp, perhaps the reason why I am often tempted to pay my children to brush my hair!

Run your fingers through your hair a few times, just gently scraping the scalp with your fingertips but not your nails. Now start to massage your scalp with your fingertips in circular motions. Don't feel that you have to massage each area method-ically. Instead, have faith in your body and let your instincts guide your fingers. Also, don't feel the need for these head massaging tools. As funky as they seem, your hands are the best healing tools. You can also use your affirmations and visualise a purple light around each area you massage.

Paschimottanasana (Seated Forward Bend), Adho Mukha Sukhasana (Easy Pose with Forward Fold) and Shavasana (Corpse Pose) will allow you to feel the peace and serenity while the Crown Chakra becomes more balanced.

Seated Forward Bend- You will start by sitting up straight with your legs nicely stretched out in front of you. Raise your hands in a circular motion up above your head as you breathe in. Slowly exhale and allow your body to fold towards your legs. You may find that in the beginning, your hands will reach your knees or your shins. Don't panic, if you do this pose each day you will soon be able to hold your ankles as you feel the stretch along your spine.

Easy Pose with Forward Fold- Sit up nice and tall and cross each leg as you bend your knees. Each foot should rest on the opposite knee. Inhale as you stretch your arms above your head and fold forward on the exhale. Lower your head towards your knees and place your hands on your mat in front of you. You will feel the stretch along your thighs but don't push yourself further than you can.

Corpse Pose- it might look like you are just lying on the floor but pay attention to pulling your shoulder blades slightly together underneath you and lift your chin upwards a touch. This pose requires deep breathing and each exhale should allow your body to sink a little more towards the floor. This is a great way to start your day, even from your bed.

AROMATHERAPY AND CRYSTAL HEALING

A lot of the essential oils we have already seen can also be used for the Crown Chakra, such as lavender, jasmine, and frankincense. You can also try vetiver. This essential oil can help you to remember your vivid dreams, sometimes signs of what our subconscious wants. Helichrysum has a high spiritual frequency and may help to reduce the strength of headaches and migraines. Spikenard will help you to find your emotional balance, enjoy a more restful sleep and assist your meditation.

The same can be said with our crystals. There is no need to go out and buy more if you already have a good selection of crystals. Nevertheless, if you are on the lookout for more, you might want to consider:

Selenite- The white stone can enable a better connection with the divine and with the high vibrations can also be used for cleansing and creating a calming space.

Clear Quartz- This is more transparent than selenite. It may help soothe pain in your nerves. Generally, it will help to harmonise the seven chakras.

Charoite- I am a real fan of the white, lavender and pearly lustre of this stone. As well as opening the Heart Chakra, it is considered to be the stone of service and altruism.

Diamond- The pure white of diamond can awaken your crown chakra and bring you greater awareness. It is a symbol of purity and love, positivity and strength.

Some people might understandably yet mistakenly see the Crown Chakra as the end of the line, maybe more so if they aren't religious. Others see this as the holy grail of chakras. Remember that the goal is to awaken each of the chakras so that the right quantity and quality of energy is flowing through our bodies. It's a process, a pleasant, eye-opening and enjoyable one that can't be rushed so that we can reach the Crown Chakra and a higher state of being. Take your time. The changes we make as we balance our chakras will last a lifetime; it's not a sprint!

CONCLUSION

A friend of mine wanted me to check her chakra healing kit that she had bought. There was a new yoga mat, there were at least ten crystals, a jewellery making kit, mala beads and more essential oils than the local pharmacy. Before we wrap up this book on modern chakras, please remember that while all of these tools can enhance the healing process, they are also not compulsory. You need your body and your mind to awaken your chakras. People get it the wrong way around and think that by popping a crystal in their pocket, they will start to see improvements in their life. We need intention.

It is necessary to begin our healing process by understanding exactly what is wrong, whether the symptoms are physical, emotional, or both. Not everyone will have symptoms that are associated with just one chakra. It's possible to have lower backache, anger issues, and a weak immune system. While the first part of this book introduces you to chakras, the final chapters will have helped you to identify your blocked chakras.

It is normal to feel slightly overwhelmed in the beginning. I remember almost feeling scared that I was going to get it wrong. By using the techniques in this book, you can't get it wrong. There is no technique or combination of techniques that will cause you to suffer. This is the main reason why I have stayed far away from the topic of opening chakras, as this runs a risk of 'too much too soon'.

The emotional journey of balancing your chakras can bring up a whole range of feelings that you might have even forgotten you had. On occasions, it might feel like there are some highs and lows as you work through each of these emotions. Keep your focus on the end goal and remember that though there may be difficult moments, you should celebrate this experience.

My other piece of advice from experience is not to try too many techniques at once. You might think that the best results are going to come about when you have your essential oils, crystal circle, ocean waves playing in the background and so on, but if you are new to meditation and visualisation, this might be distracting. To master skills like meditation and visualisation, I think it's better to start simple. Go and sit in a field or lay in your garden. Not all of the chakra techniques have to be done at the same time. Play around with aromatherapy, massage, the crystals, and even the mantras, until you start to feel that you are gaining from each part of the healing.

Needless to say, I am not a doctor. Everything in this book is completely natural, but that doesn't mean to say the alternative medicine can be used with the current medication you are taking. Please check with your physician if you have any doubts. The same is said for those who are pregnant, check with your midwife first. We are all different and have different conditions so to be on the safe side, just ask before you try.

I am convinced that no matter what gender, size, or age you are, yoga is going to become your new best friend. Yoga is easy to include in your daily routine and just five or ten minutes before you start your day can really boost your mood. If you are unsure of any of the positions or that you are getting them right, it would be wise to sign up for a few classes, even if it's just until you start to feel a little bit more confident. Again, pregnant ladies and those with medical conditions, please check with your doctor first.

As you begin to feel the energy flow up through your body, take some time to stop and look around. Reassess your goals, so that you are continuing to strive for new things, but don't forget to be grateful for what you have at this moment.

Back in the 90s, I went to Glastonbury, the festival and the town. You do notice something special there. To say you feel the love might sound a little hippy, but you can. It's a positive place where people smile, they are polite and genuinely happy. I have also been lucky enough to go to Lake Titicaca and Mount Kailash. It's impossible to describe the raw beauty these locations have—a beauty so pure that it translates into power. Each breath of air in these majestical places fills you with power and peace.

My visit to Lake Titicaca was before I had learnt about the Earth's chakras. Once I put the pieces of the puzzle together, I had one of those moments: "That's why I felt so good there!".

One of my goals is to visit all seven and if you ever get the opportunity even to visit one, take it. Don't worry about your mantras, your crystals, or your yoga mat. Just get the best view, sit down, and be present in that moment.

If I had to leave a final message it would be to explore your chakras. Learn what works for you and what can be saved for a different time in your life. Don't be afraid to try new things and delve into concepts that you haven't uncovered yet. Just because you haven't experienced a higher connection yet, doesn't mean it isn't there waiting for you.

Coming to the end of a book, I often feel a little sad, like I am going to miss writing to you. On the other hand, I can be excited because I can begin my next project. I hope you have enjoyed this book. You can also have a look for my book *Healing Mantras* if you want to learn more about the ancient Hindu practice of healing through sound vibrations. Good luck with your journey; I know you are going to excel!

REFERENCES

B. (2020, February 26). Everything to Know About Earth Chakras, and How to Heal Through Them. Retrieved from https://www.bemytravelmuse.com/healing-earth-chakras/

Bear, Y. (2017, July 30). Balance Your Sacral Chakra with These Yoga Poses. Retrieved from https://www.rte.ie/lifestyle/living/2017/0727/893438-balance-your-sacral-chakra-with-these-yoga-poses/

Benton, E. (2019, March 27). Kundalini Yoga: Everything You Need to Know. Retrieved from https://www.prevention.com/fitness/workouts/a26907922/kundalini-yoga/

Cirino, E. (2018, December 4). Reflexology 101. Retrieved from https://www.healthline.com/health/what-is-reflexology#safety

Clalit Health Services. (2018, January 25). Effects of Brief Guided Imagery for Chronic Pain in Patients Diagnosed with

Fibromyalgia - Full Text View - ClinicalTrials.gov. Retrieved from https://clinicaltrials.gov/ct2/show/NCT02846194

Cultural Chakras. (2019, November 8). Retrieved from https://www.bearmckay.com/blog/cultural-chakras

Embong, N.H., et al. (2015) Revisiting reflexology: Concept, evidence, current practice, and practitioner training. Journal of Traditional and Complementary Medicine 5 (4) pp. 197-206

European Society of Cardiology. (2004). Visualising a safe place reduces procedural pain. Retrieved from https://www.escardio.org/The-ESC/Press-Office/Press-releases/Visualising-a-safe-place-reduces-procedural-painace   reduces   procedural   pain (escardio.org)

Flood, Gavin. (2006). The Tantric Body: The Secret Tradition of Hindu Religion. I.B. Tauris.

Samuel, Geoffrey (2008). The Origins of Yoga and Tantra. Cambridge University Press.

HeereJawharat.com. (2015, June 1). Jupiter Nature. Retrieved from   https://www.heerejawharat.com/astrology/planets-significance/brihaspati-jupitar.php

Hillary on HubPages. (2011). Retrieved from https://hubpages.com/@greenlotus

History of Yoga. (2020, June 11). Retrieved from https://www.yogabasics.com/learn/history-of-yoga/

Houston, D. (2020, April 29). How to Program Crystals. Retrieved from https://meanings.crystalsandjewelry.com/how-to-program-crystals/

How To Heal Your Body and Mind With Reflexology. (2020, September 2). Retrieved from https://thewhoot.com/health/reflexology

Inam, H. (2019, December 3). What are affirmations and how to affirm yourself? - Broftware Labs. Retrieved from https://medium.com/broftware-labs/what-are-affirmations-and-how-to-affirm-yourself-e079500c732c

Jeffrey, S. (2020, August 28). How to Ground Yourself | 9 Powerful Grounding Techniques. Retrieved from https://scottjeffrey.com/how-to-ground-yourself/

Kundalini Yoga - Key Mantras. (n.d.). Retrieved from https://www.kundaliniyoga.org/Mantras

L. (2019a, November 26). Guide to the Chakras for Beginners and Healing Practitioners. Retrieved from https://www.chakras.info

L. (2019b, December 4). Understanding the 12 Chakras and What They Mean. Retrieved from https://www.chakras.info/12-chakras/

L. (2019c, December 5). What to Do When Your Crown Chakra Is Blocked. Retrieved from https://www.chakras.info/blocked-crown-chakra/

Leadbeater, C.W. (2013) [1927]. The Chakras. Quest Books.

Lynch, J., et al. (2018). Mantra meditation for mental health in the general population: A systematic review. European Journal of Integrative Medicine (23) pp. 101-108

Mallinson, James; Singleton, Mark (2017). *Roots of Yoga*. Penguin Books. pp. 178–179.

Marfan Syndrome | Hartford HealthCare. (n.d.). Retrieved from https://hartfordhealthcare.org/services/heart-vascular/conditions/marfan-syndrome

McGinley, K. (2020, August 12). 7 Chakra Meditations to Keep You in Balance. Retrieved from https://chopra.com/articles/7-chakra-meditations-to-keep-you-in-balance

mindbodygreen. (2020a, January 30). The Transformative Powers of "Bija Mantra" Meditation. Retrieved from https://www.mindbodygreen.com/0-5930/The-Transformative-Powers-of-Bija-Mantra-Meditation.html

mindbodygreen. (2020b, April 21). Kundalini Yoga 101: Everything You Wanted to Know. Retrieved from https://www.-mindbodygreen.com/articles/kundalini-yoga-101-everything-you-wanted-to-know

Molinari, G., et al. (2018) The Power of Visualization: Back to the Future for Pain Management in Fibromyalgia Syndrome. Pain Medicine 19 (7) pp. 1451–1468

Moon, H. (2019, December 23). Crystal Vibration Numbers Made Simple. Retrieved from https://hibiscusmooncrystalacademy.com/crystal-vibrations/

Provisions, G. (2018, July 18). Open your Crown & Third Eye Chakras with Head Massage. Retrieved from https://blog.goddessprovisions.com/crown-chakra-massage/

Raghunathan, R. (2013) How Negative is Your "Mental Chatter"? Psychology Today UK. Retrieved from https://www.psychologytoday.com/gb/blog/sapient-nature/201310/how-negative-is-your-mental-chatter

Rataic, T. (2020, March 3). Your Heart Chakra: 5 Quick + Easy Tips to Heal Your Center of Love + Compassion. Retrieved from https://thereikiguide.com/your-heart-chakra-5-quick-and-easy-tips-to-heal-your-center-of-love-and-compassion/

Science Wire from the Exploratorium and Public Radio International. (n.d.). Retrieved from https://www.exploratorium.edu/theworld/sonar/trythis.html

Sehra, N. (2018, September 10). Use These 7 Mantras to Clear Your Throat Chakra and Speak Your Truth. Retrieved from https://www.yogiapproved.com/om/throat-chakra-healing-mantras/

Sharma, V.K., et al. (2013). Effect of fast and slow pranayama on perceived stress and cardiovascular parameters in young health-care students. Int J Yoga 6 (2) pp. 104–110.

Sharma, V.K., et al. (2014) Effect of Fast and Slow Pranayama Practice on Cognitive Functions in Healthy Volunteers. J Clinical and Diagnostic Research 8 (1) pp. 10–13.

studio2108. (2013, March 26). What is the origin of the chakra system? – Indigo Massage & Wellness. Retrieved from https://indigomassagetherapy.com/uncategorized/what-is-the-origin-of-the-chakra-system/

Terrell, J. (n.d.). Awakening You Chakras (Energy Centers). Retrieved from https://www.awakenment-wellness.com/chakras.html

The Importance of Visualization in Sports. (n.d.). Retrieved from https://www.peaksports.com/sports-psychology-blog/sports-visualization-athletes/

Tseng, J. and Poppenk, J. (2020). Brain meta-state transitions demarcate thoughts across task contexts exposing the mental noise of trait neuroticism. Nature Communications 11.

What are Affirmations? (n.d.). Retrieved from http://power-thoughtsmeditationclub.com/what-are-affirmations/

What is Reiki? (2019, September 11). Retrieved from https://www.reiki.org/faqs/what-reiki

White, D.G. (2001). Tantra in Practice. Princeton University Press.

YJ Editors. (2018, December 4). How to Use the Seven Chakras in Your Yoga Practice. Retrieved from https://www.yogajournal.com/yoga-101/a-guide-to-the-chakras

MODERN TAROT

THE ULTIMATE GUIDE TO THE MYSTERY,
WITCHCRAFT, CARDS, DECKS, SPREADS, HOW
TO AVOID TRAPS AND UNDERSTAND THE
SYMBOLISM

5 Exciting to use Tarot card spreads, covering:

- Relationships
- Mental Health
- Career Challenge
- Self-Confidence
- Self-Care

Get this free PDF quickly so that you can immediately start to work on your newly discovered talent.

To receive your free PDF scan the QR code with your phone camera:

INTRODUCTION

Can you remember the TV adverts throughout the 90s that offered free psychic readings? We would see a caller having their tarot cards read and we would hear shrills of disbelief at the accuracy of the psychic. Millions of people called in, some felt their reading was a life-changing help, despite not being free. Others felt like they had been completely scammed.

Tarot cards have gained a bad reputation through no fault of their own. Luckily, I was already quite fascinated by spiritualism and I had started to appreciate the importance of astrology in Eastern philosophy and in my own life. Because of this, I was more open-minded to the idea of my first tarot card reading, but that's not to say there wasn't still an element of scepticism. Like most teenagers, my friends and I had dabbled in ouija boards, magic spells and tarot cards to decipher our futures. Needless to say, our lack of understanding caused us to read all of the messages incorrectly. In fact, had those experiments with divination come true, I would have become an empress who married a magician, whose name starts with the letters W and N.

"As the poet plays with words, the musician with sounds and the painter with colours, so the tarotist plays with the interaction of tarot cards and the psyche"

— - *PHILIPPE ST GENOUX*

What a beautiful, yet practical way of explaining tarot reading. Each artist has the tools to create their work. Each type of work brings a sense of peace to the viewer. As a terrible artist with absolutely no ear for music, I decided that tarot would be my art.

My doubts weren't related to the power of the cards. I knew that the symbology was there to help me answer important questions that I needed to figure out the answers to. My concern was more to do with the intricate link to magic and witchcraft. Rather than fall victim to the usual stereotypical assumptions that people make of that which they don't understand, I decided I would open my mind and embrace the unknown.

I had several readings over the space of one year. I wanted to make sure I met with as many readers as possible and with readers of different backgrounds. I wanted to get a feel for how each person interacts with their deck of tarot cards. I suppose that to an extent, I wanted to see if I could spot a fraudster after seeing so many genuinely passionate and caring readers. More than anything, I wanted to draw on the energy of those who either are gifted or have dedicated time to improve their psychic abilities.

We are faced with so many questions in life, so many doubts that seem like there is no right answer. We can spend days, even months, listing the pros and cons of each decision, waiting to see if there will be a better moment, asking friends for advice, or just doing nothing. Even those who are normally quite confident in making decisions will reach a point where the answers aren't clear.

Others feel that there are questions that perhaps they are afraid to ask, but knowing the answers may guide them in the right direction, even prevent them from making mistakes. I know that I went through several stages in my life when I had to ask "Why me?", "What else am I going to have to face" or things like "How am I going to handle this next hurdle?".

In this book, we are going to feed our intrigue as we work through divination practice. We will understand the roots of tarot cards and how they became part of divination. The first part of this book will be about getting to know tarots and the system. We will take a look at the history of tarot and how they have become a tool to help us understand the answers to many of today's difficult questions. I also want to take a little time to bust a few of those myths that are so easy to believe.

We will dedicate a chapter to the reading session. We will look at what you can expect from a reading from a psychic and how to prepare for reading your own cards, or carrying out a friend's reading. You will also need to start learning about what the different colours and images mean, as well as the various spreads or layouts you can try.

Towards the end of Part 1, you can look forward to understanding the relationship between tarot and witchcraft. We will explore the tarot cards that can help you with your spells and some of the extra materials that may also help. After all, as the tenderhearted Aunt Jet Owens said in the movie, *Practical Magic*, "There's a little witch in all of us" and this chapter will help develop the witch or wizard in you.

Once we have an amazing understanding of everything from how to choose the right deck for you to asking the right questions, we will take each tarot and understand their meanings for love, career, and finance. It even matters whether the cards that are drawn display the right way around (upright) or upside-down (reversed), and we will look at the implications of those positions.

I understand how not everyone is ready to believe what the cards are telling them. If you have read my other books, *Healing Mantras* and *Modern Chakras*, you will know that there have been many areas of alternative healing, spiritualism, and the supernatural that I began as a complete non-believer. At no point am I going to tell you what works and what doesn't, as this is down to the individual. I never burn herbs, because the smell irritates me, but that doesn't mean that it doesn't help others. My job is to present my findings in a non-biased way, offer my advice after nearly two decades of experience, and provide you with the knowledge and confidence to enjoy both tarot reading and the relationship with the supernatural.

As always, I want us to have some fun as we are learning and to this end, I will share some of the mistakes I have made along the way, for amusement and in the hope that you don't do the same. Let's begin by understanding what divination is and the role of tarot.

PART I

Prepare to feel like a student again, but if the very idea of that brings bad associations for you, let's clear those away. Here you are studying, of your own free will, a topic that you find interesting and intriguing, and you may find that it brings more improvements to your life than any French or Geography class ever did.

The next few chapters are going to focus on how the tarot cards came to play such a significant role in occult practices. We will start to look at the importance of the Major and Minor Arcana cards, how the suits represent the four elements and the incredible imagery in the cards. We will look at how to use the cards in the right way and how to choose your spread. By the end, you will be shuffling your tarot deck with the right intention, the right question, and the right frame of mind.

Everyone learns in different ways. If only I could read something once and it would be engraved on my brain... Feel free to make some audio recordings of aspects that are important to you and then replay them when you need to, or take a pen and paper and jot down some notes. Some readers may have a little (or a lot) of experience and this will be a great refresher for them. If you are completely new to the amazing world of tarot, I'm really excited for you!

UNDERSTANDING THE TAROT

After my year of various readings, I knew that I wanted to learn more about tarot cards and how to read them. It wasn't until I started to carry out my own readings that I began to understand the full scope of the benefits of tarot reading.

If you have read my books on mantras and chakras, you will already know that I have great respect for our own energy and how this energy interacts with the energy of our planet and beyond. By learning how to read the cards, I was able to further work on my energy. Pulling a card lets you take your thoughts and emotions and visualize them as a symbol. In a way, it makes it less personal and easier to separate yourself from everything that isn't helping you in life. You can use the cards to see what energy is holding you back and what is propelling you forward.

On a similar note, putting some distance between yourself and your emotions makes it much easier to see things from different perspectives. tarot cards can tap into your imagination and provide solutions to problems that you may not have considered otherwise. This can really bring about a sense of clarity and peace in your life, something I find is essential for our mental health.

It's true that learning about tarot cards can be a way to help foresee aspects of the future, but really, it is associated with much more than that, specifically, divination. To fully appreciate tarot cards, let's begin with a closer look at what divination is.

WHAT IS DIVINATION?

In very simple terms, we could say that divination is the practice of finding and understanding hidden meanings in events through different techniques, perhaps natural, psychological, or supernatural. Those who are able to uncover these hidden meanings are known as diviners and this might be a shaman, priest, or another type of holy person. It can also be a witch. A diviner is a person we turn to when we want to understand more about the mysteries of life.

Divination can be of three main varieties—inductive, interpretive and intuitive. We will take a closer look at the difference so that we are better able to see the role of tarot in divination.

Inductive Divination

Looking to the skies and nature for our answers is what's known as inductive divination. Astrology has a long history in many religions and cultures from the Mayans to the Chinese and even among Westerners. Diviners are able to see messages in the weather; lightning is seen as messages from the gods; clouds are interpreted as "castles in the air" for those celestial beings in Hinduism. Even the migrational patterns of birds can tell people more about the cycles of time and what the future may hold.

Interpretive Divination

In this method, the diviner will receive information through physical means and then extract meaning from this. These events are manipulated and often subject to interpretation. Two examples would be pyromancy (using fire for divination) and hydromancy (using water for divination). With fire, one may see messages in flames, or throw objects into the fire so the diviner can interpret the reactions. Reading tea leaves is considered interpretive divination.

Intuitive Divination

This is what some refer to as a sixth sense. The person receives information via the senses or they will react to stimuli. Those whose intuition is highly developed are often referred to as psychics or mediums. Necromancy is the ability to talk to the dead because of this sixth-sense. Divination by intuition is highly energised and could be interpreted as messages from the gods or spirits.

If you think about the ability to read tarot cards, you will need a combination of interpretive divination (understanding a message from a physical object) and intuitive divination (a well-developed sixth sense). You may see tarot readers with other objects, but quite often this is just for show. The two things that you really need are your intuition and your deck of tarot cards.

That being said, there is one other key thing we need for divination—an oracle.

THE ROLE OF AN ORACLE IN DIVINATION

Many would find a more delicate way to say this, but an oracle is like the middleman or the vehicle for the message. There are so many examples that we can see. When a fortune teller sees a message through a crystal ball, the crystal ball is the oracle. It can also be a person who receives a message for another person, perhaps from the spirit of a loved one who has passed away. Other examples can include oracle bone—pieces of ox scapula—historically used by the Chinese.

If we focus on an oracle being a person, it is someone who can remain true to themselves and their origins. They have an immense amount of healing energy that can be used in their own lives and to help others. They are able to communicate with plants and animals, not necessarily in a language the average person can understand, but in a way to successfully interpret the message.

So where do tarot cards come into this? Well, tarot can be regarded as an oracle, as an object that transmits messages from the divine (or the universe, depending on your understanding) to the earthly. However, for those who master tarot reading, they can also use this oracle to become an oracle themselves, to interpret the symbols and messages to make better choices in life.

Bear with me as I go over the background and history of tarot. I know that some people are just aching to get straight into their first reading, but others like to gain a complete understanding, often because it improves a person's understanding and therefore confidence. I promise it will be worth the short wait.

WHAT ARE SOME OTHER METHODS OF DIVINATION?

Imagine all of the different cultures over time and how each culture and even era may have had their own interpretations of divination. There is no one way that will work for everyone and once you start appreciating the benefits of tarot readings, you might want to take a closer look at one or more of the following methods of divination.

Celtic Ogham

This is a popular method for Celtic pagans and Wiccans and comes from Ogma/Ogmos, the Celtic god of eloquence and literacy. There are twenty-five sticks, each with a symbol etched into it representing a letter or sound from the Ogham alphabet.

Norse Runes

The runes were considered a gift from Odin, a Norse god and are an ancient alphabet used in Germanic and Scandinavian countries. They are often used by people who have a specific question that relates to a present situation. Runes have no history on paper, but there are numerous carvings of the alphabet in stone, which is why you will find sets made of stone. Germanic tradition has them made of wood.

Tea leaves

Before the seventeenth century, fortune tellers would use the patterns of lead or wax splatter as the oracle. When tea was introduced to Europe, the older methods were replaced with tea leaf reading, officially known as tasseomancy or tasseography. You might want to start with a special cup and saucer that has symbols marked to help with the reading, and there are certain teas that are considered to be better. Stick to Earl Grey or other teas with larger leaves.

Pendulums

If you have ever been pregnant, you may have heard of hanging a crystal or stone on a piece of string to create a pendulum and seeing which way it spins above your belly, which is supposed to determine the sex of the baby. Pendulums are probably one of the easiest methods of divination, because the querent (the person asking the questions) only needs to focus on yes/no questions.

Bones

Osteomancy is the study of bones to find divine messages, as we saw with the Chinese using ox scapula as an oracle. You will often see bones mixed with other objects, like coins or feathers. This is a personal choice for a divination method. Not everyone is comfortable handling animal bones and it's not always easy to find them. Still, the practice has survived for centuries and there has to be a good reason for this.

Numerology

In Modern Paganism, numbers can have amazing spiritual significance and magical meanings. Again, whether you choose to believe in lucky or unlucky numbers is up to you, but there are multiple superstitions throughout history related to the number thirteen. Numbers are also closely related to the planets and astrology.

Palm Reading

There was another phase back in school when we practiced something that really does give divination a bad name... Overnight, we all became palm readers, just because we could spot one line on our palm and decide if it was long or short and then determine if we would live a long life or not! Needless to say, palmistry is more complex than that and can be used to better understand personalities and what may happen in the future.

HOW ARE TAROT CARDS USED FOR DIVINATION?

First of all, let's clear up this idea of tarot cards being a pile of hocus pocus. A lot of my research has been into the fake tarot card readers, as more often than not, this is where the hocus pocus imagery comes in. I've been inside dark rooms that needed curtains, wind chimes, and crystals spread all across the room, and the most bizarre smells that I am too scared to describe. It's that typical sort of image you see on the TV and although some people may use other tools to enhance their intuition, it is not necessary. All you really need is a deck of cards.

Each of the seventy-eight cards has symbols, signs, images, colours, and together with the reader's intuition, the reader is able to use the cards as a guide to understanding likely outcomes. Sometimes, the message is clear, and other times we need to focus a little more to extract the right message. There are some cards that are easy to misinterpret because of their name or harsh images, Death being the perfect example. Pulling the Death card doesn't mean you are facing an early death, which is why it is important to take the time to fully understand the meaning of each card.

A deck of tarot cards is divided into Major Arcana and Minor Arcana. There are twenty-two Major Arcana cards and fifty-six Minor Arcana cards. We are only warming up to the tarots at the moment, so we will just take a brief look at the meanings of each. In Part 2, I want to really get into the symbolic meaning of each card. For now, let's understand the story behind the cards, starting with the Major Arcana cards.

Of the twenty-two Major Arcana cards, all but one are numbered. The first card is the Fool, which has no number, and the following cards are numbered from one to twenty-one. It is the Fool who is the lead character of our story. The other cards represent stages of his journey through life and the significant lessons he learns.

If your tarot reading contains a Major Arcana card, it points to some life lessons that you need to reflect on. If the spread has a large number of Major Arcana cards, the life-changing experiences you are going through are going to have an impact long into the future.

It is worth pointing out that a tarot card can be drawn in an upright position, or reversed (upside down). Again, in Part 2, I will talk about the specific meanings of each card when reversed, but for now, please bear in mind that a reversed tarot doesn't mean the opposite of the upright meaning. The Major

Arcana cards being reversed suggest that you aren't paying attention to those life lessons that the world is trying to teach you.

So, we start with the Fool. This card doesn't imply that you are stupid. It points to innocence and new beginnings. This free spirit is ready to take his first steps into the world. Here are the characters he meets on his journey and a brief meaning:

I- The Magician- The Magician has power, but he is also resourceful. He puts on a show and he inspires action.

II- The High Priestess- Her divine feminism represents intuition and sacred knowledge. This card highlights our subconscious mind.

III- The Empress- Another card of great femininity, the Empress is nurturing and reflects nature. She is a sign of beauty and abundance.

IV- The Emperor- He is a figure of authority and often represents a father figure. This card is a sign of establishment. We see the need for structure when the Emperor is drawn.

V- The Hierophant- The Hierophant points to tradition and conformity. He has spiritual and religious wisdom.

VI- The Lovers- Naturally, this card has strong connections to love and harmony, but it also reminds us of our choices and the need to ensure that our values are aligned.

VII- The Chariot- This tarot tells us about our willpower and control. With determination and action, we can find our success.

VIII- Strength- The woman is accompanied by a lion, a symbol of strength and courage. We also appreciate our compassion and the influence that we have on others.

IX- The Hermit- While spending time alone, the Hermit takes time for self-reflection and searching the soul for inner guidance.

X- Wheel of Fortune- It is a positive card, a symbol of good luck and destiny. The wheel also looks at life cycles and karma. It can be a turning point in your life.

XI- Justice- She teaches us about the truth and fairness, often regarding the law. But she also has lessons on cause and effect.

XII- The Hanged Man- The man hanging upside down from a tree points to a pause, a pause so that we can consider new perspectives and let go of things that are holding us back.

XIII- Death - Despite the powerful imagery, we don't have to fear this tarot as much as the name implies. Death represents the end of something, or changes and transformations.

XIV- Temperance- Temperance shows us the importance of patience, balance and our purpose in life.

XV- The Devil- The Devil highlights our attachments and even addictions. This card also explores our sexuality and some of the things that restrict us.

XVI- The Tower- There are sudden changes when the Tower is drawn and this can create chaos and disruption. However, there will be a revelation that will help you continue your journey.

XVII- The Star- The Star is a sign of hope and faith. There is an element of spirituality and renewal as we find our purpose again.

XVIII- The Moon- There might be a reason to be anxious or fearful. This card is also related to illusion, our subconscious and our instincts.

XIX- The Sun- The Sun is a fun card that fills us with warmth and positivity. We can appreciate its vitality and can point to success.

XX- Judgement- Judgement shows us the need to forgive. It also represents rebirth and an inner calling.

XXI- The World- The last of the Major Arcana cards points to the completion of the journey and an accomplishment. It also represents travel and integration.

Obviously, there is a lot more to each card. If it were that easy, we would all be reading tarot cards, but this is a good summary to give you an overall picture. Next, let's take a look at how the Minor Arcana cards are organised.

The Minor Arcana tarots are divided into four suits—Wands, Swords, Cups, and Pentacles (sometimes referred to as Coins). There are ten numbered cards in each suit and four court cards —the Page, Knight, Queen and King.

The Wands Suit

The Wands are associated with the element of fire. They are symbols of passion, determination and inspiration, which are three themes that you will see throughout the journey of this suit. The Wands are energetic cards and encourage action and the creation of new plans. Here are a few words that will give you an idea of the meaning of each of the Wands:

Ace of Wands- Willpower, desires, creation

Two of Wands- Leaving home, decision making, planning

Three of Wands- Looking forward, growth

Four of Wands- Home, a sense of community, festivities

Five of Wands- Discussions, competitiveness, rivals

Six of Wands- Triumph, success, public recognition

Seven of Wands- Perseverance, keeping control, safeguarding

Eight of Wands- Fast decisions and action, momentum

Nine of Wands- Strength, hardiness, durability

Ten of Wands- Success, a heavy burden, responsibilities

Page of Wands- Liberty, discovery, joy

Knight of Wands- Bravery, movement, adventure

Queen of Wands- Courage, happiness, determination

Kings of Wands- The bigger picture, conquering obstacles, a leader

The Cups Suit

The Cups are linked to the element of water and are linked to our feelings, our intuition and our creativity. Often, the Cups will explain things about our relationships, be they romantic, partnerships, or friendships. They will also provide insight into our imagination and inner voice.

Ace of Cups- New emotions, intuition, spiritualism

Two of Cups- Coming together, connections, partnership

Three of Cups- The community, joy, friendships

Four of Cups- Indifference, observation, a lack of connection

Five of Cups- Loss and grief, defeatism

Six of Cups- Fond memories, familiarity, recuperation

Seven of Cups- Decisions, looking for your purpose, daydreams

Eight of Cups- A rude awakening, walking away and leaving things in the past

Nine of Cups- Gratification, stability within your emotions, splendour

Ten of Cups- Internal joy, self-realization, wishes becoming a reality

Page of Cups- Pleasant surprises, idealism, sensitivity

Knight of Cups- A romantic, listening to your heart's desires

Queen of Cups- Understanding, tranquility, comfort

King of Cups- Compassion, control, equilibrium

The Swords Suit

The element of air is linked to the Swords Suit and it reflects our intelligence, reason, and truth. This suit also helps us to better understand communication and conflicts that arise. We all have the ability to use the power of our intellect, but at the same time, the swords are double-edged, so we have to be careful about how we use this power.

Ace of Swords- A sharp mind, clear thinking, developments

Two of Swords- Tough decisions and indecision, impasse

Three of Swords- Broken hearts, pain, grief

Four of Swords- Taking a break, mending, scrutiny

Five of Swords- Uncontrolled ambition, cunning, the need to win no matter what

Six of Swords- Change, moving forward, leaving things behind you

Seven of Swords- Deceit, dishonesty, scheming

Eight of Swords- Self-victimising, restrictions, confinement

Nine of Swords- Trauma, stress and anxiety, despondency

Ten of Swords- Fiasco, disappointment, collapse

Page of Swords- Intrigue, energetic mind, restlessness

Knight of Swords- Standing up for your beliefs, action, haste

Queen of Swords- Intricacy, mental clarity, perception

King of Swords- Self-control, head over the heart

The Pentacles Suit

As the Pentacles are also known as the Coins; there is a theme here of finance, business and career and this suit often points to things in the long-term future. The Pentacles are associated with the element of earth and so this suit also informs us of our stability and health, even our feelings of sensuality.

Ace of Pentacles- New ventures and opportunities, wealth

Two of Pentacles- Weighing your options, prioritising, adapting to change.

Three of Pentacles- Working together, creation, team efforts

Four of Pentacles- Preservation, thriftiness, security

Five of Pentacles- Necessities, insecurity, financial hardship

Six of Pentacles- Charity, sharing, giving

Seven of Pentacles- Hard work and attention to detail, perseverance

Eight of Pentacles- Enthusiasm, high expectations, apprenticeship

Nine of Pentacles- Reap the benefits of your hard work, luxury, rewards

Ten of Pentacles- Birthright, inheritance, collecting

Page of Pentacles- Drive, hard work, passion

Knight of Pentacles- Diligence, responsibility, efficiency

Queen of Pentacles- Comfort, financial security, possibility

King of Pentacles- Plenty, wealth, stability

This is barely scratching the surface of the seventy-eight tarot cards: it's like peeling back just one fraction of a corner and you can probably understand now why it can take years to fully master the art of tarot reading. As I said, there is no need for you to start memorising each of the short descriptions I have given. In Part 2, we will describe the images and symbols of each card so that it becomes easier to appreciate the messages, both upright and reversed.

CHOOSING THE RIGHT TAROT DECK FOR YOU

This is such a crazy question and I can only relate it to choosing crystals for healing. You have so many options and people will recommend different ones, but with so many different tarot card decks, it can be difficult to know which one is going to be right for you.

To name a few examples, there are tarot decks for witches, Gothic tarot decks, Renaissance decks, mermaid, fairy tale, mystical, Manga, and I kid you not, I have even seen an Edgar Allan Poe tarot set. There are large-sized cards, mini sets, traditional and modern. The number one rule, like in many areas of divination and spiritualism, is that you have to choose a tarot deck that you have a connection with. There was (and some still believe) a superstition that you should never buy your own tarot cards and that someone should give them to you. Many people, me included, prefer to choose their own deck to make sure it has meaning to them. For example, each different style will have different image designs and it's important that these images tap into your intuition. If you can, look at every card in the deck. I've seen a few that have amazing Major Arcanas but the Minor Arcanas leave a lot to be desired, and vice versa.

The size and quality of the deck are also worth considering. My family laughs at my tiddly hands and a large tarot deck looks completely out of place, plus I don't feel comfortable with them. Personally, I like decks that are a similar size to a standard deck of cards.

My final bit of advice for finding the right deck is to go for quality, because it will be worth the extra investment. Because of the time it takes to learn the different tarot meanings, it makes more sense to buy a deck that will stay with you for years. Once you gain confidence with your go-to deck, you can start adding to your collection.

Despite so many options, for the sake of this book, I am going to stick to my first deck, the Rider Waite tarot set. I fell in love with the colours, and the imagery and symbols in these cards were real eye-openers for me.

I'm sure you are still keen to dive straight into your readings, but in the next chapter, we are going to take a more specific look at what tarot is good for, beyond making predictions of the future.

WHAT IS TAROT GOOD FOR?

Because many of us have been given the wrong impression about tarot, it's easy to understand why we might assume it's just a method for fortune-telling. The next logical assumption from here is that the future is unpredictable and therefore, tarot readers are just out to earn a quick buck.

As I was exploring the sad world of psychic scammers, I came across a perfect example of why non-believers feel that tarot is not good for anything. I signed up for a free online tarot reading just this year. This was not because I wasn't confident in my own capabilities, but more out of curiosity. I was dealt my three cards and the first one said, "You are in for a difficult and unpredictable year", but if I wanted to find out more, I would have to register with the site. Well, first of all, we are in the midst of a global pandemic right now so it is unlikely that anyone will disagree with this statement. Second, this tarot reading was probably not good for anything, because I didn't want to be bombarded with further emails from them.

You might find it weird why such a dedicated tarot reader would discuss this rather negative side to tarot, but it is only fair that you appreciate that I am able to see things from the point of view of the believer and the non-believer. I have had readings which have literally been no good and others that have surprised me beyond belief. Just remember, that when you hire a contractor for your home or try a new hairdresser, even a restaurant, the same thing can happen. We can be amazed or disappointed by our experiences, but it's not to say that every provider follows the same ethics and standards.

Knowing that tarot cards can bring about a wealth of good made me more determined to learn the art myself, so that I knew I would be getting the most amount of benefit from the cards.

As I briefly mentioned, tarot cards can be used to gain a greater understanding of the bigger questions in our lives. We can use them to help us make decisions regarding love and romance, our education and careers, as well as our health (both mental and physical). The cards can convey advice about travel, moving home, or even a change in country. Used in the right way, tarot cards can offer spiritual guidance that helps us learn more about who we really are and what we want to achieve in life.

Regardless of why you want to explore this form of occult reading, I am going to ask one thing of you. From here on in, try to have an open mind and after reading this chapter, I hope you can appreciate the full range of benefits that the cards can offer and not just see them as a way of telling you what lies ahead. A very wise spiritualist once told me that the psychic practices are there to light our path and help us to see through the mist and the darkness; they aren't there to determine our path. If you think of tarot in this way, it can be compared to asking for help from an online recipe; the chef isn't going to make the dish for you.

TAROT CARDS AND THE TRACKING OF PERSONAL INFORMATION

Though it feels like I am always trying to defend certain practises, there is a method to my madness. So many techniques in life are portrayed by society in a certain way that it can put us off even before we have begun to consider the possibilities. Journaling is another one of these techniques. Some may see it as something young teenage girls do just to write about their latest crush. As someone who started their first journal at around that age, I can confirm that this is true, but as the years went on, my journal became my own therapeutic retreat.

Let's start out with a fact to get us all a little more intrigued. A study published online by Cambridge University Press showed that those people who wrote about a traumatic, stressful, or emotional event for fifteen to twenty minutes on three to five occasions had significantly better physical and psychological outcomes than those who didn't. It was the psychologist, James Pennebaker, who carried out the extensive studies on journaling and its benefits, one of which was that those who had participated in the study and wrote about the things they would never dream of telling anyone else had fewer medical appointments in the following months.

The language of the journal entries changed over time. "I" statements were often replaced with "he" or "she", which suggests that the writers were beginning to see things from different perspectives, considering how others think and feel. There were also more "because" statements, suggesting better reasoning of situations. Journaling is an effective way to heal both the old wounds that you thought you had laid to rest and the more recent ones that still sting.

Before looking at the relationship between tarot readings and journaling, here are a few other reasons for writing down your emotions:

- Writing improves your language learning and encourages you to expand your vocabulary, improving your **verbal intelligence**.
- Journaling lets you explore your emotions and those of others. It enhances **self-awareness** and therefore your emotional intelligence.
- Working on both your IQ and EQ will have a positive effect on your verbal **communication skills**.
- When writing in a journal, even when writing about the past and the future, it helps you to pull yourself back to the present and concentrate on how you feel in that moment, a great tool for **mindfulness**.
- Writing recomposes our thoughts and ideas and can help to boost the **memory**.
- When you include your **goals** in your journal, they become more real and important once on paper, like

you have committed to them, and so you become more determined to achieve them.

- At first, you may feel like you don't have anything to write about. You will be surprised by how much **creativity** you have once you actually start writing, not because it is forced, but because when you open the 'Pandora's box of feelings', they will flow.

- You will start to **heal.** Getting all of this weight off your chest and onto paper is such an immense relief and you can start to see the positive in things, even if it is just small steps.

- When you learn how to write about both the good and the bad, your confidence begins to grow, especially when you spend some time journaling about your achievements.

For me personally, I found journaling and tarots to be the perfect combination for three reasons. First, they helped me to improve my self-discipline. Before, despite knowing that journaling was helping me mentally, I would only pick it up once in a while, maybe even only once every few months. Second, tarot reading helped me to explore new ideas, each new image would give me something fresh to contemplate or remind me of a past experience that I felt I should understand better. And so, third, I started to write more frequently, including it as one of my healthy habits.

Reflecting on my feelings and becoming more aware of my inner self was a great help for taking the images and symbols of the cards and deciphering how they related to my personal journal and my destiny. At the same time, these striking images helped me to see the role of other people in my life and to see problems from a different angle. Instead of there only being one solution, tarots allowed me to see alternative routes to achieving my objective, and more often than not, in ways more practical than I would have thought of without the help of the cards. Between the tarots and journaling, I learnt that the easy road wouldn't necessarily reap the greatest rewards, but the two tools showed me the best way to face the more challenging road and the greater rewards.

Of course, there are still other ways that you can explore your creativity with the help of tarots. I know an amazing artist who will draw and paint her interpretations of a reading. Her work is fascinating, because although I recognise certain elements of the card, I can see how the final result is truly unique to her. If I had drawn the same cards in a reading, I probably would have a completely different interpretation, but that's the beauty of tarot.

TAROT AND PSYCHOTHERAPY

It may surprise you to learn that divination and science have not always been on opposite sides of the court. Carl Jung was one of the most respected psychiatrists and psychoanalysts of the twentieth century. Aside from his extensive work as the founder of analytical psychology, Jung was also interested in spiritualism and the paranormal and occult. Jung felt that tarot cards had potential as a tool in psychology for unlocking the unconscious mind.

In a 1933 seminar, Jung said:

"These cards… are psychological images, symbols with which one plays, as the unconscious seems to play with its contents. They combine in certain ways, and the different combinations correspond to the playful development of events in the history of mankind…

For example, the symbol of the sun, or the symbol of the man hung up by the feet, or the tower struck by lightning, or the wheel of fortune, and so on. Those are sort of archetypal ideas, of a differentiated nature, which mingle with the ordinary constituents of the flow of the unconscious, and therefore it is applicable for an intuitive method that has the purpose of understanding the flow of life, possibly even predicting future events, at all events lending itself to the reading of the conditions of the present moment."

By learning how the present has evolved from the past, he felt that it was possible to make intuitive predictions on the future. Just as many of Jung's theories were contentious, not everyone would agree with the use of tarot cards for psychology, but there are many who followed his work and you will still find some of his followers today using tarot cards to encourage clients to better understand aspects of their lives.

But why is this? They are visual images and visual images are frequently used in psychology to discover underlying thoughts or feelings as well as those thoughts that we find more difficult to express. How many times have you got into a pickle because you haven't found the right words for a certain situation? You know your boss wouldn't look at you with that weird look if you could just present your findings in a PowerPoint. Sometimes a little note from your partner with a smiley face and a heart means more than the words "I love you".

Tarot cards can be used as a tool, just like psychologists would use the Rorschach Test or the Thematic Apperception Test. You have probably seen the Rorschach Test in films—

this set of ink blogs are shown to patients to understand a person's perceptions better. The Thematic Apperception Test uses a set of images that the patient/client uses to tell a story, again, highlighting certain aspects of the person's personality, beliefs, and inner conflicts.

Visual images are crucial in psychology because, in layman's terms, they help us to find our words. In the situations where we know what is troubling us, a tarot card can spark a light that jogs our brain into focusing on what we are thinking and how we are feeling. These images can essentially remind the brain of what we are feeling or even what we want to say.

Take, for example, a person who is overwhelmed with life, there is so much going on that everything is bundled together and they can't make sense of it. There are people ready to help them, but at this point, they don't even know what they want or need. If you show this person an image of nature, a green forest untouched by humans, their mind immediately understands peace. An image of waves gently rolling onto the shore instils a sense of calm. The person knows that they need a break, but either of the images specifies that they need to find some tranquility in their life and, quite probably, some time alone. I can only testify to this, because this is how I have felt in the same situation, looking at the same images and when talking to others in need of help who have felt the same way.

If we take this one step further, it doesn't matter if you are the boss or the employee, the parent or the child, there are times when we know what we need, but we struggle to verbalise this, for fear that we will upset the other party. Tarot cards provide a comfortable way to express how we feel.

For me, this is far more relevant with tarot cards than with the Rorschach Test and the Thematic Test. Don't get me wrong, I have also appreciated the benefits of these tests, but with the help of professionals. With tarot cards, I was able to experience similar benefits without studying for a career in psychology. I know a lot of people who were too shy to talk about their deepest feelings with a psychologist and even more who were just embarrassed. The cards help to unravel these feelings by yourself, which is incredibly empowering.

Tarot cards are a massive help when people are stuck. I hate to make assumptions, but it's very possible that you are reading this book because you are 'stuck' in life. Even non-believers can relate to moments in life when they don't have the answer. When you get the point where you can't see the solution, tarot cards can zone in on the areas that you are having problems with. The cards that you draw can give a new, refreshing perspective that you may not have thought about before.

TAROT AND THE CHAKRAS

For further benefits from the cards, it is worth understanding how they correlate with our chakras. We have seven chakras starting at the base of the spine and going up to the crown of our head. These spinning energy wheels can help you connect with the energy of the cards. Here's how:

The Element of Spirit

The Major Arcana, as the cards that teach us the bigger lessons in life, are the most spiritual. Psychoanalysts influenced by Jung believe that our unconscious contains a number of archetypes, which is where we get our insights from. The Crown Chakra is also related to life's lessons, while the Third Eye Chakra sparks our intuition so that we are better able to understand the spiritual information we receive.

The Element of Air

The Swords suit is linked to the element of air and it focuses on creating ideas and thoughts and then how we communicate these creations. Considering the position of the Throat Chakra, you can see how it enables us to improve our communication and to speak the truth.

The Element of Water

The Cups is a water suit. Water is a sign of our emotions, love and the relationships we have. The world depends on water as much as we depend on our hearts. The Heart Chakra is obviously tied to love and other powerful emotions we feel.

The Element of Fire

The Solar Plexus Chakra and the Sacral Chakra are located in the lower part of your back. They are associated with action and fertility, respectively. The internal power that we have, our passion for life and our pleasures, burn like a fire inside us. The Wands suit is also about fertility.

The Element of Earth

At the base of our spines, you will find the Root Chakra and as you can imagine, it is what keeps us grounded. We relate this chakra to our survival instincts and the material things that we need in life—food, shelter, etc. It makes sense that the Pentacles, associated with the earth element, is also linked to the Root Chakra.

I find that it helps if you meditate with your tarot deck, especially as you concentrate on the energy that flows up throughout your body. Your chakras will absorb the energy of the cards, making connections between the suits, the elements, and the messages that you are being shown.

TAROT AND WITCHCRAFT

As we have seen, there are competing ideas about the power of tarot and where its claimed insights originate. Some view tarot and/or the reader as an oracle, acting as a conduit for knowledge from the divine or from the universe at large. Others, like Jung, view tarot as symbolic tools to uncover what is hiding in our own unconscious minds. There are also some who believe that each card has a special power and a magic ability behind it. The great thing, in this understanding, is that we can unlock this magic without actively knowing so. Tarot spellcasting is a way of using creative visualisation, with the help of images and symbols in cards, to develop powerful intentions. The idea is that certain cards will help you with these intentions, depending on what it exactly is that you desire. Remember that the suits can be used for certain benefits: the Swords will help with your way of thinking, the Wands tap into your creativity, the Pentacles are related to wealth and wellbeing, and the Cups are for emotions. Let's look at some of the Major Arcana cards and their purported magical uses.

The Magician- a logical place to start, the Magician channels energy with his wand and directs it with his pointing finger. You can cast a spell to ask the Magician to protect you.

The Star- you can use the star to receive good things, gifts and blessings. You can cast a spell to help you open up and be prepared for what you are asking of the universe.

Death- Death is an amazing card for tarot spellcasting. It can bring an end to all kinds of things, so that you can make way for new, brighter things. You can cast a spell to put an end to bad habits or relationships that you want to say goodbye to.

Wheel of Fortune- a wheel constantly turns, like the planets moving in our solar system. If you are frustrated that things aren't moving quickly enough for you, you can use the energy of the Wheel of Fortune to get the movement you wish.

If you are looking for more good reasons to use the tarot cards, witchcraft and tarot spells are the perfect examples. There is an infinite number of spells that you can cast and this doesn't necessarily have to be for your own good. These powerful intentions can also be used for the good of others. Naturally, if you are suffering or struggling, you will first want to concentrate on your own healing, but when you start feeling stronger, look for ways that you can use tarots and spells to help people in your life.

The main takeaway is that when you learn how to read tarot cards correctly, you will be able to unlock an immense amount of information about your life, the past and the future. You will be able to see things with so much more clarity that it becomes easier to make the more difficult decisions in life. You can see things from new perspectives which opens the door to a world of new opportunities.

Because of this, you can see how tarot readings aren't just a tool for predicting the future. The cards are an invaluable tool that helps someone understand more about what is burning through their minds; they help us to find words when we aren't sure how to express feelings, and they can be used to draw upon the energy in the universe, and even to help others. Before I started my exploration of the cards, I had no idea that there was so much good to be found!

A LITTLE HISTORY OF THE TAROTS

Despite it being decades ago, I remember hating history and having to study dates of things that were going to serve no purpose in my life. When I first got hooked on spiritualism, it was because I was a skeptic and began looking into ways almost to disprove the practices. This is how I actually got excited about history and learning about the origins of tarot cards was just as fascinating.

As we go back through time and understand how the tarots became what they are today, we also get to look at some of the typical myths that surround them, why they came about and how they aren't true.

Uncovering the Egyptian Gods Myth

One of the biggest myths that you will hear is that the tarot cards were written by Egyptian gods. This is because Antoine Court de Gebelin, a French Freemason, published a rather complete guide of the tarots in 1781. He stated that the symbols of the cards came from secrets of Egyptian priests, which came from the Egyptians gods. Now, nothing of what Gebelin wrote was based on any evidence found. As open-minded as I am, I am not inclined to believe in something without some form of proof. So, let's move on.

Are the Tarot Cards European?

We Westerners have a habit of claiming fame for, or at least popularising, things that were in existence before. We have done the same with things like yoga and chakra healing, both of which have been around for thousands of years. While we aren't as bold as to say that we invented such practises, we still find ways of making just a slight modernisation to call it our own. The same thing happened with tarot.

If you look to the twelfth century, the Chinese played games with strips of bamboo in their hands. Eventually, the bamboo was replaced with round, square, or rectangular paper or papyrus. By the 1300s, these cards had made their way to Egypt. The first concepts of playing cards came from Egypt, but the original idea of a game of cards played in the hands was Chinese.

Tarot decks were first documented in Italy in the mid-fifteenth century. The name of tarot derives from the Italian *tarocchi*, which itself is of uncertain origin. However, in the medieval period, *taroch* was used to mean 'foolishness', and of course we still have the Fool as the tarot protagonist, so this seems a reasonable explanation for the name.

In the sixteenth century, tarot was still seen as a game and one for the wealthy. Needless to say, without printing, the cards were hand-painted and the Italians with money had their own sets of cards painted with images of family members and friends. The Italians used these cards to play a game called 'carte de trionfi', the cards of triumph. A player would be dealt cards and then use the imagery to create a story. In the fifteenth century, the Spanish also started hand painting cards, although the imagery was very similar to that of the Italian, as both were considered the Latin deck. As the Spanish had a great influence on various South American countries, the cards soon made their way to these cultures too. Even in France, in the 14th and 15th century, the cards were used for purely entertainment purposes and not for divination.

It wasn't until the mid-18th century that cards began to gain a mystical reputation and people started using them for divination. At this point, the Queens had been added and the terms Minor and Major Arcana had been established. It is also at this point that things start getting a little controversial. The printing press was well established by this point, so it wasn't only the wealthy that could get their hands on a deck of tarot cards. As the cards became more popular, more theories of their origins and meanings started to arise.

We have already discussed the myth of the Egyptian gods by Court de Gebelin. Other scholars followed the path of Gebelin. Jean-Baptiste Alliette wrote a book on *the Art of Reading Cards* in 1791, and he believed the cards originated with the Book of Thoth, which belonged to the Egyptian god of wisdom. Throughout this period, the cards were seen to be esoteric, only understood by a small group of people, and the game converted into a complex set of images that required special knowledge to fully understand. Alliette and de Gebelin are nonetheless credited with popularising the use of tarot for cartomancy, and Alliette created the first known deck specifically for this purpose.

As the Victorian era came to an end, spiritualism and the occult had reached a new level of popularity with the upper classes. Parties may have been held with palm readings and tea leaf readings, and of course, a deck of tarot cards would be present.

As the tarot has evolved and new variants emerged in symbolism and usage, disagreements have inevitably arisen over what is authentic or correct. People have argued about the court cards, the originals and the various replacements. Then, more recently, we have Jung and his influence on the tarot cards, archetypes and psychology, steering the cards away from religion and more toward psychoanalysis. In the twentieth century, Rabbi Steven Fisdel peeled back all non-Jewish imagery from the cards and was left with a set of cards with numbers and Hebrew letters. This highlighted the link between the tarot and Kabbalah—the ancient Jewish tradition of mystical readings of the Bible.

While people choose to disagree on certain aspects of the tarots, this is perfectly normal and there are plenty of other things in our world, both scientific and spiritual, that we may not see eye to eye on. Rather than using this to discredit the art and even the magic behind the cards, I decided this was another reason to learn how to read your own cards. The personal interpretations of the cards are what is going to help you understand more about your life. I love history but more out of curiosity and not to prove which scholars are right or wrong. Really, I can see a valid point in a lot of what they have to say.

HOW THE DIFFERENT DECKS DEVELOPED OVER TIME

From the simple images yet the intricate gold design of early cards to the Harry Potter or the witty Silicon Valley tarot, there have been countless adaptations of the tarot cards. It's impossible to mention all of the designs, but here are some of the most significant that have impacted the evolution of the cards.

The Lenormand-style decks from the 1860s were the first to incorporate chromolithography, or multi-colored prints. These decks were a combination of the standard playing deck (hearts, clubs, diamonds, and spades) and fortune-telling images.

Prior to the Lenormand cards, a British company printed a different set of cards that had images and little snippets of advice on the bottom, such as "Be always on your guard; he who easily believes is easily deceived." Though the images aren't like those of the tarot cards, they did come with a booklet of instructions on how to use the cards, much like the Lenormand cards.

Three of the most common tarot decks that we see today are the tarot de Marseille and the tarot of Nouveau, the Rider-Waite-Smith, and the Crowley-Harris Thoth set. It's worth looking into these in a little more depth.

The Tarot de Marseille

Many of today's tarot decks still follow the same pattern of the tarot de Marseille. When the French conquered Italy in 1499, they most likely took the tarot back to France with them and then when it was reintroduced to Italy, it had the Marseille design.

The actual deck has the same structure as other decks, but each suit is known in its French name: Batons- Wands, Épées- Swords Coupes- Cups, and Deniers- Coins. To complete the Minor Arcana cards, there are four face cards, the Valet (Page), the Cavalier/Chevalier (Knight), the Dame (Queen) and the Roi, (King). The main difference you will notice with the Major Arcana cards is the Roman numerals, which are additive (the original system of ancient Rome.

Tarot Nouveau

The Tarot Nouveau was never intended for divination, which is why the French call this deck the tarot á jouer, or playing tarot. It uses the symbols we see on a standard playing deck (hearts, diamonds, spades and clubs) but the Ace card is numbered 1. Also, instead of the Page, we have the Jack.

Interestingly, the Major Arcana cards have an urban and rural representation. So, taking the first card, which we would see as the Fool, for the urban representation, we see a sad clown, and the rural representation is of a fool and a ballerina. The other significant difference is that the Roman numerals have been replaced with Arabic numerals (digits).

Crowley-Harris Thoth Tarot Deck

Aleister Crowley had the idea of a short project to update the tarot. He worked with Lady Frieda Harris, who painted the deck. The task was more demanding than originally expected, and in the end, it took around six years, finishing in 1943. The images became much more detailed, with symbols of science, philosophy, and the occult. In 1944, Crowley finished writing a book that was intended to be used with the deck.

Only the Queen remained the same out of the court/face cards. The King was changed to the Knight, the traditional Knight became the Prince and the Page was portrayed as the Princess in the Thoth tarot deck. There were also some name changes with Major Arcana cards:

- The Magician- The Magus
- The High Priestess- The Priestess
- Strength- Lust
- Wheel of Fortune- Fortune
- Justice- Adjustment
- Temperance- Art
- Judgement- The Æon*
- The World- The Universe

*According to the religion of the Thelema, which Aleister Crowley founded, history can be separated into aeons and each aeon has a form of magical and religious expression, a key to appreciating Thelemic Magick.

Rider-Waite-Smith Tarot Deck

I have worked with the Rider deck ever since I got the tarot bug, so to speak. For me, it's the deck that is richest in imagery and symbols and it made it easier for me to understand tarot as a whole. It was a combination of the talents of A.E. Waite, the academic who wrote the instructions, and Pamela Colman Smith, who illustrated the cards. They were first published in 1909 by the Rider company.

I won't go too much into the imagery now, because there is a chapter dedicated to this. It's important to know that the Rider-Waite-Smith (hereon known as the Rider deck) doesn't have such a strong Christian meaning, which makes it that more universal. For example, the Pope in the Rider deck is called the Hierophant. Smith also added much more imagery to the Minor Arcanas and Waite made some changes so that the Major Arcana cards had a stronger correlation with astrology. He put Strength before Justice so that Strength was linked to Leo and Justice to Libra. He removed one of the Lovers to tie in with Gemini.

Theme-Based Tarot Cards

Whether we like it or not, everything has the ability to become commercialised. I think to some extent, the commercialisation of tarot cards has not been a bad thing. As tarot has entered the modern world, the different decks available today make it more appealing to the many. You now have the option to select a deck of tarot cards that reflects your personality or your hobby.

If you are interested in healing, you may like the deck that is aimed at herbs and their healing abilities. If you want to explore the supernatural, you have a Ghosts and Spirits Deck.

The Modern Witch tarot has images of women of all races, shapes and sizes as the main figures in the cards. You will like this modern twist as it has a funky biker on her 'chariot' and the Emperor has a nice power trouser suit; even the Hermit appears to be closing her laptop.

For the male readers, don't worry, there are also decks that have been designed with you in mind. The Everyman tarot is based on the Rider deck, but cleverly depicts how a modern man copes with the experiences of today's world.

BUSTING THE TAROT MYTHS

If I have done my job correctly, you will hopefully know that tarot cards do not require a dark room with a crystal ball and a crystal layout around you. You also don't need to pay a fortune, have a degree in psychology or be a practising witch. Now that you know tarot is about using your intuition, you also know that you don't need to be a psychic.

Another typical myth I have heard so often is that tarot is evil or dangerous. Throughout history, man has been gifted with intelligence. People have used this for good and for evil. Tarot cards can be used for evil, but this comes down to your intention, not the cards. The cards themselves are neither evil nor dangerous. This myth may have come about because when people see certain aspects of their unconscious, it can scare them. But, it's not really fair to blame our unconscious or our fears on tarot.

I know I have touched on this but I just want to remind everyone again, not because you weren't paying attention, but because it is such a widely believed myth that it's worth reiterating. The cards are not predicting your future. They can be used to see what might happen if you continue on the path that you are on. That being said, you have the ability to make any changes you want. The guidance the cards offer you can provide hope, but they were never intended to be a tool to fix you.

Life is funny sometimes! I consider myself to be extremely confident at tarot readings, I would even go to call myself an expert, but I feel too big-headed. That being said, I recognise that there are lots of different approaches to, and interpretations of, tarot and I am only proficient in one particular tradition. The scholars over the last centuries have all had their interpretations, some based on opinion, others on fact. It's still been a great trip through time to understand some of the most significant moments of the tarot cards.

Now that we have looked at what the tarots are not, it's time to gain more insight as to what a reading looks like from start to finish.

A TAROT READING

There are so many different settings for a tarot reading. I have been in little rooms in the back of a holistic shop, in my own home, in the psychic's home, in a field at a festival, in a shopping center, you name it, I have tried it. It's easy to blame the tarot reader for hearing something that we don't want to, or for not finding the answers we were hoping to, but the setting has a very key role in the reading. If you go for a massage, would you prefer to be in the middle of a field in a rock concert or in a beauty parlour? You wouldn't ask your doctor for your blood test results in the middle of a supermarket, and so on.

When getting the right setting, I always run through a checklist of my four spaces, the physical, mental, emotional, and spiritual. Let's touch a little on each of these.

- **Your physical, safe space**

Basically, this is everything in your setting that you can touch, from the comfort of your seating to the texture of your table, or the tarot cloth you lay down. Some people like candles and crystals and I admit that I will also use them on occasions, but only when the mood takes me. Sometimes, all I feel the need for is my deck, sometimes I like to sit in the garden, other times on the living room floor. Your physical space has to be the right balance between comfort and privacy. You will need some privacy so that you feel in a safe place where you will not be interrupted.

- **A calm mental space**

Clarity and focus are the goals here, but we all know that this is a challenge. Busy lives tend to occupy our minds and it's hard to put aside the list of things we have to do. It's a great idea to start with a short meditation or even some deep breathing to start to clear the mind. You will notice that knowing exactly what your questions are will help to slow down your racing mind and get more out of your reading. Another thing to remember is that some people like having the herbs, candles, crystals, etc., while for others, this feels like clutter and a cluttered physical space can lead to a cluttered mind.

- **A peaceful emotional space**

As well as feeling safe prior to your reading, you also want to ensure that you are feeling positive and that your emotional baggage is left behind. Negative emotions could cause you to read the cards in the wrong way, possibly even to see things that aren't there. As you use deep breathing for your mental space, exhale the negativity and inhale the positivity.

- **An intuitive spiritual space**

The spiritual space is what will allow you to tap into the energy of the universe and of the cards. Making sure your chakras are balanced is a good start for boosting your energy and creating a stronger connection with your spiritual self. If you are looking for an alternative to meditation, you could use mantras or affirmations to increase your confidence and the faith in your own intuition.

One of my more amusing errors early on was dedicating too much time to the physical space and not enough on the mental, emotional, and spiritual. My spare room was converted into the perfect image of a supernatural den. The colour scheme was spot on, the enchanting smells filled the room, my meditation CD was playing and there were more candles than in Ikea. I found it bizarre in those first few weeks that there seemed to be an energy wall around me that prevented me gaining the necessary spiritual connection. That's when I dialed it right back and focused more on preparing myself and not my environment.

As with anything new in life, don't worry if you don't feel that you have the right space straight away, because it might take a few sessions before you decide what feels comfortable for and what doesn't. It's not like making a mistake will harm you. It's about finding that perfect space for you so that your intuition is enhanced and your reading is clearer. Your attitude, however, is something that you should get right from the outset.

HAVING THE RIGHT ATTITUDE AND INTENTIONS FOR YOUR TAROT READING

It sounds a little harsh, but if you just want to know what is going to happen in your future, you might be better off having someone read your tarots for you. This is only because it takes quite a bit of time and dedication to learning about tarot cards and the result is far more than simply fortune-telling.

Your intentions should be to find a greater level of truth regarding your life, more guidance, and direction. The cards are a tool that should be used for personal growth and to learn more about yourself and your role in the universe. Imagine the cards as a bridge from your physical being to your spiritual self.

Like any divination tool, the tarot cards mustn't be used to control your life's decisions. Instead, they are to help you provide wisdom and insights on things that you already have information on. Let's say your question is whether or not you should go for the promotion that is available at work. If the cards indicate that the new role will require more hours at work, it's a sign that you shouldn't take it. It indicates that you need to consider if you have available time, if you can free up additional time for your hobbies and whether or not there is enough compensation for these extra hours. If you take the job because "the cards told you", you have the wrong attitude about the practice. You have to take responsibility for your own life and your actions.

You also need to remain objective at all times. A negative attitude will more than likely lead to an unsatisfactory reading. If you have a question, but you have already made your mind up about what you think the answer or solution is, then your reading will be biased.

One thing that many aren't aware of is the importance of urgency. If there is a movie on TV this weekend and you have wanted to watch it for absolutely ever, you are more likely to sit down and watch it. If the movie is 50/50, there will be something more interesting to do. If the answer to your question is urgent, you will find that the insights you read are more direct, clearer, and conclusive.

I promise you, the more readings that you do, the more confident you will be with your readings. This continuous effort drives your intuition to new levels and over time, you start to see more about your interpretations. Like an athlete pushing themselves to the next level, your rewards will surprise you and encourage you to learn even more about your inner self.

THE ART OF FORMING YOUR QUESTIONS

A genie appears in front of you and instead of three wishes, you can ask three questions. Would you know which questions to ask? If the same genie appeared on a Sunday morning or one month before Christmas, would those questions be the same? Sometimes, planning your questions can be trickier than the actual reading, mainly because you can't change your mind halfway through the reading or things just won't make sense. First, let's look at the different types of questions that you can ask:

- Questions about the present
- Questions about the past

- Questions about the future
- Questions about making decisions
- Open-ended questions
- Yes/no questions- bear in mind that this type of question won't lead to a direct yes or no, because the answers aren't always quite as simple. When you learn more about the specific symbols on the cards, you will be more prepared to understand complexities and find your yes/no answer.

Here is a guide to formulating the perfect tarot questions:

1. **Begin with open-ended questions.**

Questions that start with who, what, where, why, how will give you a chance to explore the options available to make a change in particular situations. Questions like "How can I get out of my financial difficulties?" allow for a more in-depth analysis of the card's meanings.

2. **Steer clear of questions that shift the responsibility**

As I mentioned before, tarot cards are to provide meaning, not to tell you what choices to make. Questions that start with 'should', 'will' or 'when' tend to move that responsibility to the cards. If you take the same question as above, but asked "When will I get out of financial difficulties?" the cards might show you a sign. If you haven't resolved your problems by then, you may end up wrongly blaming the cards.

3. **Discover more about your general life direction**

If you don't have a particular question, you can still carry out a reading to learn more about the path you are on right now or about the energies that you feel are around you at this time. These types of questions are good to not only learn more about your life in general, but you may discover ways to enhance your life across the board.

4. Be careful how you phrase your questions

Much like avoiding those questions that shift the responsibility, you should also choose vocabulary that will encourage the most amount of guidance. Conditional questions are good for this; for example, "How will my partner feel if I decide to take the promotion?" Your reading will focus more on the emotions of your partner, rather than whether or not you should take the promotion, as that decision is your responsibility.

5. Consider everyone involved

The main goal is to learn more, so that you can make decisions to improve your life, but you still need to consider those who may also be affected by the decision (as with our conditional question). Going back to the promotion, it is likely that the promotion will help get out of the tight money spot. But what if this has negative consequences on your relationship or your other family members?

6. Ask about the advantages and disadvantages

Probably in the past, you have made a list of pros and cons to help you make an important decision. Tarot cards can help you gain better insights into what could be on these two lists. Asking the cards what the advantages and disadvantages of the promotion will provide alternative perspectives.

7. Look for areas of improvement

Maybe you want to expand your skillset, take up a new hobby, or get in shape physically. I know that there is always an area of my life that I would like to work on. Use your readings to ask how you can reach these improvements.

8. Break larger questions down into smaller ones

If you get overwhelmed at the thought of finding a solution to your money worries, it is probable that these emotions will roll over into your reading. Break down the question, so you might want to ask "How can I reduce my spending?" or "What are the advantages of selling this or that?" etc.

9. Keep your questions positive

Even if life isn't going as you had hoped and you are struggling to see the positive in life, you need to keep your readings positive. To help you do this, change any negative questions into a positive. So instead of saying "Why can't I find love?" change the question to "What can I do to find love?".

10. Take notes

There might be things in the reading that you don't understand or that lead you to more questions. It is a great habit to get into making notes of your thoughts and feelings during a reading so that you can reflect on them later. As you are reflecting on your reading, you may discover new questions that you would like further guidance on in the next reading.

You can imagine that it's impossible to list every question you may want to ask in a tarot reading. Each of us has our own concerns, circumstances, and life decisions. We all need to find the questions that will help us on our individual path. Aside from the questions we have seen in the guide above, here are a few more that may give you some inspiration:

- What do I need to be aware of to help me make the right decision?
- What am I missing or ignoring in my life right now?
- What am I doing now that will help me in the future?
- Which steps are the best to take if I want to achieve X,Y,Z?
- What can I learn from my past that will change this situation?
- What do I need to pay more attention to at the moment?
- What is preventing me from achieving my goals?

THE TAROT SPREAD

I can feel the build-up, we are so close to breaking open the deck and giving the cards that all-important shuffle. How do you shuffle tarot cards? Pretty much the same way as a standard deck of cards. I love the way the pros split the pack and fan them together. I tried it and it looked like a game of '78-card pick up'. So, I stick to the over-the-hand shuffle. You can cut the deck into different piles and restack them or just spread them all out on the table and scoop them back into a new pile.

Later on, we will go into more detail about the spread. This is the layout of the cards that are drawn. The simplest layouts are the three-card spread and the five-card spread. Once you get a little more experienced, you can look at the Celtic Cross. You can then have a three-card spread for love, a three-card spread for careers, for understanding the past, etc. When we discuss each card in detail, we will also learn how to read it if it is drawn in the reversed position and its specific meaning.

You may feel that the selection of your cards is a sheer coincidence, but it's far from it. Intuition plays a huge role, even at the point of choosing which cards to draw. This is known as synchronicity or 'meaningful coincidences'. Synchronicity was coined by Jung and he speculated that it was a law of nature that formed part of each person's spiritual development.

It refers to one thing happening at a certain time that has a certain quality or meaning. In Jung's own words, it is the "meaningful connection between the subjective and objective world". He also defined synchronicity as coincidence that appears to exceed random probability.

Examples of what some would say are like a wink from the universe would be dreaming of something specific and then seeing it the following day, seeing repeated numbers, symbols, or colours, even being in the right place at the right time. A few months ago, I was driving when the truck in front of me stopped. Just in front of the truck, there was a horrendous accident. Just minutes earlier, that could have been me, and it wasn't me because I had forgotten my glasses and had to pop back home. I saw this as a sign.

From Jung's point of view, our worldly perceptions and experiences are synchronous with our soul and the images on the cards we draw are intermediaries between ourselves and our spiritual energies. So, even if you consciously try to choose a random card, your current energy will draw you to a particular card and its energy.

WHAT IS THE SIGNIFICATOR?

Though it may sound like something from a sci-fi film, the significator is a card that the reader will choose before a reading. It's certainly not necessary, but for those that are new to tarot, it often helps to draw a deeper connection with the cards, because they can see some meaning in that particular card. This is the card that represents the querent or the thing/person they are asking about. It may even represent the situation you are facing.

In some cases, you might want to choose your significator with intention. With this card next to you during the reading, you will find it easy to relate to the cards. There are a few different ways for you to choose a significator—only if you want to and you feel it will add more value to your reading.

Based on age:

- Children and young adults- A Page
- Young males between 18 and their 30s- A Knight
- Women over 18- A Queen
- Men over 40- A King

Based on astrology:

- Water signs: Cancer, Scorpio, Pisces- Cups
- Fire Signs: Aries, Leo, Sagittarius- Wands
- Air Signs: Gemini, Libra, Aquarius- Swords
- Earth Signs: Taurus, Virgo, Capricorn- Pentacles

Based on appearance:

- Fair skin, blonde hair, blue eyes- Cups
- Rosy complexion, red hair, blue/green eyes- Wands
- Light complexion, light or grey hair, blue/green eyes- Swords
- Dark complexion, dark hair, brown eyes- Pentacles
- Naturally, if you are working on the above descriptions, you can also combine them. In this way, a mature female with blue eyes would choose the Queen of Cups whereas a young man whose star sign is Aries would select the Knight of Wands. If you prefer to choose your significator based on the situation, here is an in-depth guide:
- Love, relationships, family- Cups
- Work, business- Wands
- Disagreements, logic- Swords
- Finance, health- Pentacles
- Fresh starts- The Fool
- Trickery, magic- The Magician
- Psychic ability- The High Priestess
- Parenthood- The Empress
- Advancing your career- The Emperor
- Religion, leaders- The Hierophant
- Love, choices- The Lovers
- Fame, success- The Chariot
- Law, moral, equality- Justice
- Self-discovery, solitude- The Hermit
- Luck- The Wheel of Fortune
- Courage, strength- Strength
- Health- The Hanged Man
- Life-changing decisions- Death
- Peace, calm, happiness- Temperance

- Addictions, obsessions- The Devil
- Unexpected shocks- The Tower
- Hope, desires- The Star
- Doubt, uncertainty- The Moon
- Happiness, family- The Sun
- A calling, destiny- Judgement
- Travel, world issues- The World

Please don't get overwhelmed with another list of meanings. It's a personal preference and you may have done many online searches about tarot and not even heard about the significator until now. My advice would be to try a few readings without one and with one. If you are taking a note of your feelings and thoughts, you will be able to go back over these to see if there is a noticeable difference in your readings.

OOPS, I DROPPED A CARD!

The five-second rule, unfortunately, doesn't apply here, and another thing that I didn't realise until I got deeper into my research is that cards have certain meanings when they are accidentally dropped. I'm also glad I found this out after dropping almost an entire deck, as I was trying to shuffle like they do in the movies. A specific number of dropped cards and whether they land face up (so you can see the image) or face down has important significance.

If you drop…

- One card face up, something related to the card will happen within hours or days.

- One Major Arcana card means you will have a surprise development or something that you haven't been considering will appear in your reading.
- One Court card or Ace points to unexpected news from or related to a relative or authority figure from that suit and you can look forward to a new boost of energy.
- Numbered cards mean a situation (be that good or bad) related to that suit will happen all of a sudden and disappear just as quickly.
- One card face down means the event will occur in the distant future.
- One card face up or down that is drawn in the reading is the absolute key to everything you need to know.
- Two cards face down suggests there will be two events in the future and one will trigger the next.
- Two cards, one face down and the other face-up means the event of the card facing up will occur beforehand and by paying attention to this, you can minimise any upset from the event of the card facing down.
- Three cards can be used in a three-card spread.

Now, if you have a fumbly-finger day like me and drop more, there is no need to panic. In this case, it's best to pick them up, take a few deep breaths, refocus your mind and start shuffling again. No one is perfect!

MASTERING THE ART OF STORYTELLING

I made it so far without saying 'a picture is worth a thousand words' but it is so true that we have to appreciate this fact. When we master the art of telling the story that appears in the cards, we are going to start seeing some incredible changes in our lives, in the way we feel and how we process our thoughts. We can take these images and use them to make sense of the events in our lives.

Each card represents an archetypal situation that we have experienced throughout our lives. This could be, for example, as the trickster, the saint, or the hero. It may also be in the form of a caregiver, a lover, an artist, or an idealist. We may not remember each of these situations with great clarity, but our experiences are there nevertheless. The art of tarot reading is to appreciate these archetypes through storytelling.

To get better at storytelling, you want to first learn to trust your instincts. You may struggle with this if you have had problems or feel like you have made the wrong decisions in the past. I know what this is like, but try to remember that you aren't the same person and you have learnt from your errors. Your instincts are probably far more in tune now than they were. The more readings you carry out, the more intuitive you will become and the more you will end up discovering. The cards don't hold the secrets, you do.

Enhancing your storytelling skills doesn't have to be limited to when you are using your cards. If you have children, you have the perfect audience. While you are out and about, look at the different situations you see and make up stories with them. Take in the environment and the symbols you may see. Even if you don't have children, you can still take everyday situations and create a story related to it.

As for the cards, don't feel you always have to use them for a reading. Sometimes, you can just select some cards and use the imagery to develop a story. This is a really good exercise for becoming more confident with the symbols and colours. As your confidence and intuition start to grow, you will find it easier to relate these stories to your own life.

In order for you to do this, it's time to take a good look at the amazing imagery of the cards and start to understand more about each specific meaning.

THE LANGUAGE OF THE SYMBOLS

In my early, skeptical days, I couldn't see how a psychic was getting so much information from one card. Let's take the Two of Cups as an example. I saw a man and a woman, two cups and a lion head with wings. I paid no attention to the small house in the distance. I never appreciated that the colours brought more meaning, as well as details right down to the displays of wealth on their heads.

Every tiny detail of each tarot card matters and this is why it can take a long time to fully master the art of tarot reading.

THE MEANING OF THE COLOURS

In my book *Modern Chakras*, we paid a lot of attention to the seven chakras and the modern emphasis on the importance of their colour with regards to spiritual healing. You will probably notice some overlaps here and the colours in tarot cards have an insightful power.

White

You may already have made the connection between white and peace, but it is also a sign of innocence and purity. White, and also silver, also represent the light of the moon and femininity. In the Death card, we see white as the colour of cleanings and rebirth, as well as of purity.

White and black

When white is paired with black, it shows absolutes that are present in archetypes. It's the combination of masculine and feminine, or passive and active. The High Priestess sits between a black pillar and a white pillar, showing us that she has found her balance.

White and red

White and red are often seen together in the smaller details, like in flowers or patterns on clothing. These two colours often point to the opposite energies of passion and innocence.

Black

It is less common to find black alone, except in Death and The Devil. It is sometimes seen as bad luck and evil but is more often associated with mystery and the unknown.

Grey

You may find grey pointing to uncertainty or an unhealthy perspective of life. It can be found in cards that have stormy weather and may suggest unhappiness or dullness. In some cases, grey can indicate wisdom.

Red

Red is a passionate and lustful colour. It represents the element of fire, as well as Mercury, Mars, and the suit of Wands. It can also suggest action and inspiration, a passion for life. Sometimes, red will be used for anger and even a strong will. Red is a representation of the conscious mind.

Orange

As a mixture of red (fire) and yellow (air), orange cand be a sign of energetic happiness. It is also a colour that points to enthusiasm, but in some cases, an orange sky could suggest challenges.

Yellow

In the Rider deck, you might see a yellow sky rather than a yellow sun. Sometimes the ground can have a slightly yellow hue rather than brown earth or green grass. It is linked to the masculine energy of the Sun. Yellow is a representation of the highest level of our conscious minds.

Green

The power of green can tell us of new beginnings, money and well-being. It also has strong ties to the element of Earth, nature, and growth. If you look at all the green in the Queen of Pentacles, you will see the link with living things.

Blue

Generally, blue is a color of inner peace and spirituality. Cards that have a lot of blue are usually related to processes in the subconscious mind. When the figures are wearing blue, it suggests that they are introspective or taking advantage of their subconscious.

Purple

Purple is a very spiritual colour associated with our Third Eye Chakra and psychic energies. You will commonly see it as a colour of wealth, luxury, and royalty.

Pink

On the rare occasions you see pink, it will most probably be in with the Cups. It can be seen as a sign of opulence, sensual pleasure, or unconditional love.

Brown

This is another colour that is associated with earth, but more in the sense of being practical, about working your way through your daily jobs and achieving material success.

Gold

Gold is an amazing healing color and is connected with revitalisation.

Rainbows

If you see a rainbow, it will imply happiness, abundance, and wishes coming true. In other decks, it can be seen as a sign of celebration.

Because there are so many different tarot decks, I won't relate the symbols to any particular card. In the Rider deck, there is no rabbit in the Queen of Pentacles but there is in the Robin Wood deck. Here, we will cover the meanings of the symbols and when we study individual cards, we will look at the symbols combined with colours and meanings.

THE RICH MEANINGS OF THE TAROT SYMBOLS

Angels- messages, divine messages, higher thought and ideas.

- Ankh (Egyptian Cross)- immortality and balance, life, the sun rising from the horizon.
- An arch- entrances, a new direction, taking initiative.
- Armor- protection, being prepared, strength.
- A bench- it's time to sit down, relax, and understand your situation.
- Birds- spiritualism, higher ideas, freedom, ascending to a higher level
- Blindfold- unwilling or unable to see facts and the truth or see things clearly.
- Boats- travel, change in direction, an important thought that will lead us to action.
- Brick wall- negative or inaccurate thinking is holding you back.
- Bridge- Moving from one phase of life to another, we have the resources to help us.

- Bull- power, force, and stability. Also stubbornness and unwillingness to change.
- Butterflies- transformation, often in thoughts, resulting in something beautiful.
- Caduceus (two snakes around a winged staff)- balance, correct moral behavior, protection, cosmic energy, joining forces, new and successful relationships.
- Castle- building strong foundations to reach our goals, shelter, or something preventing us from reaching our goals.
- Cats- perception, a watchful eye, psychic abilities, seeing things from all perspectives.
- Chains- restrictions, conflict, a slave to our own ideas, addition.
- Children- new starts, hope, promises, a sign of the future, a new venture or literally, the birth of a child.
- City or village- centers and people, thoughts, and energies coming together in a group effort. Protection, the need for teamwork and tapping into the energy of others.
- Clouds- confusion, clouded judgement, higher thoughts, divine messages, or the contrary, a revelation or epiphany.
- Dogs- loyalty, honesty, righteousness, often a sign that we are on the right path or that we need to question our loyalties.
- Doves- purity, hope, ascending, love. When the dove is pointing down, it reminds us to be grounded before we take to the sky.
- Falcon- higher vision, vibrancy, power, we may question whether or not we are reaching our potential.

- Fire- energy, passion, ambition, and power. It has the power to destroy and create.
- Fish-emotions, intuition, unpredictable motion in our subconscious, abundance is you can control our passions.
- Flag- the announcement of a change, but the change will depend on the imagery on the flag.
- Flowers- unfolding and opening up, receiving joy and love, the beauty that is all around is.
- Globes- the union of the cosmic and the physical, achievement is nearby, seeing the bigger picture, completion and cycles.
- Grapes or grapevines- this fruit has powerful meanings for different religions: fertility, redemption, hospitality or youthfulness.
- Hammer- hammer your point, hammer the detail, force, action and masculinity.
- Hand- giving and receiving from one hand to the next, power, domination and protection.
- Heart- aside from love and affection, truth, the center of our being and existence.
- Hoe- hard work and effort, resourcefulness, we reap what we sow— the good and the bad.
- Horn- a triumphant or victorious announcement, or possibly a warning.
- Horses- strength, action, vitality, a symbol of spirituality and incorporation of the elements.
- A house- our own sacred place, where we hold our closest secrets, safety and protection.
- Ice- isolation, distance, patience, profound contemplation, growth that won't be seen till later.

- Keys- unlocking our knowledge, intellect, wisdom, potential, or is our potential being locked away.
- Lantern- illumination, truth, a symbol of life, vigilance, clarity.
- Lemniscate (infinity symbol)- infinite energy that can't be created or destroyed, thoughts and actions where the consequence could be infinite.
- Lightning- instant divine intervention, a creative spark, the creator and the destroyer.
- Lily- purity, fertility, health, growth, vulnerability, confidence to be ourselves.
- Lion- strength, courage, royalty, protection, spiritual valor, our saviour or our destroyer.
- Lizard or salamander- renewal, rebirth, enlightenment, vision, small conscious efforts lead to big changes.
- Lobster, crab or crayfish- lunar symbols, cycles, rebirth, casting shells, protection.
- Moon- femininity, levels of awareness, intuition, reflection, phases, a powerful influence.
- Mountains- obstacles, success, attainment, realization, endurance, everlasting, consider our place in the universe.
- Ocean- vastness, depth, infinite possibilities, the power that surrounds us, a reminder that we aren't always in control, possibilities.
- Path- direction, phases of life, beginnings and endings, small steps make progress.
- Pillars- balance, diplomacy, strategy, things aren't black or white, the middle way can provide new perspectives.
- Pitcher- a vessel, the contents of our mind or heart, the need to be a pure vessel.

- Plowed fields- We reap what we sow, the efforts we make impact our harvest, patience, time.
- Pomegranates- plentiful, fertility, love, female sexuality, feminine power, luxuries and wonders in the world.
- Rabbit- grounding, social, good judgement, fast-acting.
- Rain- cleansing, wash away the old to make way for the new, providing life.
- Ram- taking initiative, action, determination, motivation, leadership, taking responsibility.
- Ropes- restriction, binding, being in a knot, state of inaction, struggling makes the knots tighter.
- Rose- beauty, purity, new beginnings, hope, thorn pricks represent potential pain.
- Scale- equality, balance, where we need to create more balance in our lives.
- Scroll- passing down of sacred knowledge, secrets, hidden facts.
- Shield- protection from what can harm us and what we value.
- Ship- journeys, water, the subconscious, emotional baggage on your voyage.
- Snail- slow and steady progress, security and happiness being carried with us.
- Snake- renewal, the need to adapt and be flexible, shed things so we can grow.
- Snow- quiet, beauty, fresh, crystally, beauty, a choice between being left in the cold or enjoying the beauty.
- Sphinx- guardianship, protecting life's secrets, using our senses, unraveling secrets.
- Staff- support by the archetypes, stability, represents the number 1, new beginnings.

- Stained glass- perception and beliefs impact our vision, clear vision or rose-coloured glasses.
- Star- illumination, guidance, direction from a higher source.
- Sun- energy, growth, expansion, the rising sun represents new beginnings, midday for creativity, setting for an ending or a transformation.
- Sunflower- looking to the bright side, positivity.
- Tomb- lay to rest the things that are no longer any use, changing mindsets.
- Triangle- balance, creativity, intelligence, the energy of love, the union of the mother, father, child.
- Wall- keeping parts of our lives separate, privacy.
- Waterfall- constant flow of emotions, emotions crashing to the ground or running away from us, the need to control our emotions.
- Wolf- primal urges, loyalty, intelligence, refocus desires, being true to ourselves.
- Wreath- victory, protection, peace, purification.

It's an incredible list when you think about it. One part of the cards is about appreciating these symbols, but the other part is then deciphering which of the possible meanings each symbol will have. This could be helped by combinations of different symbols on a tarot card or the cards that come before or after.

MINOR ARCANAS AND THE SIGNIFICANCE OF NUMBERS

Some people have lucky numbers. For example, some won't change their lottery numbers, because they are "the lucky numbers"—despite never winning! Others count magpies, because the number they see is a sign (remember '1 for sorrow, 2 for joy'). I know people who won't stay in certain hotel rooms because of the number, even hotel owners who skip room numbers. Whether you believe in numerology or not, numbers have and will continue to play an important role in our belief systems. Here is what the numbered cards mean in a tarot deck:

The Ones- The aces are represented by the number one and are a sign of pure energy. This energy needs to be shaped and you have to take great care to do so that you gain the most from it. Without care, the power of this energy can overwhelm you.

The Twos- The solitude of the ace is left behind as we move onto unions between two people. More often than not, twos represent a peaceful joining of two people, even when the forces are opposite. There are occasions when the connection between two people is so strong that it is hard to break free from it when certain decisions have to be made.

The Threes- Like in many religions and cultures, three signifies a group, whether that's people, objects, or ideas. We frequently associate three with grouping in order to complete a phase, but lookout for creative moments.

The Fours- Before you can build a house, you need the four corners of the foundation. The same can be said for many things, that the fountain is crucial for growth. The fours are telling us that endurance is necessary for us to progress, despite the disappointments we may have.

The Fives- The theme of pushing forward continues from the threes. The fives often tell us that change or turbulence is

present. There is a need to take our energy and use it to overcome conflicts and the reasons that cause us to doubt change.
The answers are more often than not found within you.

The Sixes- Our disagreements with ourselves or with others
are about to convert into solutions. If you draw a six, you may
have to resolve issues you have with people or learn how to let
go of things that no longer benefit you. A six is a sign of positivity after times of difficulty.

The Sevens- One of the sevens in a reading suggests your best
course of action might be some time to yourself to reflect on
what it is really is that you want to achieve. Take some time for
introspection so that you consider if you are on the path you
should be on.

The Eights- You can expect a second phase to come to completion, because you are mastering your skills. There may even be
an achievement that will help to further your growth. Your
success might be a physical one or an emotional one, and you
may find that it comes about when you least expect it.

The Nines- Though close to the end and these cards may
suggest the end of your cycle is near, they could also be a sign
that this is a pause before the final change or achievement.
Life's events may level off before you reach your goal. There
may be more to come.

The Tens- Drawing a ten is another sign of moving forward,
but in these cases, it is because your cycle has reached competi-
tion. The full circle has come around and now it is time to look
forward to those new beginnings.

It's true that the Major Arcanas also have their individual numerical numbers, but rather than create another section here, I think it is better to cover this when we look at each card individually and in more depth.

A SUIT FOR EACH ELEMENT

I have already touched on the different elements for each suit, but because it has been embedded with other information, I'd like to save a mini section to help reinforce what we have already seen, plus to outline the link between each one and the seasons.

The Cups are related to the element water, and this ties in with our emotions and intuition. The cups often point to our relationships and creativity. There is often a great amount of joy with the Cups as they represent summer, the warmth of those longer days and feeling complete.

As the earth element is seen in the Pentacles, we can appreciate a link to material wealth, healthy finances and careers. Things start to manifest when the Pentacles are drawn. There is a logical connection between the Pentacles and autumn/fall as this is the season when we can harvest our plentiful crops.

Air is the known element for the Swords and this suit is a sign of thoughts and intellect. Furthermore, it is a sign of truth and communication. There is a lot of sadness in the images of these cards, some are cold and lonely, and so the Swords represent winter.

As the cycle of the seasons comes back around, the Wands, represented by the element of fire, are symbols of spring.

Spring is a time for enthusiasm, energy, and new beginnings. Notice how new life blossoms from the Wands.

TAROT SYMBOLOGY AND WITCHCRAFT

Black cats, tall hats, and bats are strung up as decorations for Halloween, but are far from the symbols that most practising witches associate with. There are plenty of examples of relationships between symbols of the tarot cards and symbols in witchcraft.

The most obvious is the pentacle or pentagram. The five-pointed star inside a circle represents the four elements (the four lower points) and the final point of the star represents the spirit. The star, sun, and moon are all present in both practices. But then, if you start to look a little closer, you will notice the link with symbols like snakes, flowers and wreaths. In many ways, the tarot cards and witchcraft complement each other.

It's been a bit of a listicle chapter, but this was necessary to get a true understanding of the depth of imagery within the cards. If, like me, you would look at a card and only see the surface, I hope that with the help of these lists, you will be able to draw more meaning from the different symbols, colours, and numbers. Now that you are aware of the powerful imagery, we can begin working on the different types of tarot spreads.

OPTIMISE YOUR SPREADS

There are numerous tarot card spreads that you can use in a reading. The main reason for such a variety is that each situation will require a different type of spread. You can't imagine a love spread providing the same insight as a sibling-rivalry spread. Even when looking at love spreads, you will be able to see a relationship cross spread, which is one of the more straightforward ones, to a ready for love spread, requiring more cards. Some spreads are designed to give you faster guidance, like the Yes/No spread, but you can also do a more detailed reading with a twelve-month spread.

Many times, one type of spread can be used with different intentions. The three-card spread can be used to uncover general insights, in which case we call it a non-dedicated spread. A dedicated spread would still have three cards, but it would be about love, your career, or something else more specific.

Like with everything else we have talked about regarding tarot cards, it is a case of practising the different types of spreads and finding which ones you find yourself connecting too more. It is better to stick to the easier spreads while you are gaining more confidence with the symbolism and then move onto spreads that require more cards.

Because the layout of the cards is so crucial, I have included some diagrams at the end of the book that you can copy or print and keep close by while you are learning. For now, I am going to rely on my creative explanations to guide you through some of the most important spreads you can try.

Before you start randomly picking cards, let's just remind ourselves of the basics. I hate being repetitive, but the preparation is essential for the right results. Things like lighting a candle, meditative music, etc., are up to you, I'm talking about the fundamentals:

- Make sure you are in a calm environment where you can focus and won't be interrupted
- Calm your mind, let go of the negative thoughts and start to bring your mind towards the question you want to ask
- Shuffle your cards (you don't have to be a pro, nobody is examining you). It is essential that you shuffle the cards before every read. This is to cleanse the cards of the previous questions

And for the new stuff... hold the cards in both hands and focus on your question. Cut the cards with your left hand and place the bottom pile on the top. From this point, you have the first card for your tarot card spread. I try not to be biased in my books and generally exclude my favourites, but in this case, I will start with two of my preferred spreads for when I was first learning. After that, I have added the most popular tarot spreads and tried to keep them in order of simplicity.

One Card Tarot Spread

It doesn't get much easier than this, but it isn't really designed to provide detailed guidance. We would use a one-card tarot spread more often in daily use. It's like a short meditation session about your day. I prefer to use this in the morning so that I can make better decisions throughout the day. Take the first card in your prepared deck and see what the images are telling you.

Three Card Tarot Spread

This is probably one of the most common spreads for beginners and for tarot readers because it can be less overwhelming. However, the forms can vary, so again, you need to have your question clear. A three-card spread might be about the past, present and future. Other spreads could focus on the foundation, problem, and advice. The Yes/No/Maybe is also a popular form. Take the first three cards and lay them from left to right. The first card may represent your concern, the second the obstacle and the resolution (as an example).

Simple Five Tarot Card Spread

It's another great option and I found there was a nice easy transition from the three-card spread to the five-card spread. By adding two more cards, you naturally get a better understanding of your question. The first card is the general meaning of the spread, the second looks to past events, and the third points to the future. The fourth one will tell you more about the reason behind the question. It's normal to find some relation between the second and forth card, like 'the penny dropped' moment. The fifth card looks at the potential within the situation.

Seven Day Tarot Card Spread

I like this one because it is like an extended version of the one day spread. You would lay seven cards from left to right and an eighth card above card number seven. Each of the seven cards represents a day, with the first corresponding with the day of your reading. The eighth card is an overview of the week. Don't forget the intention of your question. Do you want a general look at the week ahead or are you looking for specific guidance to your job?

Seven Card Horseshoe Spread

Those with experience drop their jaws as I talk about this spread before others that are more common, but I have always felt that this is still incredibly insightful, but just a tad less daunting. The seven-card horseshoe spread starts with the first card positioned at the top left of the spread and the following cards are positioned in a horseshoe shape or 'V' with the fourth card being the tip of the 'V'. The first card looks to the past and the second at the present. The third card points to hidden influences and don't worry if you find it hard to see the significance straight away. The fourth card is a representation of you whereas the fifth focuses on the influence of those around you. The sixth card indicates what you should do and the final, seventh card implies the outcome.

Six Month Tarot Card Spread

It's very similar to the seven day spread, but for a longer period of time. As the layout is the same, it is essential that your focus and intention are for the full six months. Cards one to six are placed from left to right and the first card shows the month you are currently in. Each card can give you insights into the months ahead. The seventh card, placed in the top right corner will help you to see the full six months more clearly.

The Romany tarot Card Spread

This spread requires twenty-one cards in three rows, seven cards in each. Despite having a lot of cards, this is still quite a simple spread which will tell you more about the various stages in your life. The first seven cards in the top row offer insight into your past. The second row of seven indicates what is happening in the present. And the bottom row points to the future if the middle row continues as it is. You can use this for both general and specific readings.

CHAKRA BALANCE TAROT CARD SPREAD

It goes without saying that I have also loved this one, because of how much I gained from learning about my chakras and keeping them balanced. So, this spread is another great tool to work in conjunction with the chakras. Cards one to seven are placed in a vertical row. The first represents the Root Chakra, the second, the Root Chakra, and so on. Each card will provide insights into whether the chakra is overactive, underactive, or balanced.

The Celtic Cross Tarot Spread

While it comes out on top for popularity, the number of cards and placements may put some beginners off. The first card, placed in the center, shows your influences at the time. The second is placed horizontally on top of the first and indicates what is blocking you. You need to place the third card below the first; this is the past which has created the foundations for where you are today. The fourth card sits to the left of the first and deals with your past from further back. Above the first card you would place card number five, a representation of your dreams, and to the right of the first card is the sixth, and this card hints to your future. To the right of the spread, you need to lay cards seven to ten (bottom to top) in a vertical row. These cards are signs of your attitude towards the situation, how others see you, your hopes or fears, and the outcome, respectively.

Snapshot Tarot Card Spread

This is a good one, because the snapshot gives you a look at your emotions, as well as aspects from your spiritual and mental life in the past, present and future, plus the opportunity to see how they are linked. Lay cards one to three from left to right on the table. This shows your emotional, mental, and spiritual pasts. The fourth card is placed above the second and looks at the power of your past. Cards five, six, and seven (from left to right) are placed above the fourth card (card six directly above). Like the first three, they look at the emotional, mental and spiritual aspects but in the present. The eighth card shows the power of the present and is placed above the sixth. The final row on top of the eighth card (nine, ten, eleven) are the emotional, mental, and spiritual aspects of your life in the future. The last card, number twelve, is placed above the tenth and is the snapshot of the life cycle you are in at present.

I always feel that when I get to the end of a chapter, I reinforce my own realisation that the cards are hard to learn. I feel blessed that I stuck at it and took the time to learn not just the imagery but also the benefits of the different spreads. That being said, I do remember a time at the beginning where I just stuck in the habit of only doing three and five card spreads. Even when my confidence increased, I still feared the idea of trying a new spread. Don't make the same mistake as I did. While it's good to practice with the easier spreads, not trying out the more intricate ones could mean that you miss out on some amazing guidance.

There is still a deeper connection between witchcraft and tarot cards, including a particular spread that I would like to explore a little more with you. If you are in touch with the witch (or wizard) inside of you, you will enjoy the last chapter in part one. If you are still a little skeptical of witchcraft, that's ok too. I only hope that you keep reading with an open mind as we uncover the incredible relationships we have with the elements and other concepts we see in the cards.

A LITTLE BIT OF WITCHCRAFT TO
GET YOU STARTED

Picture this, you learnt Spanish at school and have tried to keep up with at least the basics. Your boss offers you the chance to move to Italy and it dawns on you that you are going to have to learn a new language. Now imagine your relief when you notice there are some similarities between the languages. The same thing happens with tarot and witchcraft: once you start mastering one, you can see the beautiful links with the other.

There is no need to rehash the links between the witchcraft, tarot and the four elements air, fire, earth and water. By now, you may have also picked on the overlap between three of the suits, the wands, cups, and pentacles. We saw the power of numbers that the cards represent and numerology is also a practice closely tied to the occult, as is astrology. There are three main reasons why you might want to consider using tarot cards along with your witchcraft practices:

1. By performing a tarot reading before you cast a spell, you will be better informed about what lays ahead for you.
2. Certain cards can be used in a spell to incorporate more energy into it. If you are planning a spell related to prosperity you might want to include the King of Pentacles or a spell to overcome the challenges you face would be helped with the Chariot card.
3. Using tarot cards when casting spells will help with your visualisation, particularly if you can relate figures in the cards to certain people.

Casting spells can be used for good and for bad. I am not here to judge or tell you what to do, but I do not use the power of the cards or spells to do harm. First of all, I have no intention of wasting my time on people who have hurt me and secondly, I don't want that negative energy around me. If tempted to put a curse on someone for their actions, try to understand where their actions are coming from. It's more than likely that they have some underlying issues in their life and this is causing them to react in the wrong way. You could choose to be the better person and try to find or create a spell that will help them. But again, it's up to you!

I have one more list for you regarding the cards you can use to help you create your spells. The following will give you a better idea of which cards are more suited to certain spells. Remember it is just a general list and I encourage you to find your own personal connections with the cards for spell casting, once you are more familiar with them.

- To create action- The Chariot, Ace/Eight of Wands
- To change a bad habit- Strength, Temperance, Judgement
- To find inspiration or creativity- The Magician, The Star, The Moon
- For success in a project-The Magician, The Sun, Ace of Wands
- For business success- The Sun, Three of Wands, Ace of Pentacles
- For a change- The Magician, Wheel of Fortune, Eight of Wands
- For fertility- The Empress, The Sun, Ten of Cups
- For help making a decision- The Hermit, The Star, Justice
- To break free from guilt and suffering- Judgement, The World, The Moon
- To bind your spells- The Hanged Man, Temperance, Two of Swords
- To promote healing and good health- The Sun, Strength, The Star, Three of Cups
- To enhance wisdom and knowledge- The Hermit, High Priestess, The Moon
- To bring about financial wealth- Ace/Six/Ten/Courts of Pentacles
- When you need protection- Temperance, The Chariot, Four of Wands
- For self-improvement- The Magician, Strength, The World
- To relieve stress and anxiety- Temperance, Ace/Four of Cups

HOW EXACTLY DO YOU CREATE A SPELL?

If you have read my other books, you probably know how much I love my analogies and cooking. So, creating a spell is just like creating your own recipe. You might find a recipe for lasagne and it turns out OK, and this could happen when you use a prewritten spell. But when you tweak the ingredients to match your own tastes, your result is going to excel—all you need is the basic outline. In this section, we are going to look at the basic outline for creating your own spell.

Your purpose and words

We have covered purpose and intention, but here we will put these into words to make sure you achieve the right outcomes. Spells rarely go wrong, but they don't always turn out as we had hoped, because we haven't taken the time to choose the correct vocabulary. A perfect example is when you cast a spell for more money and the next day your boss asks you to do overtime— you got more money, but probably not how you were thinking!

Avoid words like will and want, pain, fear, no, and contractions (can't, don't, etc.) Imagine how you would feel and what you would be doing if you were in the situation you wish to use the spell for. Your spell and your heart might say "I don't want to be fat", but a more specific and positive spell would be "I am strong and I am healthy".

Note the use of the present tense. When we cast our spell into the universe, it isn't able to decipher between the past, present, and the future. For the universe, all we have is now. The present tense tells both your subconscious and the universe that you are ready for this change now. For more inspiration, you can see the section called Affirmations in Healing Mantras.

This is not a Disney film, or any other spell to entertain the viewers, so don't feel that it has to rhythm or sound good to a tune. Spells are best not shared in case the energy of the person in some way impacts the spell.

Once you are happy with your words, say the spell out loud and get a sense of how it sounds to you. If you like it, write it down. Bit by bit, you can create your own personal book of spells, some you will be able to adjust for different moments in the future.

The materials you can use

I can't stress this part enough: materials will help, especially if you are a little skeptical or if you feel like you need some extra help from components that you can use in a spell, but they are not necessary. It hurt me to see one young gentleman spend practically all of his income on materials for his spells and he ended up in more problems than before. Build up a spell kit slowly—a herb here and a candle there. And if you can't afford it, all you need is your mind. In fact, psychic spells never require objects or even words, just focus! Here are some things that you may want to gradually add to your kit:

Stones and crystals- Each crystal has its own energy and power (red jasper for strength, black tourmaline for protection, amazonite for confidence). You can use them in protection circles and at the altar and later carry them around with you. Look for crystals that are attractive to you. Each type of crystal will come in different shapes, textures and tones. Also, you need to cleanse your crystal before you use it and recharge it. You can do both of these things by running your crystal under water or submerging it in fresh saltwater and then leaving it in the sunlight and moonlight to recharge—only if it isn't sensitive to water or light.

Herbs- I killed two birds with one stone and grew a little herb garden for spells and cooking, but many people find it more convenient to use dried herbs. Spearmint is ideal in spells for courage, garlic wards off negativity, and witch hazel can help mend a broken heart.

Essential Oils- Both oils and incense work in a similar way to herbs. As we breathe in the scents, our brain receives certain messages. Aromatherapy has been used in healing for centuries for the positive effects it can purportedly trigger.

Candles- The best thing about candles is that we all probably have one or two in our homes anyway. It is also very easy to buy such a huge range of candles, so you can choose curtain ones that really compliment your spell. A red, rose-scented candle is perfect for a love spell. You can also combine candles with essential oils to create your own scented candle. If you are calling upon the element of fire, a candle may help.

Other tools- I say the word cauldron and it immediately causes people to laugh and, because of commercialism, some people feel that it is a bit gimmicky, but it is the perfect tool for mixing herbs. You may choose to use a chalice instead. Again, a Tupperware pot will also work, so don't feel compelled to buy these tools if you can't or don't want to.

THE TIMING OF YOUR SPELL

Not every situation will allow us to wait for the perfect moment to cast a spell. This is more of a little bonus idea that can give your spell a boost of power. Also, not every spell will correlate to an ideal time. Each day of the week corresponds to a celestial body in the solar system and each planet has its own energetic properties:

- Monday- the Moon- psychic abilities, dreams, feminine energy, fertility, family
- Tuesday- Mars- energy, motion, independence, overcoming obstacles, handling conflicts
- Wednesday- Mercury- knowledge, creativity, communication, education, careers
- Thursday- Jupiter- business, finances, prosperity, legal issues
- Friday- Venus- love, relationships, sexuality, marriage, social status
- Saturday- Saturn- meditation, binding, overcoming habits, discipline, protection
- Sunday- The Sun- health, happiness, strength, general success

Finally, certain spells will benefit from the phase the Moon is in.

- New Moon- fresh beginnings, health and beauty, personal and/or professional growth
- Waxing Moon- motivation and inspiration, friendships, healing, personal strength, luck

- Full Moon- creativity, romance, love, fertility, psychic abilities and divination
- Waning Moon- overcoming bad habits or addictions, ending unhealthy relationships

BRINGING YOUR SPELL TOGETHER

Not wanting to moan about the negative impact of the film and TV industry again, but casting a spell isn't just about lighting a candle and chanting a rhyme. From start to finish, from my intention to researching the particular materials, I am rarely able to create a new spell in less than twenty to thirty minutes. Sometimes, it can take hours to get it right. Maybe those who practise spells and consult their own book can do it faster, but everybody would agree, you can't rush his process. Here is how I created a tarot wish spell:

I was having some difficulty with a friend and we couldn't see eye-to-eye on a moral matter. I wanted to bring some more harmony and joy back into our friendship. First, I collected:

- The Three of Cups card
- A white candle
- A clear quartz crystal
- A piece of white string

I felt that the following words summed up how I wanted our friendship to be:

"We are kind, intelligent, loving people and we understand each other's points of view".

Next, I tied the string around the card and placed it next to the candle that I then lit. I held the crystal in my hand and imagined myself and my friend in a happy celebration. Once I could clearly see us in this place, I said my spell. Then I left my crystal on top of the card until the candle burnt down. For the tarot Wish Spell, you need to put the card under your pillow while you sleep until your wish comes true.

A TAROT SPREAD FOR WITCHCRAFT

Another perfect union of tarot cards and witchcraft is the Pentagram spread. This spread looks at the four elements, plus a fifth—the spirit—which completes the five points of the pentagram.

Place the first card in the center. This card is the significator. The next five cards will be placed on each point of the star around the significator, say one o'clock, five o'clock, seven o'clock, ten o'clock and twelve o'clock. The card at one o'clock is the earth element and looks at our security. It will represent the problem you face. At five 0'clock, you have the element of air and relates to communication. It can provide insight into what others are telling you or how they are influencing you. The card at seven o'clock is connected to fire, and don't forget its ability to both create and destroy. This card may point to the doubts you have, an internal conflict, or even ways that you are destroying your own goals. Next, at ten 0'clock, we have water, the element of wisdom. There are things you can learn from this situation, more so when you listen to your intuition. Finally, at the highest point of the pentagram, we have the spirit element. This card will show you the end result of all your influences and ultimately the result if you remain on the path you are on.

USING TAROT CARDS TO HELP WITH CIRCLE CASTING

Circle casting or a magic circle is a little bit like a safety bubble. It's a psychic boundary that is cast for protection, but also serves for other purposes. Your magic circle will protect you by filtering the negative energies and only allowing the positive energy to pass through. It can also help by protecting you from distractions. This protective barrier will also help to contain your energy and even amplify it.

It is not necessary to cast a circle before a spell, but it is a ritual that many people follow, especially in the early days when we are developing our focus and intuition. If you do decide to cast a magic circle, here are the steps to follow:

1. Find a flat space that allows for a circle of about five to six feet in diameter. Indoors or outdoors is fine but it has to be somewhere quiet.
2. Identify the four cardinal points. Remember the sun rises in the east and sets in the west, or cheat and use the compass on your phone.
3. Take one tarot card that represents each of the four elements and place them on the corresponding cardinal point.
4. In each of the following, take a deep breath, relax, and feel a connection with the words:

- Face east and say, "Spirits of Air, I call on you"
- Turn south and say, "Spirits of Fire, I call on you"
- Turn west and say, "Spirits of Water, I call on you"
- Finally, face north and say, "mother Earth, I call on you", then draw the energy of the cosmos into your body and say, "Father Sky, I call on you".
- Finish by showing your gratitude and say, "Thank you, the circle is cast, blessed be".

1. Your sacred area is now ready for you to focus on your magic.
2. Once you have finished, be sure to repeat step four but instead, thank each of the elements, for example, "Air, you were here, and I thank you for this". When you have completed your circle of gratitude, the magic circle will release the energy that has been contained within it.

Congratulations on this mammoth amount of information you have taken on. As soon as I started to see the power of the images and symbols combined with the complexities of different spreads, I began to understand why seasoned professionals charged what they did for a tarot reading. Though it might feel like you are back at school and you will never remember it all, trust me, you will and it won't be long until you start to feel your intuition growing and you feel more confident in the decisions you make that will keep you on the right path to achieve your goals. Don't forget to have fun while you are doing this and to make it enjoyable, explore different methods and tools. The possibilities are infinite!

PART II

In the following part of *Modern Tarot*, we are going to break down each card and look at their general meanings. It will then be up to you to combine the general meaning with the information in Part 1, so for example, your particular question and spread.

When it comes to adding crystals, oils, herbs and candles, I am going to encourage you to do your own research. This isn't because I am lazy or I don't know. But from experience, when someone tells me this or that works, I go out and buy it, because my brain thinks I must need it. I don't want you to hear seventy-eight different crystals, oils, herbs and candles and feel an obligation to buy them. There are also many tools that can be used for more than one intention and so with your own experience and research, you will be able to create a personalised kit.

Don't forget that I am using my trusted Rider-Waite deck to describe the figures and images in each card. With that in mind, let's begin!

THE MAJOR ARCANA TAROT CARDS

The twenty-two Major Arcana cards are representations of our bigger life events or decisions. They represent a story of personal development and growth. The beginning of our journey starts with the innocence of youth.

The Fool

Don't assume the young man in the card is an idiot. The term 'fool' refers to his innocence or lack of judgement, emphasised by the puppy at his feet. Notice the white rose in his hand, another symbol of innocence and purity. He is not scared of anything on the edge of the cliff and the bright yellow sky radiates positivity. The bag over his shoulder suggests he is about to go on a journey, which could relate to your situation.

Reversed- Innocence comes with its problems. One more step and the Fool could be in danger. You should fear the next stage you are about to take on, but you should pay close attention to everything that is around you.

The Magician

The colours red and white are very predominant, along with the yellow background. The red and white show the purity of his magic. The Magician represents balance, with one hand pointing to the sky and the other to the earth, and completion, seen in the infinity symbol over his head. There is a cup, wand, sword, and pentacle on the table to his right—the righteous side. He is confident that he can bring these four symbols together as he looks ahead to the future. Like the Magician, you may have learnt new skills.

Reversed- The new skills you have learnt might be of the manipulative kind or perhaps you like to show others skills that you haven't mastered yet. If you know someone in your life who likes to control you, now might be the time to keep some distance.

The High Priestess

The High Priestess sits on a throne between a black and a white pillar, a sign of the beginning and the end. The High Priestess is a wise woman, seen by the large pearl on her crown. But this wisdom isn't necessarily what the world has taught her. Her robes are blue, the colour of intuition. This card points to our inner wisdom. Behind the throne, there is ripe fruit, a symbol of fertility and even prosperity. If you want to reach this place, know that your journey will have to take you through the pillars.

Reversed- In this position, you may find you aren't listening to your intuition or other people's opinions are having too much sway over you. Maybe someone has too much power over your thoughts and feelings, stopping your creativity.

The Empress

Just look at all of the symbols in this card! There is a stream, a field full of life, the symbol of Venus. The pomegranates on her robe are ready to harvest and her crown is made of stars, her link to the higher world. The Empress is comfortable with her beauty, her sexuality, and her creativity. While this card is often a sign of fertility, it also reminds us of the beauty in the world. It can also indicate the growth of material goods.

Reversed- We often assume that the reversal means a lack of fertility, but it is more likely that you are struggling to appreciate your femininity. If you draw this card upturned, you may need to start putting your needs before those of others.

The Emperor

The curved, comforting thrones of the High Priestess and the Empress have been replaced with a stone throne with straight, solid edges, much more masculine. The sky is a darker red, more like fire. The scepter in his right-hand looks like an ankh. The Emperor is obviously wiser than the Fool. There is a combination of intuition (just a hint of blue clothing) and protectiveness (his armour covering his feet and legs). This card means that you have probably gained and even though this might not be much, it still needs to be protected. You have what it takes to achieve your goals.

Reversed- Never abuse the power you have gained or be careful of acting as if you have more control over things than you actually do. Make sure you are setting the right example and not expecting others to do things you aren't willing to do.

The Hierophant

The Hierophant is the leader of the religious world, represented by the three tiers of his crown and the closeness to heaven. Two monks face him, one wearing a robe of red flowers, the other white. The Hierophant wears a combination of red and white. He seems to be educating the monks, perhaps performing a ceremony. Your education is important when this card appears. You may have a strong mentor in your life who will guide you on your journey.

Reversed- Depending on your situation, you might feel the need to rebel against the tradition that we often see in long-standing institutions. If your mentor doesn't have your best interests at heart, you may need to look in other directions for guidance.

The Lovers

It's hard not to see the correlation with Adam and Eve before the fall: they are naked, but show no shame, the trees are full of fruit and the snake is wrapped around the tree behind the woman. Some will see the river as a sign of the lovers coming together, others see the mountain between them as the challenges that keep them apart. The Sun offers warmth and the angel who towers over them has large red wings and purple robes. More often than not, this card points to romantic relationships, but it can also point to the other relationships in your life that are equal.

Reversed- Your relationship might be lacking balance, one of you may be feeling a lack of appreciation. Equality isn't limited to tasks in the house, it also extends to your love and caring for each other.

The Chariot

The man in the chariot looks as if he has accomplished things on his travels and you could see this as a sign that you will too. He is strong and determined, as well as in touch with his spiritual side. He has made his way alone and if you are determined, so can you. Will power drivers the chariot. On the front of the chariot, there are blue wings and in front, a black and a white sphinx. Look very closely at his shoulders. His armored suit appears to have two moons, one happy and the other sad.

Reversed- If you aren't moving at full speed, you might need an extra dose of courage, focus, or determination. Don't depend on others or material objects. The tie spent in looking for other people's approval could be better spent alone.

Strength

I love the combination of the beauty of the female figure with the masculinity of the lion. This combination is the key—we can all have a wild side and a feminine side. Despite being the king of the jungle, the lion still has his tail between his legs. Once again, we see three key colours, the woman is wearing white, the lion is red, and the sky is a bright yellow. Strength in this card doesn't come from tools or weapons but in will and kindness. You may be tempted to run from your challenges, but if you can be calm, you can succeed.

Reversed- Most problems we can overcome, but upturned, your troubles may be getting the better of you, because you don't feel like you have the power or ability to overcome them. Take care that the lions in your life aren't draining your strength.

The Hermit

There is a noticeable difference in the colours used in this card. The white hair suggests he has become wiser, while the white snow reminds of our innocence. His gray robes suggest he can now see things in more than just black and white. The Hermit is very much alone and although the scene looks quite dull, he is taking the time to self-reflect. The wand in his left hand suggests he knows things that others don't. This card often means you need to take a step back from the hustle and bustle so that you can find some peace.

Reversed- On the contrary, in the reserved position may imply that you are too focused on yourself. You may have alienated people, because you feel you are above them, but the Hermit chooses to be alone.

Wheel of Fortune

Where do we begin? You can see the four elements in the middle of the wheel, letters around the rim, four figures in the corners, each having a relationship with a zodiac sign. Hermes, a snake, and a sphinx are all balanced on the wheel. As the wheel turns, evil will fall as wisdom rises, but because life is one big cycle, as the wheel turns, evil will rise again. You will have ups and downs, but your luck will change, so it's important to stay positive.

Reversed- If you feel like you are down on your luck, you need to take responsibility for your actions to make a change. Some people get stuck in the past and aren't able to change. Be careful of negative attitudes and self-fulling prophecies.

Justice

Justice wears a rich red robe and a golden cloak. Her crown has just one blue gem in the middle and this is in line with the blue gem in her cloak—a more subtle sign of balance. In her left hand, she has the signature balanced scales, in her right, a double-edged sword. She is the definition of fairness, but the white shoe just appearing from under her robe is a reminder that we are innocent until proven guilty. If you feel like you have been treated unfairly, this might be rectified soon. Those who lie and cheat will get what is coming to them.

Reversed- I assumed that it would mean injustice, but no, it actually still implies justice, but that this isn't always clear and there may be a price to pay. Justice is the right thing, but it may come at a cost or a sacrifice.

The Hanged Man

The name always brought a bit of a chill down my spine, but don't assume the worst. First of all, the young man is hanging from one foot. He has gold shoes, red trousers and a blue shirt. A halo glows around his head. The sky is quite bleak, but there are green leaves growing off the cross he is tied to. The card can have different meanings for different readers. Some will assume that his hands are tied behind his back and it's a helpless situation. Others feel that he doesn't look distressed. The halo suggests he is spiritually aware, but he could be difficult to trust with his hands behind his back. His bent leg looks like the number four, a symbol of the four elements.

Reversed- You need to free yourself from what is restricting you. Perhaps you feel like you don't have what it takes to untie yourself. If you don't take action or make a decision, some else may do it for you.

Death

It's normal to think the worst—both the name and the imagery can be shocking. Drawing the Death card isn't a sign that someone is about to die! Instead, it points to the end of something or that you are heading for a big change. Death is riding a white horse and the black banner has a white rose, signs of purity. Although the people seem to be working through the stages of grief, there is still plenty of life in the imagery. There is a river, trees, and the Sun still rises, so life goes on even after a change. The King is dead, but looking at the bigger picture—a new King will take his place. This card is an important message to accept change.

Reversed- A change is still coming and as with death, you can't try to bargain. You might be scared of the change and so you try to avoid it. Burying your head in the sand could mean you aren't prepared for the change.

Temperance

Temperance has one foot in a river, in touch with her emotions, and the other is grounded. She is wearing a long white robe and has large red wings. She has a triangle on her chest and a circle on her forehead. She is pouring water from one cup to another. A path goes up through the middle of a field to the mountain where the Sun rises. Temperance wants you to focus on a path that doesn't take you to either extreme, neither too much of something nor not enough. This is how you will find the knowledge you need and peace.

Reversed- It is possible that this card is pointing to an imbalance or lack of harmony.

You should look at ways to fix this before trying to make other changes in your life. Don't get stuck in a situation where you do nothing, because you don't want to rock the boat.

The Devil

Like Death, we often jump to the wrong conclusion with this card. The Devil is half man, half goat, with the face of a lion and bat-like wings. You can also see an inverted pentagram above its head. There is a man and a woman in front of the devil. They are chained to the chair the Devil is perched on. They both have horns and tails, although the woman's tail has grapes and the man's tail has fire. Some may see this as signs of food and sex, or lust, two of our main desires. The Devil isn't trying to control the people. The black background is a reminder that we all have a dark side, but it's up to us to create balance, rather than ignore it.

Reversed- Don't assume it's a sign that you aren't lustful or passionate. In fact, it could be that you need to learn how to control your sexuality more. Relationships might be hard for you because of this.

The Tower

If you thought Death and the Devil were bad cards, the Tower will shock you. The images are shocking and this is the least favourite of all the tarot cards. The tall tower is situated on top of a mountain, which is falling away. It has been hit by lightning and the fire is causing people to fall from the higher windows. A rich man and a poor man are falling, a sign that nature knows no boundaries. Changes are coming and they will be disruptive, but can make way for a fresh start.

Reversed- You could probably be dealing with your problems in the wrong manner and it might even be making things worse. Even bad situations have something that we can learn.

The Star

The Star is refreshingly positive after the Tower. The bright blue sky has a large

eight-pointed star with seven smaller stars around it. There is a naked woman and, like Temperance, she has one foot in the water. She is pouring water from one of her jugs onto the land and new life is growing. I love this card, because the meaning is simple. If we have nothing to lose, there is nothing holding us back. If you share the little you have, you will be rewarded with more.

Reversed- You should feel more confident about your plans and decisions, maybe it would help if you listened to your instincts more. This will also help shift the feeling that you are stuck.

The Moon

The Moon has very similar colors to the Star. There is water, green land and a bright blue sky. The Star has been replaced with a Moon and the face is the Moon is looking down on the world. There are two towers with a very narrow path from a dog and a wolf leading to the middle of the towers. These animals represent our tame and wild sides. There is a crawfish leaving the water heading towards the dog and the wolf. Depending on your situation, you may be feeling brave or unaware of the danger that might be in front of you.

Reversed- If you are worried, nervous, or confused, you need to work through these feelings. Keep your feet on the ground because not being in touch with the real word may cause you more problems.

The Sun

It makes sense that the Sun is such a positive card: I know I feel better on a sunny day! Even the young boy riding the horse looks as if he is full of happiness. It seems like he is celebrating that he has made it over the wall behind him. On the wall, there are four sunflowers, all facing the boy. The boy is holding a large orange banner. This card often means you have succeeded in overcoming an obstacle. Your problems are behind you and you can look forward to some fun in life.

Reversed- If you are lacking confidence, you should know that trying new things can help. If your confidence is a little too high, remember that it may not last. Don't get trapped dwelling on the negative, because you might miss all the good in the world.

Judgement

All the people on Earth are ashen grey and looking up towards an angel in the sky. They are all naked and they have no possessions and are therefore equal. What has happened in their lives is now irrelevant. The angel has red and purple wings and blue clothes. He is wise, pure, and calm. His trumpet has a St. George's flag and it is traditionally a trumpet that sounds for announcements. This is a period of resurrection, reflection and new beginnings.

Reversed- There is probably a lot of self-doubt and you are possibly being too hard on yourself. It's likely that you are making the wrong decisions. Don't forget that your actions have consequences and at some point, you will have to face Judgement.

The World

The final card completes the cycle. A woman floats in the center of the card, the sky blue behind her. Her legs are facing the right, but she is looking to the left. She is surrounded by a green wreath with a red ribbon on top. More symbols include the angel's head, the ox, the eagle and the lion in the four corners. They represent the four Gospels, four of the zodiac signs and stability. You have reached a significant time in life and this cycle that you have completed has made you stronger and better.

Reversed- Quite literally, in the reverse, you may have things that are incomplete or that you have missed opportunities that were offered to you. Sometimes this is because of your own fear or doubts, but it could mean there is someone in your life who is preventing you from moving forward.

I have just touched on some of the images in the Major Arcana cards. Each card can have a different meaning for you, depending on your question. Just remember that these cards are more related to those bigger questions in life, so aim to look at the bigger picture.

THE CUPS SUIT

A spread that is dominated by cups is pointing to your emotions; perhaps there are conflicts that need to be resolved, matters of the heart. The cups are related to the element of water and I like to imagine our emotions being able to flow as water does. There may be relations with those who have a water zodiac sign—Pisces, Cancer, and Scorpio.

The Ace of Cups

One cup sits in the palm of a white hand that seems to be coming out of a cloud. Water flows out of the cup into a body of water below. Pay attention to the five streams of water leaving the cup and the twenty-five droplets. The white dove is carrying a Eucharist in its beak, maybe like it is going to drop it into the cup. There is a W on the cup, or it could be an M— woman or man. Lilies float in the water and there is green land in the distance. This card encourages you to use your imagination, instead of only looking from your own perspective.

Reversed- It's possible that you are hiding from your true feelings or struggling to express them. There might be someone in your life who can't control their emotional outbursts.

The Two of Cups

It's a happy scene between a man and a woman. It seems like a ceremony; it reminds me of when couples link arms to drink champagne on their wedding day. The woman wears blue and white, while the man is in yellow and black, a less frequent combination. This card is very much about the bond between two people, as there is nobody else in the card. Not only are there two cups but also two snakes and the lion head has two wings.

Reversed- Unfortunately, upturned often points to problems in a relationship. The disagreements might be so bad that if you don't make a change, there is little hope.

The Three of Cups

The Three of Cups is reminding us not to forget the groups and communities in our lives. Three women are dancing in a circle. Instead of the handbags in the center, the focus of the women is their raised cups, arms linked to show the closeness of their friendship. At this moment, the women have all they need to be happy, and that is each other and so you shouldn't be trying to achieve things alone.

Reversed- It could be that you are feeling lonely or that the dynamics of your group aren't quite right and you feel left out. Don't feel like you should change to fit in with the crowd.

The Four of Cups

We go back to solitude with the Four of Cups, but not in a bad way. A man is sitting under a tree, with crossed arms and legs. He looks like he is contemplating things and doesn't pay attention to the hand coming out of the cloud, offering him a cup. The other three cups are in a row in front of him. Often, this card points to missing out on opportunities, because we aren't able to look beyond ourselves. It's good to spend some time alone, but not so much that you aren't able to see the amazing things that are in front of you.

Reversed- Like the man, you might be ignoring emotional ties. You may have an emotional opportunity in front of you, but you need to make an effort to get it.

The Five of Cups

There is a bit of a darker scene with this card, both in colours and meaning. The sky is now grey and a woman wearing a long black robe has her head bowed low and her back to us. Three of the cups have been knocked over, and red and green liquid pours out of them, a sign of loss of life and magic. It indicates a loss of some kind or maybe a failure, but there is a great deal of pain as a result. The woman could refill the cups or cross the bridge to go home, but instead, she takes the time to grieve her loss.

Reversed- You have moved past this time of grief and it's time to start moving on. It's normal to still feel sad, but the other two cups are still upright, a sign that you should concentrate on them.

The Six of Cups

There is so much yellow in this card that you can instantly see a different tone to the Five of Cups. There is a boy offering a girl a cup with a white flower in it. There is another cup behind him and four more on the ground, all with a white flower in them. I like the mixture of innocence and purity, yet the children are in a city and there is a guard walking away from them, so there is still the need for protection. This card reminds us of the joy of children and the simple things in life, like having fun.

Reversed- Somebody may have a habit of crushing spirits, because they are so skeptical of everything. It can also suggest a childhood that wasn't quite so happy. Know that holding onto your past isn't healthy.

The Seven of Cups

The Seven of Cups is all about the choices that we have in front of us and how they can be rather intimidating at times. A man is facing seven cups in a cloud, although we can only see a silhouette of him. Each cup has a different symbol, a female head, a person covered in a white cloth, a snake, a dragon, a wreath, gems, and a tower. It's difficult to decide which is the right cup to choose because there could be positive and negative consequences with each.

Reversed- The choices you have aren't as varied as you think. You might be chasing a dream or perhaps doubting what it is that you really want.

The Eight of Cups

I have mixed feelings about this card. There are five stacked cups and another three in a different pile. The five represent sadness and the three happiness, so all is not lost. The Sun sits in the crescent of the Moon. The face shows no emotion. A man wearing red has crossed the river and has left the cups behind. He is about to start his new journey and it feels like he has accepted that he needs to leave the emotional baggage in his past.

Reversed- I feel a connection with the Seven of Cups. You might feel like you have made the wrong choice and you are trying to move forward the best you can. You may not be ready to start a new phase in life or just refusing to start.

The Nine of Cups

There is a man sitting with a semi-circle of nine cups behind him. He is wearing a white robe, yellow shoes and a red hat. He is happy and because the cups are about emotions, it's not material things that put the smile on his face. He doesn't keep his cups close to him or even look at them. He is happy to share because he isn't worried that his good fortune can be taken from him. He isn't a king, so he has had to work hard to get what he wanted, and so will you.

Reversed- You may well be missing something in your life or you haven't got what you wanted. You might be putting on a show trying to convince others of your happiness and success, but this comes at a cost, maybe even an obsession or addiction in other areas of your life.

The Ten of Cups

This is probably my favorite of the Cups suit. There is a huge rainbow with ten cups in it. The rainbow shines over the roof of a house, a river, a sandy beach and a family. The man holds the woman around the waist as they reach up to the sky. The children are happily playing nearby. The family have received good fortune, dreams have come true and they are grateful for this. They have had their difficult times but everything turned out all right.

Reversed- You may have had a string of bad luck and or your idea of success is slightly off and it's impossible to feel happy. Start looking at the smaller things in life to find happiness.

The Page of Cups

A rather elegant-looking man dressed in blue and pink is standing on a sandy beach with the water behind him. The cup is in his right hand but more interestingly, there is a blue fish inside the cup. It even looks as if the two are having a conversation. The fish is a symbol of new beginnings, creativity and imagination. Listening to the fish is like listening to the inspiration that pops up in us every now and again.

Reversed- More often than not, in this position, you are lacking creativity or you are using it for things that you shouldn't. It's important that you concentrate your efforts in turning the dream into a reality.

The Knight of Cups

The knight in shining armor riding a white horse is a cliché, but there is a lot more detail t0 this image. First of all, he is the most romantic of the four knights; the red fish on his cloak shows his creativity and passion. But the wings on his helmet and boots point to his connection to the spiritual world. The land around him is dry, with just a river in his path. Perhaps in preparation for his long journey, he is going to fill up his cup.

Reversed- Take care not to ignore the feelings of others because you are wrapped up in your emotions. You may feel like you need to be more creative or it's possible that you have some imaginative impulses that are making you uncomfortable.

The Queen of Cups

The Queen sits on a throne that might be on an island. Her throne is engraved with cherubs, another connection to children, angels, and the higher world. She is wearing blue and white and she holds her cup in her hand. The cup isn't the same as the other cups. Maybe I am a little too imaginative, but it looks like a little robot. The point is that the cub has a lid. It is mysterious and maybe she wants to keep a lid on her thoughts and feelings. The Queen looks at her cup lovingly and will love and help those around her.

Reversed- Sometimes, this position points to someone who isn't in control of their feelings or their imagination. Other times it shows a person who struggles to understand other people's emotions, this may cause problems like manipulation and emotional vacuums in relationships.

The King of Cups

For a court card, it's not as royal as you would think. The King sits on a throne that is in the middle of a rough sea. The ship and the fish are being thrown around. He is wearing a blue robe and a yellow cloak with red trimmings. He has a cup in one hand and a scepter in the other. He is not bothered by the rough waters around him; in fact, he seems quite calm. One foot is close to the water. He doesn't fear his emotions; quite the reverse, he is in control of them. He is thoughtful and will listen to the thoughts and opinions of others before making a decision.

Reversed- Remember the importance of boundaries and not getting your feelings confused with those of others. This could be a sign that you need to increase your emotional intelligence so that you are better at coping with other people's emotions.

So, the main theme that runs through the Cups suit is our emotions and learning to find balance in expressing them. Our imagination and creativity are also important. The strongest colour throughout the cards is blue and we can see this with both the clothes and the water. There are other smaller details, like the wings and angels, that remind us of the importance of spirituality.

THE PENTACLES SUIT

These fourteen cards look at the day-to-day parts of our lives, such as our health, career and financial situation. On a deeper level, they can explain more about our self-esteem and how we view ourselves. The Pentacles are associated with the earth element, being grounded and our own growth. The Pentacles can give insights into those in our life who are earth signs, like Taurus, Virgo and Capricorn.

The Ace of Pentacles

As with the Ace of Cups, we see another hand appearing from a cloud with a pentacle cupped in it. The hand is white while the cloud blends in with the blue sky. The pentacle looks like it could be the Sun and even the hand shines brightly. There is a path between green fields and it leads to bushes with an archway. The pentacle could be leading the way to something better on the other side. You should think about what you can hold in your hands and what this will enable you to achieve.

Reversed- In the upturned position, you might have missed opportunities or turned a blind eye to small opportunities that you thought weren't worth it. Don't underestimate the value of money.

The Two of Pentacles

It's the ridiculous-looking hat the man is wearing that you may spot first. This is loosely related to the ships on the rough waves behind the man. Regardless of the troubles behind him or what others think of him, his concentration remains on keeping his pentacles balanced. His clothes are red and orange, meaning magic and enthusiasm. The green infinity loop around the pentacles is a sign of life. If he can maintain control over his pentacles, he can stay happy.

Reversed- There could be some imbalance in your life, financially, career, home life, or even your emotions. Rather than worrying what others think of you, take some time to figure out how to get more control again.

The Three of Pentacles

There is something about this card that reminds me of a Ken Follett book. A young man is standing on a bench working on a cathedral arch. The three pentacles are at the top of the arch. He is talking to a monk and perhaps an architect as he has plans in his hands. There is a balance between wisdom, age and skill. If you draw this card, it shows that you may need to listen to others if you want to create something amazing.

Reversed- The warning here is "more haste, less speed". If you go at things too quickly, you are unlikely to succeed. You should also listen to the advice of those who know more. If you feel like people don't listen to your advice, you need to work on your confidence.

The Four of Pentacles

This is another card full of balance and control. A man is sitting on a stone in front of a colourful city. He has one pentacle on his head, another between his arms and one under each foot. It's hard to tell if the man is taking control of the pentacles or if they are preventing him from going anywhere. It's clear that he doesn't want to share his wealth, but this doesn't make him greedy. It may suggest that he is more concerned about material possessions than he should be.

Reversed- Money can't buy happiness and it shouldn't be more important than your loved ones. If you aren't that well off financially, it doesn't mean that you aren't fortunate, and at the same time, don't overestimate what wealth you do have.

The Five of Pentacles

Until now, we have seen images of people managing their wealth, but the Five of Pentacles has two poor people struggling through the snow. What's more, the man is on crutches. They are wearing the right colour clothes—blue, green, orange and red—but they are torn. The five pentacles are in a stained-glass window, maybe a church. They almost look like they are in the form of a tree. Without wealth, life is hard, but there is help, if the couple chooses to go inside the church.

Reversed- You have probably gone through the worst of your hard times and although it's not quite over, there is light at the end of the tunnel. If you are becoming more financially stable, you can learn to be a little more relaxed with your spending.

The Six of Pentacles

The couple on the floor are dressed the same way as the couple in the Five of Pentacles, but there is no snow and they have learnt how to ask for help. A man is giving them coins, but in his other hand, he holds scales. The six pentacles are in the sky around him, however, they aren't balanced. This card isn't necessary about balance, but more about appreciating the fact that not everyone is equal.

Reversed- You may be working incredibly hard, but someone else is spending your money. This could lead you not to trust this person and stop being so generous. It could also mean you are gaining wealth but a loved one is losing it.

The Seven of Pentacles

I find this quite a reassuring card. There is a man looking over his grape vines. Maybe he is watching them grow or maybe he is trying to decide if it is the right time to harvest the grapes. The pentacles are on the grape vines. One pentacle is one the ground, perhaps a sign that they are almost ready. This card is all about patience. He has his tool, he has worked hard and things are growing. Now it's about waiting for the right moment.

Reversed- It is quite the opposite when upturned—a lack of patience or hard work. Instead of focusing on one thing, you might be trying to juggle too many and you aren't seeing the rewards.

The Eight of Pentacles

A carpenter is working on a pentacle. Six are already placed on a tree and the eighth is on the ground, ready to be put up next. His blue shirt suggests he is calm, while his red stockings imply he is passionate about his work. He is alone, but this only enables him to focus more. We don't know if he will keep the pentacles or give them to someone. The point is that he is making an effort and he takes pride in his work. It may also mean that you need to keep perfecting your skills until you get your work right.

Reversed- Watch out for becoming a perfectionist: you may end up going overboard and destroying your hard work. In this position, it might suggest that you need to work on developing your skills.

The Nine of Pentacles

This time, we see a woman with the pentacles on grapevines. This difference is, the man only had one bush, whereas the woman has a field full of ripe grapes, a sign of plenty. The falcon on her hand points to her complete control and because of her control, she is able to create so much. She is happy, and for the time being, she can enjoy her rewards. But a tiny snail is moving towards her crop. It has the ability to destroy it, so remember that nothing lasts forever.

Reversed- You can't wait for others to provide you with wealth or you need a little more self-control to succeed. Enjoy everything you have right now rather than concerning yourself too much about the future.

The Ten of Pentacles

My OCD kicks in a little with this card. There is an awful lot happening and there seems to be tons of imagery. Plus, the pentacles are just on the card, not randomly placed (look for the shape of the Kabbalah Tree of Life) but almost like they are stickers you want to peel off to see what's underneath. Probably the most significant symbol is the old man watching his family. He has worked for his wealth and you can see this by his extravagant cloak. Now it is time to sit back and enjoy his family. His faithful dogs look up to him respectfully.

Reversed- You haven't found the stability in life you are hoping for. There could be problems with your wealth because of your family or your business/career. It may also indicate that someone doesn't want to pass the baton on to the next person, whether that's in terms of knowledge or wealth.

The Page of Pentacles

A young man stands in a green field with a forest in the distance. To his left, there is bare land, ready for him to sow his seeds and plant his dreams. Behind the care field, you can see a mountain, a symbol of stability. He is holding his pentacle high, perhaps planning his fortune. The sky is the same colour as the pentacle, a good sign that fortune surrounds him. This card shows all the signs of new life. The man is young, but that doesn't mean that he can't achieve his dreams, as long as he stays focused.

Reversed- This is a strong indicator that you are being impractical, that your goals are too high or you don't have the confidence to achieve them. Don't allow yourself to take the easy road, or feel defeated when faced with obstacles.

The Knight of Pentacles

The Knight of Pentacles shows the next step after the Page. The fields have been ploughed and the dream is becoming a reality. The Knight of Pentacles still has to work hard to take care of them, but his black horse shows that he is serious about his work. The horse has a sprig of oak on the front of his head, a sign of courage. Both knight and horse stand determined, maybe even stubborn to succeed. The choices have been made and now it is a case of sticking to them.

Reversed- You need to find the motivation or courage to take the first steps. You might not be ready for the hard work ahead of you. If people around you don't share your enthusiasm, don't be disappointed.

The Queen of Pentacles

There are similarities with the Queen of Cups, but instead of the water, the Queen of Pentacles is surrounded by land and flowers. She also holds the pentacle a little more lovingly, almost maternally. Like with the page and the knight, the pentacle is the same colour as the sky. The red roses growing match her red robe. She has everything that she wanted and feels stable within her own life. Now she is dedicated to caring for something else.

Reversed- This is about not being in the right position to care for someone else or for the responsibilities that come with being an adult. You may also feel like you are giving so much, but not receiving an equal amount.

The King of Pentacles

The King's robe blends into the flowers that are growing all around him. He is sitting on a black throne, a connection maybe to the knight's black horse. The castle behind him emphasises his wealth. There are two gold oxen on his throne, a sign of his stubbornness. The pentacle rests on his knee. His armour shows that he is an active king. He has worked, he has practiced control and now he can enjoy his wealth. The same is available to you, if you work hard like the king and remain humble.

Reversed- it is possible that you are acting like the king but you haven't behaved in the same way. Look for solutions to your problems and don't let fear or pride get the better of you.

While the general theme of the Pentacles suit is money, I think that when you start to relate the various images, it goes beyond what's in your bank account. This suit is about our ambitions and in a few readings, I have got the sense that the cards reinforced a goal I had, but encouraged me and even helped me to see if I needed to work on my abilities or my self-esteem. It's also a good suit to remind us that sharing, helping, and giving to others is an important part of our journey.

THE SWORDS SUIT

In this chapter, we are going to take a closer look at the mind, thoughts and beliefs and the balance between intellect and power. There is a lot of action associated with the Swords and this action can be used for either good or bad. Because the Swords are linked to the element of air, they reflect Aquarians, Libras and Geminis.

The Ace of Swords

Our hand is back, holding a sword that points straight up. Unlike the other clouds that the hand appears from, this cloud is darker than the sky. There is a crown around the top of the sword and laurel leaves hang from the crown. The crown isn't held in place. Only the tip of the sword goes through the crown, highlighting the sharpness of the mind. The hand could be offering the sword or it could be challenging someone to take it. If you choose to take it, you hold the power to create or destroy. Your journey should include the search for truth.

Reversed- You might find it hard to clearly visualise your goals. You are intelligent but you may not be using it in the right way. Organise your opinions so that you have the confidence to share them.

The Two of Swords

Despite the two swords, I still feel that the images are quite calming. There is a woman dressed in white with yellow shoes, she is sitting on a white stone and the ground is also white. The blue water is separated from the sky by just a small amount of raised land. Only the Moon is in the sky. She has a sword in each hand, her arms are crossed and she is blindfolded. She has a decision to make but she has to rely on her intellect and intuition.

Reversed- The decision you need to make will be harder because all the information isn't available. If you feel you aren't brave enough to make the right decision, have faith in your intelligence.

The Three of Swords

It's true that this is not a good card, but remember that tarot guides only provide insight: they don't determine your future. There is a heart in the grey sky, and it's raining. The three swords are going straight through the heart. This card points to loss, possibly a death, or maybe it's the knowing that you won't be able to achieve your goals. It's hard to know what to do next when there is so much sadness.

Reversed- Unfortunately, there is still a lot of sadness, but reversed would indicate that you don't want to accept the situation. You keep going over your memories and it's probably going to leave you feeling exhausted.

The Four of Swords

After the Three of Swords, you might be nervous about the tomb in this card. The tomb is of a man, it's gold and there is a sword on the side. The other three swords are on the wall, but look as if they could hurt him if they fell. There is a stained-glass window, perhaps happy memories of his past. This card isn't about death, it's about taking a moment to be alone, step back and process what your mind is telling you, learn what you actually want before moving forward.

Reversed- Your mind is working overtime, which makes it difficult to take the break you need. Others won't leave you in peace to think. You might even be scared of what you find out if you take time to process your thoughts.

The Five of Swords

There are three men, one wearing green, red and orange, and the other two yellow. The man in green holds three swords, the other two are lying on the ground in front of the other men, who are walking away. The smile on the man's face suggests he has won this battle. The irony is, what can he do with three swords when he only has two hands? The other men are still alive, so the battle has more likely hurt their pride or social standing. The message here is that even if you are stronger and smarter than others, you can't risk pushing them out of your life.

Reversed- As with the double-edge of all the swords, winning this battle might mean that you have lost another—or even the metaphorical war. Perhaps you have reached a point where you don't want to be alone.

The Six of Swords

It's another card that is a little bleak. Even the water isn't blue, but rather an icy grey. There is a man paddling a boat with a woman and child sitting in front of him. We can't see their faces. The six swords are stood upright in front of the boat, but they haven't caused a leak. To the left, the water is calm, to the right it's rough, hinting at mixed emotions. The family has no possessions and we can't see what is ahead of the boat, but they know they need action to move forward.

Reversed- The only way is forward, but you are reluctant; maybe you even have a slight hope of going back to how things were. It's also possible that there are things preventing you from moving forward.

The Seven of Swords

The Seven of Swords is brighter and even a little amusing. There is a man with five swords in his arms. He is either running or maybe tiptoeing. There are two swords behind him. It's hard to tell if he is looking back at the swords he has left behind or the camp he has left. He hasn't spotted the three soldiers in the distance, so perhaps he hasn't completely escaped. This card shows determination, perhaps betrayal, selfishness and that you shouldn't be too quick to assume you have gotten away with things.

Reversed- There might be some disagreements ahead of you and the outcome may not be positive. Watch out for passive-aggressive behaviour, creating drama so that people can see you aren't happy.

The Eight of Swords

We are back to the grey sky with the Eight of Swords. A woman is tied up and blindfolded. The eight swords look like a fence behind her, but she isn't tied to them. Although there is water under her, her feet aren't touching it, implying her problems aren't related to her feelings. It's obvious that the woman is restricted in her choices, but if she wants to break free, she will touch the water and therefore her emotions. Her mind might be blocked but her legs are still free. We shouldn't always rely on our intelligence to solve problems.

Reversed- In this position, it's likely that you've been through a situation where you needed something other than your intelligence. You may have tried something and it didn't work out as you had hoped. Don't be scared to try again.

The Nine of Swords

Our first thought is of the woman who is sitting upright in her bed as if she has had a bad dream. The swords are lined up behind her, but you can't tell if they are in the black sky or they are hanging on a black wall. There is a lot of symbolism if you look closely: the blanket is covered in roses and astrological signs, the bed has carvings of a fight. Her pillow is yellow. Still, the main point is the nightmare, the fears we can't control.

Reversed- One meaning could be that you now understand what you are scared of or what is troubling you. Alternatively, your negative emotions are so overwhelming that you can't get out of your distress.

The Ten of Swords

Again, not the most positive-looking card. There is a man on the ground, the ten swords stabbing him from his head to the base of his spine, and there is a red cloth draped over him. The mountains are blue and the yellow sky is being overtaken by the black clouds. The worst really has happened and this is the end of the tragedy. Whatever you have been doing mentally hasn't been working and it's time to make a change.

Reversed- The worst has still happened but you are not facing this. Try not to waste your energy fixing something that can't be fixed and remember that you need to move on from the suffering instead of getting stuck there.

The Page of Swords

We are back to a positive image with the Page of Swords. A young man stands on a hill, the wind in his hair and his sword held up ready for action. He may have had to fight to get to where he is or maybe he is ready to defend his position. This position on top of the hill is an advantageous one. His yellow clothes show his intelligence and his red boots, passion. This card represents the creation of thoughts and new ideas. It represents honesty and searching for justice. The page will need courage for his journey, through the wind and to find the truth.

Reversed- You may need to work on your mind to develop your thoughts. If you can learn new things, you will see a great improvement in your self-esteem and stop feeling like you don't match up to others.

The Knight of Swords

The knight is full of action and it's motivating. His horse is at full speed and he holds his sword high in the air. He is full of courage and nothing is going to stop him. The knight passes the same windblown tree that was behind the Page of Swords. The knight has his idea and he is determined to see it through. This card is telling you that if you want a change or something new, you will need the same enthusiasm and drive as the knight.

Reversed- You might have the idea but you need to be focused more to take the first step. You are lacking the bravery that the knight has, or perhaps you listen too much to people who don't believe in your abilities.

The Queen of Swords

The Queen of Swords is different to the other queens. There are no flowers or greenery growing and she doesn't look at her sword lovingly. The queen sits on a throne, and her hand is raised as if she is addressing the crowd. The throne is white, so are her robes. There are clouds behind her, making her look like a goddess. The river behind her implies her decisions aren't affected by her emotions. She relies on her own intelligence and people respect her for this. If you draw this card, you should find the same confidence the queen has.

Reversed- In this position it might be a sign that you find it easier to follow others than make you own choices. You might not always be honest and perhaps put your foot in it at times.

The King of Swords

It's almost like we are looking at a front-on version of the queen. The king is sitting on his throne with his sword in the same hand and same position as the queen. The angel in his crown shows his connection to the divine. He is intelligent and fair, but he also looks quite stern. He doesn't put up with people who are going to waste his time. He is aware that he needs to set the right example. Like the queen, he will not consider emotions when making choices. He will look at all perspectives to make decisions.

Reversed- It might be possible that you are using your intelligence for the wrong reasons. Unlike the stern king, you take the rules so seriously that you may appear a little bullyish.

There are a lot of ups and downs with the Swords suit. There is some amazing imagery that inspires and makes you want to get up and create new plans. There are also quite a few dark cards, but I think it's so important not to jump to the wrong conclusions. I know how easy it is to assume the worst, instead of taking a moment to look closer at the symbols and messages and relate them back to your questions. I suppose the whole point of the Swords suit is to use your intelligence over emotions and this applies to the positive and the negative cards.

THE WANDS SUIT

The wands are all about what makes us who we are, our consciousness, our ego, and our energy. They give us insight into our strengths and ambitions, as well as highlighting our intuition and even our sexuality, which makes sense, as they are linked to the element of fire. This suit can represent the fire zodiac signs—Leo, Sagittarius and Aries.

The Ace of Wands

Our familiar white hand appears from a large gray cloud holding a wand. New leaves are sprouting from the wand and the scene below is inviting. There is a river flowing through green fields. There are mountains and maybe a castle in the background. The river separates the hand from the mountains. The wand is an offering, an offering of a new beginning that is different from the path that others are on.

Reversed- Even though you know the right thing to do is start afresh, you are worried about this because you are going to have to overcome your fear of doing new things. You might not feel you have the time or the knowledge but don't listen to these excuses.

The Two of Wands

A man holds one wand in his hand and another stands upright next to him. He is standing at the top of what looks like a castle and I like to think it's the castle in the Ace of Wands, because there is also a green field and a river. The man has a globe in his other hand. What might be more important are the roses and lilies below the wand, the balance between passion and purity or between our determination and letting things go. This card wants us to think of the plan behind the action we are about to take.

Reversed- Try not to rush things and end up making mistakes, but then don't go to the other extreme where you are trying harder than necessary and it takes longer. Even reversed, this card points to balance.

The Three of Wands

The sky is bright gold and so is the land, but there isn't the same growth as before. A man stands overlooking the dry land, one wand is to his left and the other two to the right. The road ahead seems more positive than with the previous wands, there are no ships fighting the waves and although this man doesn't hold the globe; the future's still bright. If you draw this card, it's a good sign to keep going, because what lies ahead is positive.

Reversed- You know your plan, but you may lack the courage to start. It is also possible that you have started a new journey, even though you aren't completely sure where you are going. Even if you aren't happy about this new direction, know that you are heading the right way.

The Four of Wands

This is a lovely card: the sky is still bright and the four wands are draped with a canopy, inviting you to the celebration. The couple might be celebrating their wedding; there are a few guests there already. The large castle in the background represents purity and stability. It's a sign of places and people that make you feel welcome. The wed couple has made the decision to be happy; you should do the same.

Reversed- Maybe you can't find peace or you don't feel welcome in certain situations. You might feel like your life is unstable because of some problems you have with people.

The Five of Wands

I always feel like there is such a huge contrast with the previous card, but not necessarily in a bad way. First, the sky is bright blue. Second, there are five men, each with a wand. It might be a fight or a game, but it's important that each man is using his wand in a different way. If they are trying to work together, it's obviously not working. This new group of people have a goal or a mission, but it suggests the first steps towards becoming organised isn't always easy.

Reversed- If you find it hard to work with a particular group, it could be because you can't concentrate or you aren't happy with the group dynamics. You might be tempted to go it alone, but if you can stay patient, you can benefit from the group once it becomes stronger.

The Six of Wands

We have lots of great colours in this card. The white horse covered in a green cloak, the man riding the horse has a red robe with a touch of yellow underneath and orange trousers. Five men to his side carry their wands, the man holding the sixth with a wreath on the top and another on his head. This man seems to have successfully organised the chaotic group of men and is now being praised for his success. If you have achieved something and are reaping the rewards, remember that it may or may not last.

Reversed- It can indicate that someone is overly arrogant about their achievements or that they are expecting recognition for something they haven't done. If this isn't you, be careful that your humility doesn't let others take advantage of you.

The Seven of Wands

The man looks as if he has been working hard to create a barrier with six wands and he is ready to place the seventh. Whatever the man achieved in the Six of Wands, this man is determined to protect. By his position, he doesn't seem to have much choice. What I love about this card is how he is balanced over a small stream, yet he is wearing odd shoes—a sign that he is confident, but that there is still part of him that is cautious. Consider all of the things you have that need protecting, even things like your reputation.

Reversed- It's likely that there have been times that you didn't defend yourself, either because you couldn't or it was easier not to. Try not to rely too much on what others think or to be too sensitive to what others think.

Eight of Wands

Like the Seven of Wands, there is a bright blue sky and green land. This is one of the few cards that doesn't have any people. There are just eight wands, parallel in the sky. We aren't sure if they are all moving down to the ground or up to the sky, but they are able to move in any direction they wish. The freedom of the wands is what we need to learn from. This card is a sign that we need to get rid of all that weighs us down so that we can be free.

Reversed- It's hard to find the right pace. You may not have the same enthusiasm to move forward as the wands do and your journey is taking too long. If you feel the opposite and things are all rushed, take a moment to enjoy the beauty in life.

Nine of Wands

The man now stands in front of eight wands as he leans on the ninth for support. He has a bandage around his head. The man looks suspicious, perhaps concerned about what the wands can do. It might be that the man is paranoid, because nobody on the card is out to get him. The bandage might be a sign of his hurt pride; the colours of his clothes suggest he has plenty to be happy about, so it might be emotional. If you receive this card, it is a sign that you may have challenges ahead, but you will be able to keep going.

Reversed- You need to find more courage so that you can face all of your problems. However, you might not see this, because you are too busy blaming others for your problems.

Ten of Wands

This man has scooped up his ten wands and is carrying them towards a village. It's hard work, but he keeps his head down and continues. His orange and brown clothes represent enthusiasm and strength, so we know he will make it with that last bit of effort. The Ten of Wands is a sign of the finish line and that your efforts will soon pay off. The last leg of this race points to success after all of your ups and downs. It might have taken more effort than others had to make, but there is no need to feel bad about this.

Reversed- The weight of the wands might be heavier than necessary, because you are carrying an additional burden. There may be too much self-pity or looking for approval from others. If the burden you carry isn't yours, it's time to get rid of it.

The Page of Wands

This card makes me smile. Maybe it's the white hat, or maybe it's the confidence the Page of Wands has. He is looking at his wand like it's the first time he has seen it and it seems like it's the source of his inspiration. He is alone, but this doesn't bother him, because he is so happy with his wand. The colours of his clothes are a mixture of innocence, magic, the higher mind and passion. His tunic is covered with salamanders. If you receive this card, it means you should be happy about going about things alone. It's time to make a new, unique path for yourself.

Reversed- The fear of being alone could be blocking your creativity or you might be being too hard on yourself. Although you don't know what is in front of you, know that repeating the same thing isn't going to help.

The Knight of Wands

The Knight of Wands is riding a brown horse rearing up ready for action. The knight is in a full suit of body armour and a yellow tunic with salamanders. The tunic is torn, maybe from the battle or maybe from trying to get it over his armour. We can't see what is ahead of the knight, but he is riding away from three pyramids or mountains, the challenges he has overcome. The Page of Wands had a dream and the Knight of Wands has the confidence to carry out the dreams. That being said, the knight is quite young. He may not have the knowledge or skill, or he may even be a little too confident for what lays ahead.

Reversed- You have skill, but you might be overestimating the level of your skills. You may be impulsive and need to take more time to think about the plan and the outcomes. In some cases, you may not have enough confidence and you are too scared to move forward.

The Queen of Wands

In one hand, the queen holds her wand, in the other, a sunflower. She sits in her throne decorated with lions, and she is wearing a yellow robe and a white cloak, a contradiction to the black cat at her feet. The cat looks straight at us, but the queen looks to one side. The queen seems to have it all—intelligence, beauty, sexuality, and a dark side. The subtleness of her toe pointing out from her robe shows that she is involved in all. This is a very powerful and feminine card to receive, a symbol of your own confidence.

Reversed- It may be hard for you to see your femininity or your confidence to get things done. Those around you might not appreciate who you truly are. Try not to let things get on top of you because you fear your own potential.

The King of Wands

You will notice a lot of salamanders in this card, on the king's throne, cloak and one at his feet. His red hair and robe point to the fire and passion of this man. You can also see lions on his throne, reminding us he is a brave man. The king looks into the distance; he is focused and not concerned about what is happening around him. His green shoes show that he isn't a dreamer and in fact is very much in touch with the real world. The way he holds his wand indicates that he is prepared and determined. Whether it's a battle or his goals, he is ready to succeed.

Reversed- You probably have a lot of ambitions, but you may not have the skills to fulfill them. The other possibility is that you have too much confidence in your skills and this is making you come across as a bit of a brag. If you are acting like a bully, it is probably a sign that you are being bullied.

Please remember that this is a guide and for a successful reading, you need to use your intuition as well. What you will probably find is that this book is a great reference to get you started while you build up your confidence and knowledge of the symbols, colours and meanings. After some time, you will get better at seeing the relationship between a card and your situations.

CONCLUSION

That's it! You now have all the knowledge you need to start reading your own tarot cards. If you haven't already, now is the time to get yourself a deck and give them a good shuffle. My advice would be to get yourself a Rider Waite to start off with. It is such a nice deck for learners and it sounds weird, but the cards feel comfortable in your hands. Maybe it's because they are the most familiar images that they are easier to relate to. Once you are into the swing of things, your familiarity with the images will make it easier to recognise the same imagery in other decks.

After going back through the rich history of the tarot cards, it's now difficult to associate them with dark, mysterious corner stores or online scams. Hopefully, I have cleared up the myths of predicting the future. The cards aren't going to tell you about your future love or whether or not you are going to win the lottery.

Now, you can use tarot cards to help you understand parts of your past, present and future. The insights that you gain can assist you in making decisions that will lead you down a better path. But nothing is ever set in stone. Never forget that these insights aren't guaranteed. Let's say that you have two career paths and the cards seem to point in favour of one over the other. It's still down to you to make that final decision. With this in mind, it's also not right to blame the cards when things don't go your way. Our destiny is always in our own hands.

It's been a rather emotional rollercoaster for me. Even after quite a few years of doing my own readings, it was a great experience to delve into the intricate details of each element, suit, and card. It also allowed me to get out some of my earlier journals and see the progress in my understanding and even how my questions have advanced. I recommend that you keep a journal as well. It's not as though the only thing we have on our minds is the next reading. As you can now see, with so much potential information, it is impossible to remember everything.

You should also use your journal to jot down any questions that come to mind before you start your reading. So often, I am driving or plodding around the supermarket and a question pops up. Not like what I want for dinner that night, but you know how your brain works!

We have also learnt of some other skills that you may have thought didn't have much relation to tarot cards. Again, I hope I have revamped the image of the teenage witch from the 90s into something more realistic and practical. Many of the techniques we looked at can be transferred to other areas of spiritualism. For example, the protection circle we create when making a spell can also be used to enhance meditation. Even in Buddhism, the protection mandala can help meditation, or creating a circle with your thumb and index finger forms a circle, a familiar symbol in feng shui. Pay close attention to the power of circles!

Another thing that I think you should bear in mind is that not every card will always have significance. A mistake I made in the beginning, which I admit made me look a bit like a crazy scientist on a whiteboard, was to be convinced I was missing something. You can see that this was probably just a lack of confidence in understanding the meanings of the cards. But I would read through books and books trying to find what I was missing. If you don't see a meaning or relate to a card, it's perfectly normal, so don't feel like you are doing anything wrong.

When this happens to me, I take note of the images and symbols in the card, just a short message to myself on my phone. The days after drawing a card that seems to have no relevance, I keep my eyes open for related symbols. An unexpected rainbow, a lion carved into a stone, and especially any signs of cups, swords, wands or pentacles. You may not see the relationship straight away, but you will be surprised when the penny drops.

This is the fun side of tarot cards— the synchronicity. You can walk through your entire life and miss these connected events or symbols. The black cat in the Queen of Wands is a classic example. Black cats are associated with black magic and bad luck. Now I see a black cat and I wonder why I am being reminded of my darker side. On a similar note, don't forget not to jump to those wrong conclusions when you see a strong card like the Hanged Man or Death. The Fool isn't an idiot and the Wheel of Fortune doesn't automatically imply you are in for good things. If you are a beginner, try to erase any stereotypical ideas you have of the cards before you start. It will help you to begin reading the cards in a more efficient manner.

Give yourself enough time for a reading—time and a deck of cards is all you need. Yes, you can buy candles, crystals and essential oils. You can set the scene, if you think it will help, but time is crucial. If you rush through, you won't have enough time to find the answers to these difficult questions. The other thing you may find is that because you rush, you feel the need to have another reading before time has passed to make sense of the first reading. Rushing anything takes the fun out of it, and the last thing to remember is that it should, above every-thing, be enjoyable.

If you are new to my books, I thank you from the bottom of my heart for choosing to read this combination of years of research and practice. If you have read *Healing Mantras* and/or *Modern Chakras*, I hope this has been as practical as the others and that like me, you can appreciate a more spiritual living and overall, a happier life. Join me on Facebook and you can contact me on my website too. Of course, I will be forever grateful if you could take a minute to leave your feedback on Amazon so I can continue my learning journey while I prepare for the next book! Good luck and I would love to hear how your readings are going.

Thank you for reading my book. If you have enjoyed reading it perhaps you would like to leave a star rating and a review for me on Amazon? It really helps support writers like myself create more books. You can leave a review for me by scanning the QR code below with your phone camera:

Thank you so much. Verda Harper

REFERENCES

Baikie, K. A. (2018, January 2). *Emotional and physical health benefits of expressive writing | Advances in Psychiatric Treatment.* Cambridge Core. https://www.cambridge.org/core/journals/ advances-in-psychiatric-treatment/article/ emotional-and-physical-health-benefits-of-expressive-writing/ED2976A61F5DE56B46F07A1CE9EA9F9F

Burroughs Cook, A. (2009). *What falls to the Floor...* tarot Dynamics. http://tarotdynamicsannacook.blogspot.com/p/what-falls-to-floor.html

Categories: tarot Readings. (n.d.). Psychic Reviews. https://www.psychicreviews.com/guides-expanded/tarot-readings/

Dore, J. (2017, September 2). *Using tarot in Psychotherapy.* Psych Central. https://www.psychcentral.com/pro/using-tarot-in-psychotherapy#1

Douglas, C. (ed) (1997) *Visions: Notes of the Seminar given in 1930-1934 by C. G. Jung.* Vol. 2. p 923. Princeton University Press.

Hammond, C. (2017, June 2). *The puzzling way that writing heals the body.* BBC Future. https://www.bbc.com/future/article/20170601-can-writing-about-pain-make-you-heal-faster

Hancock, P. (n.d.). *tarot Spreads.* Psychic Revelation. https://www.psychic-revelation.com/reference/q_t/tarot/tarot_spreads/

Jones, J. (2017, September 1). *Carl Jung: tarot Cards Provide Doorways to the Unconscious, and Maybe a Way to Predict the Future.* Open Culture. https://www.openculture.com/2017/08/carl-jung-tarot-cards-provide-doorways-to-the-unconscious-and-even-a-way-to-predict-the-future.html

Labyrinthos Academy. (2017, February 26). *tarot and Numerology: What do numbers in tarot Mean for the Minor Arcana? (Infographic).* Labyrinthos. https://labyrinthos.co/blogs/learn-tarot-with -labyrinthos-academy/tarot-and-numerology- what-do-numbers-in-tarot-mean-for-the-minor- arcana-infographic

Michelsen, T. (n.d.). *Colour Meanings on tarot Cards – tarot Moon.* tarot Moon. https://tarotmoon.com/colour-meanings-on-tarot-cards/

Moon Phases for Doing Spells. (n.d.). Free Witchcraft Spells. https://www.free-witchcraft-spells.com/moon-phases.html

Nguyen, T. (2017, December 6). *10 Surprising Benefits You'll Get From Keeping a Journal.* Huffpost.Com. https://www.huffpost.com/entry/benefits-of-journaling   -_b_6648884?

guccounter=1&guce_referre   r=aHR0cHM6Ly93d3cuZ29v-
Z2xlLmNvbS88&guce   _referrer_sig=AQAAAN2lpR5KmOyO-
ezRS1AelU7zVREqNoIWSwr1Tgt30IkEq-pdy-   D5xgUugI_C-
s7JtymaMifLOLkjGtQAyb1Nvee   H1qx39daqsQTRWHIJ0du-
l6valHQ_ wFVjGskXjzUCBIFSoIxqsVfzl6g5xu6vR 14gxAwv-
LIkAofqynYZG4tz0y

Oatman-Stanford, H. (2015, December 4). *tarot Mythology: The
Surprising Origins of the World's Most Misunderstood Cards*. Mental
Floss.   https://www.mentalfloss.com/article/71927/tarot-
mythology-surprising-origins-worlds-most-misunderstood-
cards

Parry, M. (2020, January 17). *3 Self-Care Benefits Everyone Can
Get from a Daily tarot Pull*. Brit + Co. https://www.brit.co/self-
care-tarot-reading/

Patterson, R. (2018, May 11). *StackPath*. John Hunt Publishing.
https://www.johnhuntpublishing.com/blogs/moon-
books/tarot-spells/

Posada, J. (2007). *What is an Oracle?* Jenniferposada.Com.
https://www.jenniferposada.com/what-is-an-oracle

Reed, T. (2019, December 18). *What are significators in a tarot
reading?* The tarot Lady. https://www.thetarotlady.com/signifi-
cators-tarot-reading/

Roos, M. (2019, November 6). *How to Connect tarot and Chakras*.
Siobhan Johnson. https://www.siobhanjohnson.com/connect-
tarot-chakras/

Sol, M. (2020, December 30). *Synchronicity: 7 Ways to Interpret and Manifest It *. LonerWolf. https://lonerwolf.com/synchronicity/

Staff, J. (2016, December 29). *tarot-Kabbalah connection not all that mysterious*. J.Weekly.Com. https://www.jweekly.com/2004/11/05/tarot-kabbalah-connection-not-all-that-mysterious/

tarot Card Meanings List - 78 Cards By Suit, Element, and Zodiac. (n.d.). Labyrinthos. https://labyrinthos.co/blogs/tarot-card-meanings-list

Whitehurst, T. (2020, August 13). *How to Cast a Magical Circle in 6 Simple Steps*. Tess Whitehurst. https://tesswhitehurst.com/how-to-cast-a-magical-circle-6-simple-steps/

Wigington, P. (2018, June 6). *Where Did tarot Cards Come From?* Learn Religions. https://www.learnreligions.com/a-brief-history-of-tarot-2562770

Wigington, P. (2019, November 27). *10 Basic Divination Methods to Try*. Learn Religions. https://www.learnreligions.com/methods-of-divination-2561764

Wikipedia contributors. (2020, December 27). *Rider-Waite tarot deck*. Wikipedia. https://en.wikipedia.org/wiki/Rider-Waite_tarot_deck

VERDA HARPER BIO

For those who are interested in discovering more about themselves and the world of Spiritualism, Verda Harper combines her years of experience with practical knowledge and a love for the topic. Her travels have taken her to India, China, Sri Lanka, and Indonesia as well as cities across the U.K and the U.S to discuss her expertise with fellow specialists.

Over a decade ago, Verda would have described herself as normal, yet after nearly two decades of research into emotional and physical healing, she shies at the word, teaching people to look for what makes them unique, their individual goals and how they can turn their lives around and strive for happiness.

Her books include Healing Mantras, Modern Chakra, and Modern Tarot and along with her own encounters, we learn about the amazing impacts of other lives Verda has touched. Her advice will help readers learn about the traditions and benefits of Eastern Philosophies.

One often leans towards certain stereotypes in this field but Verda Harper has broken them all. This spiky short-haired woman is well-grounded, centred, and logical in all of her books, neither scientific nor religious, but factual. Each book is a journey with Verda Harper offering advice for each step of the way.

Printed in Great Britain
by Amazon

67672671R00271